INTERCULTURAL COMMUNICATION
A Perceptual Approach

MARSHALL R. SINGER
University of Pittsburgh

Prentice-Hall, Inc., *Englewood Cliffs, New Jersey 07632*

Library of Congress Cataloging-in-Publication Data

Singer, Marshall R.
  Intercultural communication.

  Bibliography.
  Includes index.
    1. Intercultural communication. 2. Interpersonal
relations. I. Title.
HM258.S487 1986   303.4′82   86-5905
ISBN 0-13-469115-6

Editorial/production supervision
  and interior design: Mary Bardoni
Cover design: Photo Plus Art
Manufacturing buyer: Harry P. Baisley

© 1987 by Prentice-Hall, Inc.
A Division of Simon & Schuster
Englewood Cliffs, New Jersey 07632

Printed in the United States of America

10 9 8 7 6 5 4 3 2

ISBN 0-13-469115-6 01

Prentice-Hall International (UK) Limited, *London*
Prentice-Hall of Australia Pty. Limited, *Sydney*
Prentice-Hall Canada Inc., *Toronto*
Prentice-Hall Hispanoamericana, S.A., *Mexico*
Prentice-Hall of India Private Limited, *New Delhi*
Prentice-Hall of Japan, Inc., *Tokyo*
Prentice-Hall of Southeast Asia Pte. Ltd., *Singapore*
Editora Prentice-Hall do Brasil, Ltda., *Rio de Janeiro*

*This book is dedicated to my Israeli son, Shepherd;
my Afghan son, Attid; and my philosopher son, Paul, as
well as to the other important young people in my life—
Margaret, Martin, Jeffrey, Mitchell, and Karen Singer—all of
whom have taught me how culturally unique every human
can be.*

*It is also dedicated to the most superb human being
I have ever known—Helen Singer—who has been mother,
sister, friend, and giving tree to us all.*

CONTENTS

PREFACE

Over a decade ago the Society for Intercultural Education, Training and Research (SIETAR) received a grant from what was then called the Office of Cultural Affairs in the U.S. Department of State to assess the "state of the art" of intercultural communication. (It is significant that the funding came from the State Department. At that time most people thought of intercultural communication as being something one did exclusively with foreigners. It is only quite recently that people have begun to realize that it is often far more intercultural for, say, an American business executive to communicate with an American high school dropout than it would be for him to communicate with a German business executive in a company selling the same product he sells.) George Renwick took the lead on the "state of the art" study, and what he found (in about 1977) was that there were over 450 courses in intercultural communication being taught across the country, mostly (but not exclusively) in Departments of Communication. He also discovered that at that time there was not a single book which could qualify as a text on the subject. Since then a number of books have appeared (many of them with titles very similar to this one), although some are collections of readings rather than texts *per se*. Few are attempts to systematically address the question of what actually constitutes intercultural communication. None attempt to explore the process—as a process—on the personal, group, and national level of analysis. This work hopes to fill that gap.

While it is aimed primarily at the student in courses in intercultural communication, it is the hope of the author that teachers and students in courses in interpersonal communication, group dynamics, group behavior, political behavior, anthropology, and international affairs will start to take into account some of the ideas discussed here. It is also hoped that with the publication and dissemination of this work increasing numbers of scholars and practitioners will begin to recognize that intercultural communication is more than just *trying to communicate with foreigners*. It is a multidisciplinary field which has as much relevance in trying to understand—and overcome—the barriers to effective communication between different people and different groups within the same country as it does to trying to deal with barriers to effective communication within large organizations such as public bureaucracies and large private corporations.

When people start to recognize that every human being is culturally unique, they will begin to realize that *every* interpersonal communication is, to some degree, also an intercultural communication. Once they recognize that, perhaps then they will start to look at the cultural differences that make each of us unique, and will start to consciously ask what they can do to more effectively overcome those differences in values, attitudes, and beliefs. At that time, hopefully, a significant start will have been made in attempting to understand both our differences and our similarities as human beings. This is not to say that because we start to communicate more effectively conflict will disappear. Certainly it will not. Rather, with more effective intercultural communication we will know what it is that we are in conflict about and can then take steps to realistically deal with the conflict.

Which brings me to the issue of power relationships. For too long communication specialists have overlooked the fact that every interpersonal, intergroup, and international relationship has a power component to it. What I hope to do in this work is to make the reader aware of that aspect of all relationships and have him or her more realistically assess those power components before entering into a conflict which they are bound to lose. If I save just one reader, or one group, or one nation, the cost and the pain of doing that (simply because they didn't know how to do it effectively), I will consider this effort to have been a success. Conversely, if I can convince just one political scientist (who is familiar with studying power relationships) that it is important to look beyond the power component and look at the intercultural dynamics of the relationships as well, I will also be happy. If I convince two, I will be ecstatic.

ACKNOWLEDGMENTS

This work has been in process for a very long time. On one level it all began in 1964, when I was asked to teach a graduate course in intercultural communication at the Graduate School of Public and International Affairs at the University of Pittsburgh and to help design an intensive summer program in intercultural communication for a group of Westinghouse Corporation middle-level managers. Much more difficult, in order to do both assignments I had to think through exactly what I understood intercultural communication to mean.

Fortunately, I had a group of very stimulating and provocative colleagues around me to goad my thinking. A. Gaylord Obern, Michael Flack, Jack Matthews, Edward Stewart, Alex Weilenmann, Richard Cottam, Carl Beck, Daniel Rich, Steven Rhinesmith, Gary Althan, Toby Frank, George Renwich, and David Hoopes were all associated with Pitt at that time. In one way or another, all of those people contributed to my intellectual development over the years. In those years Pitt was *the* place in America where intercultural communication was being thought about. It is not an accident that when the Society for Intercultural Education, Training and Research (SIETAR) was founded, many of those people were on the governing council.

Specifically, this book owes its genesis to David Hoopes, of the Intercultural Press, who suggested that I write it back in 1977. In part, it grew out of an article I wrote in 1965 entitled "Culture: A Perceptual Approach," and partly it is an extension of the ideas I published in the first three chapters of *Weak States in a World of Powers* in 1972. I am indebted to the Free Press for giving me permission to expand on and develop that work here.

I have been teaching courses in intercultural communication for more than twenty years now and can't begin to list the names of all the students who argued with me in those classes and helped me clarify my views on the subject. I'm not certain they are aware that they taught me at least as much as I taught them. To all of them I am very grateful.

I can name the students who helped me with library research and who proofread successive drafts for hours on end. My deepest thanks go to Michael Usnick, Cathleen McInerney, Ligaya Angeles, Dan Whitmeyer, Jim Duffett, and Charles Kwarteng for all the hours of grief they put up with and for all of their constructive suggestions. I am also indebted to many people for typing assistance, including Willadean Bailey, Barbara Wells, and Gracie Schetley, but particularly to Joyce Valiquette and Kathy Rud, who stayed late and came in weekends just to try to meet the publisher's deadlines. Clearly, without them this book couldn't have been completed.

I am particularly indebted to Richard Cottam, Alex Weilenmann, Bulah Rohrlich, Felipe Korzenny, and David Hoopes for reading the manuscript and making invaluable suggestions. They tried to help make it better. Errors of either fact or judgment are, of course, my own.

CHAPTER ONE
THE ROLE OF CULTURE
AND PERCEPTION
IN COMMUNICATION

INTRODUCTION TO PART I

In an essay on humor, the noted writer and humorist E. B. White wrote: "Humor can be dissected, as a frog can, but the thing dies in the process. . . ."[1] Since I love to communicate interculturally, I would hate to hurt a process I love. Fortunately, the communication process is not the same as either frogs or humor. The more we understand it, the better at it we are likely to become. Hence, this work is undertaken with a sense of love and enjoyment of the process. My hope is that by dissecting the communication process and coming to understand it better, the reader will not only become better at communicating across cultural barriers but will also enjoy it more.

Back in the 1960s I argued that every identity group has a culture of its own.[2] I also argued then that every individual is a part of perhaps hundreds of different identity groups simultaneously and that one learns, and becomes a part of, all of the cultures with which one identifies. I will make those same arguments in the pages that follow.

At the time I wrote that article some anthropologists said that I was destroying the concept of culture. If it was to have any meaning it had to be applied only to very large groups like total societies or large language or ethnic groupings. As I saw it, the way the anthropologists viewed the problem forced them to describe the

1

large degree of cultural variation that exists *within* every society as being "sub-cultural." For me that didn't seem to be a logical or useful way to deal with the problem—particularly when I realized that I was in some ways much closer to some "subcultures" in other societies than I was to many within my own. It seemed to me then—and still does today—much more logical and useful to talk about the culture of each group and then to examine—for each total society—the groups that comprise it. Each society is certainly different from every other society, but that is because no two societies contain all of the same groups and only those groups. I suppose it's a little like looking at two different kinds of cake. A chocolate cake is certainly quite different from, let's say, a fruitcake, yet they are both still cakes and as such have more in common with each other than either does to, let's say, a chocolate candy bar. But that does not distract from the fact that the chocolate in the cake and the chocolate in the candy bar are much more similar to each other than they are to any of the other ingredients of either the cake or candy bar.

Culinary analogies notwithstanding, over the course of the decades anthropologists themselves have now independently come to take a position very similar to the position I took then. Certainly they have not done so because of me but rather because of the compelling logic of the argument. In any event, in the pages that follow I hope to show the reader how the individual interacts with the groups of which she or he forms a part and how both the individual and the groups affect each other.

Now with this work, I am about to anger some anthropologists again, because I am pushing the concept still further. I am now going to argue that because no person is a part of all, and only, the same groups as anyone else and because each person ranks the attitudes, values, and beliefs of the groups to which he or she belongs differently, *each individual must be considered to be culturally unique.* Notice that I am *not* arguing that every person is a culture unto herself or himself. Culture is, after all, a group-related phenomenon. What I will argue is that each individual in this world is a member of a unique collection of groups. No two humans share only and exactly the same group memberships, or exactly the same ranking of the importance, to themselves, of the group membership they do share. Thus each person must be culturally unique.

If I am correct in this assertion—and I hope to be able to convince the reader in the pages that follow that I am—this means that every interpersonal communication must, to some degree, also be an intercultural communication. The implications of this conclusion, if true, are rather enormous. Some may have difficulty in accepting it. I hope the argument I make is sufficiently convincing that over the course of the next decades most scholars—regardless of discipline—will come to accept this way of viewing interpersonal and intergroup interactions.

There is another important concept I will introduce here. I will argue that every communication relationship has a power component attached to it, and we might as well deal with it openly and consciously. Until now very few communication specialists have been prepared to deal with the power aspect of the communication process. On the other hand, most political scientists until now have failed to recognize the importance of cultural differences in the situations they study. It is one of my most deeply held convictions that the study of intercultural communication informs the study of political behavior. It is also my contention that any study of communication relationships that ignores the power aspect of those relationships is one that misses a very important element of all communications.

It is a further contention of this study that we are talking here about processes that are applicable on all levels of analysis. That is why in the second part of this book I have chosen to attempt to apply to the personal, group, and national levels the concepts developed in the first part. I hope I have been successful.

One additional point that must be made: I do not believe that "better communication" is a panacea. Conflict at every level of analysis has always persisted and probably always will. I am convinced that to the degree that interpersonal, intergroup, or international communication can be facilitated (a) there is likely to be less misperception and fear of other actors, and (b) at least the actors can be certain, if they are in conflict, that they both agree on what the conflict actually is about.

In many ways the world is shrinking at an incredible rate. Strange and often frightening groups are coming into contact with each other at ever accelerating rates. Isolation is unthinkable. More people are living and working and studying among people of differing cultures today than at any previous time in history. That experience can be made easier, more productive, and more satisfying if we better understand the processes at work. And while intercultural communication may be a difficult task, it is not impossible.

THE ROLE OF CULTURE AND PERCEPTION IN COMMUNICATION

Let me begin my discussion of culture by relating a true story. Just before teaching my first graduate course in intercultural communication many years ago, I decided that I would like to do something to dramatically illustrate to the class how all-pervasive cultural norms are; how much we take them for granted; and how upset we become when they are violated. I hit upon an idea and asked my wife what she thought about it. Her reaction was *extremely* negative. She became terribly upset at just the thought that I might actually do what I proposed. She begged, she pleaded, she implored me not to do it. Indeed, her reaction was so intense it convinced me that I had hit upon exactly the kind of illustration I wanted.

The next day before class, I dressed very carefully. I put on a male athletic supporter, underpants, and swimming trunks and was careful to wear a shirt that had long tails I could tuck into my trousers. (I did not want to be accused of indecent exposure.) Then, just before walking into my class, I unzipped my fly. For twenty minutes I paced in front of the room. I sat on the desk. I paced again. In general I tried to behave, nonverbally, as normally as possible, while at the same time not letting the class forget that my fly was open.

The reaction of the students was marvelous. They were terribly uncomfortable and embarrassed. They squirmed in their seats. They blushed. They would glance at my fly, then quickly look away. Some avoided eye contact. Others locked their eyes onto my face and refused to let their eyes go anywhere else. Though not one of them said a word about it, it was perfectly clear that they were very uncomfortable. Throughout this entire period I continued to talk as though I had noticed nothing unusual. Finally I said to them that I was sensing a high degree of discomfort in the class, and that I thought it might be related to the fact that one zipper on my person, which in our culture is normally always closed in public, was open. There was a look of stunned disbelief on their faces. One of them actually blurted out: "You mean you know it's open?" "Of course I do," I answered. "I did it to illustrate how much we take cultural norms for granted and simply don't even think about them until they are violated." I then explained to them what I had worn that morning, and why I had done what I did. The expression of relief on their faces was profound. There were smiles, laughter, sighs, and general good feeling. We continued the discussion on the role of culture in molding accepted and expected norms of behavior for another ten to fifteen minutes, but I intentionally still had not zipped my fly. Finally one of them shouted out, "Close the goddamn fly!" I did, and then we discussed why having my fly open was so distressing even knowing what I was wearing and that I had opened it intentionally.

Before we proceed any further, let us take a closer look at what is involved in cultural conditioning.

CULTURE: WHAT IS IT?

Of all the animals known to exist, the human animal is perhaps the most social. Particularly in our earliest years, but throughout our entire lives as well, people exist—and must exist—in relationships with other human beings. Each of the humans with whom one comes into contact brings to that relationship his or her own view of the universe. More important, perhaps, each of the groups in which one has been raised or in which one has spent a good deal of time will have conditioned the individual to view the world from its perspective.

As animals, all of us must eat, drink, sleep, find shelter, give and receive affection, and meet all of the other biologic requirements "that flesh is heir to." But what we eat, when we eat, and how we eat are all behaviors we have learned from the groups in which we have grown up. Not only the language I speak and the way I think but even *what* I see, hear, taste, touch, and smell are conditioned by the cultures in which I have been raised.

Benjamin Lee Whorf, the noted linguist, has written:

We are thus introduced to a new principle of relativity, which holds that all observers are not led by the same physical evidence to the same picture of the universe, unless their linguistic backgrounds are similar, or can in some way be calibrated.[3]

I would go a step further and substitute the word *cultural* for the word *linguistic*.

Every culture has its own language[4] or code, to be sure, but language is the manifestation—verbal or otherwise—of the perceptions, attitudes, values, beliefs, and disbelief systems that the group holds. Language, once established, further constrains the individual to perceive in certain ways, but I would argue that language is merely one of the ways in which groups maintain and reinforce similarity of perception.

Genetically, we inherit from our parents those physical characteristics that distinguish us as their offspring. Admittedly there is a good deal of individual variation physically and experientially, but there is a good deal of similarity. Given two white parents the overwhelming probability is that the offspring will be white. Given two English-speaking parents the overwhelming probability is that the offspring will speak English. The difference is that physical identity is—within a given range of probability—fixed, while cultural identity is not. The son of two white parents will always remain white no matter what happens to him after birth, but the son of two English-speaking parents may never speak English if immediately after birth he is raised by a totally non-English-speaking group. Thus while physical inheritance is relatively immutable, cultural inheritance is ever changing. The fascinating aspect of cultural conditioning, however, is that while there is theoretically an almost infinite number of possibilities, in fact, the number of group-learned experiences to which most individuals are exposed is amazingly limited. Thus for example, while there may be a whole world to explore, if not an entire universe, the incredibly overwhelming majority of individuals who inhabit this planet never stray more than a few miles from their place of birth. They will, in all probability, speak the language that their parents spoke; practice the religion that their parents practiced; support the political parties that their parents supported; and in broad outline accept most of the cultural perceptions that their parents accepted. In sum, they will perceive the world in a manner strikingly similar to the way their parents perceived the world. That is precisely what makes them a part of the same broad cultural groups of which their parents formed a part. All will deviate from the perceptions of their parents, of course (some only mildly, others more radically), but that is inevitable because every individual is unique. So too are the experiences that every person has. While most of those experiences will be learned from other groups into which the individual will be socialized in the course of his or her life, some of those experiences will not have been group related.

What is more, cultures themselves are constantly changing (in part because the environments in which people live are constantly changing), and thus people's perceptions of the world around them are also constantly changing. Further, some people—particularly in Western societies—rebel against the attitudes and values of their parents and adopt different group values for themselves. Though most people in the West go through a period of rebellion while in their teens, by the time they are adults the vast majority seem to have returned to the cultures of their parents. Each of us is a member of a finite number of different identity groups (which will be defined and discussed in the next chapter), but it is a comparatively small number compared to the incredibly large number that exist in the world. A very large number of the most important groups to which we belong are the same groups to which our parents belonged.

It is a most basic premise of this work that *a pattern of learned, group-related perceptions—including both verbal and nonverbal language, attitudes, values, belief systems, disbelief systems, and behaviors—that is accepted and expected by an identity group is called a culture. Since, by definition, each identity group has its own pattern of perceptions and behavioral norms and its own language or code (understood most clearly by members of that group), each group may be said to have its own culture.* Since these first three chapters are about perception, identity, and communication, and how they affect each other, in a very real sense these chapters, collectively, are about culture and how it operates.

Years ago Ruth Benedict said:

> The life history of the individual is first and foremost an accommodation to the patterns and standards traditionally handed down in his community. From the moment of his birth the customs into which he is born shape his experience and behavior. By the time he can talk, he is a little creature of his culture, and by the time he is grown and able to take part in its activities, its habits are his habits, its beliefs his beliefs, its impossibilities his impossibilities. Every child that is born into his group will share them with him. . . .[5]

And while she was referring there to total societal groups, everything she said then still holds with reference to all identity groups.

The early cultural anthropologists wanted to collect data on how different groups met their biological needs and related to their environments. In order to do that they felt that they had to find remote, isolated, "primitive" groups that had not been "contaminated" by contact with Western societies. Thus they went to the South Pacific, to isolated American Indian reservations, to the Latin American mountains and remote jungles, and to the Asian subcontinent looking for people who were presumed to have been so isolated that they would have been living and doing things the same ways for millenia. In the process they created the impression that it was only those "quaint" and "primitive" peoples who had cultures that were clearly differentiated from one another. Later anthropologists corrected that misconception by rightly demonstrating that all peoples have unique histories, belief systems, attitudes, values, traditions, languages, and accepted and expected patterns of behavior, and that these ensembles constitute culture. But even there the notion persisted that one had to look at a total society in order to understand its culture. Thanks most, perhaps, to the work of Benjamin Lee Whorf and Edward Sapir, the tremendously important role of language in shaping patterns of thinking—and thus the relationship between language and culture—were established. But in so doing they also created the impression that only peoples who spoke distinctly different languages—not dialects—had distinctive cultural patterns. Only in very recent times have scholars come to accept the notion that *every group* that shares a similar pattern of perceptions—with all that implies—constitutes a culture. Since every identity group has somewhat different learned cultural ensembles, in greater or lesser degree, then every identity group may be said to have its own culture.

C. T. Patrick Diamond paraphrases as follows a statement of P. Kay published in *Current Directions in Anthropology:*

> The worlds of café society, ethnic and sexual minorities, the social elite, professional or occupational groups and age cohorts each represent a shared but distinctive perspective that orders the respective field of experience to provide identification and solidarity for its members. Such groups possess sets of implicit assumptions or bases for discrimination. These conventional understandings provide their culture or their tacit theory of the world.[6]

Thus at least some modern anthropologists also share the view that every group has a culture of its own.

Why the importance of making this distinction? Because looking at it this way enables us to apply the tools and techniques of intercultural analysis and communication to all interpersonal, intergroup, and international interactions. Further, it enables us to look at any totality—a small informal group, a large organization, a city, or a tribe or nation[7]—and ask, What are the identity groups present in that unit of analysis? To what degree are there linkages among the groupings? To what degree are the unit identities stronger than the group identities that comprise it? To what degree are the group identities stronger? How can communication between groups be encouraged? These and dozens of similar questions must be answered if the effectiveness of personal, group, or national communication is to be increased. And the effectiveness of those communications will be increased if we constantly keep in mind the cultural differences that must be dealt with.

Henry Hoijer has said:

> . . . to the extent that languages differ markedly from each other, so should we expect to find significant and formidable barriers to cross-cultural communication and understanding. . . .
> It is, however, easy to exaggerate . . . the . . . barriers to intercultural understanding. No culture is wholly isolated, self-contained, and unique. There are important resemblances between all known cultures—resemblances that stem in part from diffusion (itself an evidence of successful intercultural communication) and in part from the fact that all cultures are built around biological, psychological, and social characteristics common to all mankind.
> . . . Intercultural communication, however wide the differences between cultures may be, is not impossible. It is simply more or less difficult, depending on the degree of difference between the cultures concerned.[8]

To this Diamond adds the following, this time paraphrasing the psychologist G. A. Kelly:

> People belong to the same cultural group not merely because they behave alike nor because they expect the same things of others but especially because they construe their experiences in similar ways. However, people are not helplessly suspended in their culture. The task is to generate the imagination needed to envision the infinity of possibilities still open to people of any group; that is to construe their way out of cultural controls.[9]

PERCEPTIONS AND HUMAN BEHAVIOR

My first conscious awareness of the importance of perceptions to human behavior began with an incident when I was still a graduate student. At that time esoteric foods like chocolate-covered ants, fried grasshoppers, smoked rattlesnake meat, and sweet-and-sour mouse tails, were the culinary fad. Upon moving into a new apartment, I received from a friend (as a housewarming gift) a whole carton of these canned delicacies. Having at that time rather prosaic food habits, I did not proceed to consume the entire carton. Indeed, it sat untouched for the better part of a year while I alternately toyed with the idea of trying one of those less-than-tempting "goodies" myself or throwing the entire carton in the garbage. One evening while putting out a whole array of cheeses and other edibles in preparation for a cocktail party I was about to hold, it occurred to me that my opportunity had arrived. Without saying anything to anyone about what I planned, I opened a can of fried caterpillars into a little white dish and set them out on the table along with the other foods. Then I waited to see what would happen. Halfway through the evening one of the unsuspecting young ladies I had invited to the party came up to me and said, "Marshall, those fried shrimp you put out were delicious." "Fried shrimp?" I asked as innocently as I could. "I didn't serve any fried shrimp." "Yes you did," she insisted. "They were in a little white plate on the table. In fact, they were so good I ate most of them myself." "Oh," I said, pausing for maximum effect, "those weren't fried shrimp, they were fried caterpillars."

Virtually the moment I said that the smile disappeared from her face, her complexion turned markedly green, and she proceeded to become terribly sick all over my livingroom floor. I realized immediately—as I was cleaning up the floor—that what I had done was a terrible trick to play on anyone, and I have never done it again. But as I reflected on that incident, it amazed me that a food that could have been thought to be so delicious one moment—when it was *perceived* to be fried shrimp—could be so repugnant the next, when it was *perceived* to be something else. Suppose they really had been fried shrimp, and I had merely been pulling her leg? Would that have changed her physical reaction? I doubt it. In this case, as in most cases involving human behavior, reality was less important than one's perception of reality.

It is not the stimulus itself that produces specific human reactions and/or actions but rather how the stimulus is perceived by the individual that matters most for human behavior. It is perhaps the most basic law of human behavior that people act or react on the basis of the way in which they perceive the external world.

PERCEPTIONS: WHAT ARE THEY?

By *perception,* I mean the process—and it is a process—by which an individual selects, evaluates, and organizes stimuli from the external environment. Perceptions are the ways in which a person experiences the world. They also determine the ways in which we behave toward it. That "world" includes symbols, things, people, groups of people, ideas, events, ideologies, and even faith. In sum, we experience *everything* in the world not "as it is"—because there is no way that we can know the world "as it is"—but only as the world comes to us through our sensory receptors. From there these stimuli go instantly into the "data-storage banks" of our brains, where they have to pass through the filters of our censor screens, our decoding mechanisms, and the collectivity of everything we have learned from the day we were born. All of the information stored in the brain—including the "program" we have learned that teaches us how to learn about new data—in turn affects (if not determines) not only what relatively few bits of data we will attend to (from the literally millions available) but also how we will interpret each bit that we do select.

Perceptions, attitudes, values, and belief systems are not all the same thing (although throughout this work I will sometimes refer to *perceptions* as a shorthand way of referring to them all), but they all affect each other and they all constantly interact.

Technically speaking, group-related, learned perceptions (including verbal and nonverbal codes), attitudes, values, and belief and disbelief systems plus accepted and expected codes of behavior, taught by the groups with which we identify, are what constitutes culture. Perceptions that are not group taught (such as individual physical differences in sensory receptors, body chemistry, or individual unique experiences) should not be considered part of cultural perceptions. Neither should physical or environmental factors that affect perceptions. The trouble is that the distinction between these types of perception is extremely blurred.

They are all closely interrelated. G. A. Kelly has argued:

> Meaning is not extracted from Nature but projected by people upon it. People's behavior can be understood only in terms of their own constructs; that is, from their own internal frames of reference.
>
> Even people's most familiar constructs are not objective observations of what is really there; they are instead inventions of personal and group culture.[10]

Hence, virtually every message to which we attend will be *at least indirectly* affected by our cultural conditioning. Further, when we have finished discussing all of the factors that affect perceptions the reader will see more clearly, I think, what a profound effect our cultures do have on the way we perceive and what a minor effect (by comparison) other factors have in most cases. Thus if I am somewhat imprecise in the way I sometimes use the terms *culture* and *perceptions* synonymously, I ask the reader to forgive me. It should be understood, however, whenever I do use them synonymously that I am referring to *group-related, learned* perceptions only. I suspect that it will be easier for most readers to forgive some imprecision than it would be for them to forgive having constantly to wade through the phrase "the totality of all of the attitudes, values, beliefs. . . ."

Take any stimulus, whatever that stimulus may be—a person, an event, an idea—it doesn't matter. On the basis of all the previous stimuli that have gone into our data-storage banks and the way we have organized those stimuli, we make judgments about the new stimulus. Those judgments are called attitudes. Something is good or bad, right or wrong, useful or dangerous, beautiful or ugly. Each of the groups into which we have been socialized (and as we shall see shortly, we are socialized into a great many) teaches us *its* attitudes toward those stimuli. Many of the groups with which we identify will teach us conflicting judgments about the same stimuli. In some cases even the same group will, on specific issues, teach conflicting attitudes. Conflicting or not, what is important to note here is that *every* group teaches its members what *its* preferred attitudes are.

A value on the other hand is a desired event or situation—something we would like to see happen. After twenty-five years of research on human behavior Milton Rokeach says of values:

> A *value* is an enduring belief that a specific mode of conduct or end-state of existence is personally or socially preferable to an opposite or converse mode of conduct or end-state of existence. A *value system* is an enduring organization of beliefs concerning preferable modes of conduct or end-states of existence along a continuum of relative importance.[11]

He goes on to argue that values can be broken down into two categories: *institutional values,* which concern "desirable modes of conduct," and *terminal values,* which concern "desirable end-states of existence."[12]

Obviously, values are closely intertwined with attitudes. We desire certain events or situations above others because we have learned that they are good, right, and/or useful. Which attitudes and values the individual will adopt as his own will depend in very large part on the ranking he makes of the various group identities he holds at any given time. Yet the complexity of the process is such that those attitudes and values, in turn, will affect our identity, which in turn, will affect how we perceive any new stimulus. *The totality of all of the perceptions, attitudes, values, and identities that we hold—and the way we rank them at any moment in time—is referred to as a belief system.* Holding a particular belief system implies, however, that there are a host of other belief systems that we do not hold. Those are labeled disbelief systems. If, for example, I believe that people are basically

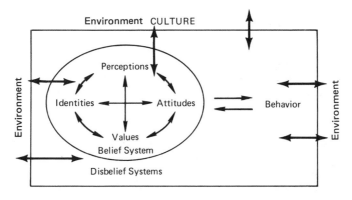

FIGURE 1.1

hostile and "out to get me," then I do not believe that people are basically friendly and helpful. If I am a Buddhist believer, I am not a Buddhist nonbeliever. Nor will I likely be a Christian, Muslim, Jewish, Hindu, or any other kind of believer.

The totality of all of our group-related, learned perceptions, attitudes, values, and belief and disbelief systems *plus the ranking we make in any specific context* of all the groups with which we identify (our identities), plus the behaviors we normally exhibit, constitute what I call our personal culture. Some—indeed, even many—of those perceptions, attitudes, values, and identities we hold may be totally (more often partially) contradictory. Despite that, we somehow manage to hold them all and to apply different ones to our behavior in different situations. Further, there are times when our own behavior can alter those very perceptions, attitudes, values, identities, and beliefs we hold. Thus what I am suggesting is a circle of causality. Each affects the other and is in turn affected by them. (See Figure 1.1.[13])

Virtually all of these processes, of course, occur completely below our level of consciousness, and they occur continuously from the moment of our birth. We are hardly ever aware on a conscious level that they are occurring at all. They are almost totally involuntary processes despite the fact that they are very largely learned. But learned they are. Particularly in those early, formative years our most basic belief systems and our corresponding disbelief systems are being formed. And once formed, they change only very slowly—or when we are confronted by some event that is so dramatic and/or so discordant with an attitude, value, identity, or belief that we have held dear that we are forced to reevaluate. Most often we are forced to reevaluate when we interact with people who have different attitudes, values, or belief systems. While the ranking of our identities change from context to context, it is probably true that once hardened, attitudes and values change much more slowly than do other perceptions. Our most basic "central beliefs" (almost always held subconsciously) probably never change at all.

We will deal with perceptions, attitudes, values, and belief systems in this chapter and with identities and behaviors (and how they interact) in the next. But please note that the separation is quite artificial since each does affect all of the others.

FACTORS THAT AFFECT PERCEPTION

There are a great variety of factors that affect perception, as we shall see in both this and the next chapter. There is no question that the learned factors are by far the most important. But before we discuss them, there are some other factors that are not unimportant, and we will discuss those first.

Physical Determinants of Perception

The only way we can know about the world outside our own bodies is by the impressions of that outside world picked up by our sensory receptors. In another chapter we will discuss the five receptors recognized by Aristotle. Later research, of course, has revealed several things. First, it showed that it is not really the eye as such that is the sensory receptor but more specifically the nerve endings in the cones and rods of the retina of the eye that pick up those visual sensations and transfer them to the brain for interpretation, organization, and storage.[14]

Second, it was discovered that, in fact, there are many more receptors than the five Aristotle mentioned. Indeed, current research has identified at least thirty-seven differentiated sensory inputs into the human brain, and there are probably many more yet to be discovered.[15]

While most of us have all of these same sensory receptors, we know that no two individuals are identical physically. For example, empirical evidence has proven that the swirls on the tips of every human's fingers are ever so slightly different from anyone else's. It must then follow that each person's sense of touch must also be ever so slightly different. Yet far more important for the way people view the universe may be the still unanswered questions of physical variations in other sensory receptors. What about the configuration of cones and rods in the retina of the eye, or taste buds on the tongue, or fibers in the ear, or any of the other physical receptors of external stimuli? *If no two individuals have identical physical receptors of stimuli, then it must follow, on the basis of physical evidence alone, that no two individuals can perceive the external world identically.*

Yet physical differences in sensory receptors, while important, may be the least of the factors contributing to differences in perception. Consider for a moment that peculiar combination of physical and psychological factors called personality or temperament that makes each of us unique. Some scholars would argue that temperament is one of the key factors determining how we perceive the external world.[16] While I'm not certain that I would place it in as central a position with regard to perceptions, there is no doubt that it is a contributing factor.

Which of the factors that go into making up temperament are physical, and which are learned—and to what degree they are learned—it is impossible to say at this point in our knowledge. Nor is it very important to this book that we do so. We know that some children are born with incredibly placid personalities, while others are born hyperactive. Certainly that is not learned. What are probably learned, however, are acceptable and unacceptable ways of coping with those physical characteristics. What is learned is that other people react to us in certain ways if we follow one behavior pattern and differently if we follow another.

Before I leave the subject of physical determinants of perception, there are a whole range of other physical differences that make us unique and deserve to be mentioned here because of the ways in which they affect our perceptions. I'm thinking here of the vast array of physical characteristics we inherit at birth. Height, weight, gender, skin, color, hair texture, physical handicaps of one sort or another all have an impact on how we will perceive the world. It is not the physical characteristics themselves that necessarily determine our perceptions but rather other people's reactions to these physical characteristics that are so important in shaping our view of ourselves and of the world.

In summary, while I do not believe that physical factors are the most important determinant as to how individuals perceive the world, what I have attempted to show in this section is that physical differences *alone* make it impossible that any two humans could perceive the world identically. That fact by itself would make it impossible for any two humans to communicate with 100 percent accuracy. As we shall see as we proceed, other factors individually and collectively make the probability of accurate communication even more remote and difficult to achieve.

We will say more about the other, more major, learned factors affecting perceptions. Before we get to that, we should pause first to consider some of the environmental factors that affect perceptions.

Environmental Determinants of Perception

No matter how good, bad, or different people's visual sensory receptors are, in the absence of sufficient light no color can be perceived; in the absence of all light no visual images whatever can be received. Similarly if a sound is made above or below the threshold at which the human ear is capable of sensing it, no sound will be heard. (It is important for us to make the distinction, as we will later in greater detail, between stimuli that are received on the conscious level and those that are received below the level of consciousness. What I am discussing here are the factors that affect the perception of the stimuli, whether at the conscious or subconscious level.)

Physical environment also affects the way we perceive things. There is increasing evidence that people who live in tropical areas of the world may see reds and oranges very differently from the way people living in the Arctic see those colors. People living in a desert environment or a rain forest will certainly have very different perceptions of water. It is not an accident that Eskimos have twenty-seven different words for snow. And indeed people who grew up in a big city probably perceive a great many things very differently than do people who grew up on a farm in the country.

Relationship of stimulus to surroundings Bernard Berelson and Gary Steiner say: "Even the simplest experiences are organized by the perceiver; and the perceived characteristics of any part are a function of the whole to which it appears

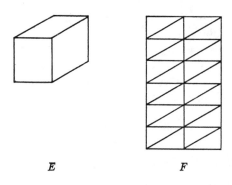

E   *F*

FIGURE 1.2 From Willis D. Ellis, *A Source Book of Gestalt Psychology,* Humanities Press, N.Y., 1967. Reprinted by permission of Humanities Press and Routledge & Kegal Paul Ltd.

to belong."[17] Observe Figure 1.2. The figure E is present in F, but it is very difficult to perceive it there consciously because of the surrounding elements in F.

What has been said thus far also applies to size. Look at Figures 1.3 and 1.4. Correct! The inner circles in both drawings in Figure 1.3 are the same size, as are the lines in Figure 1.4. Once again the surrounding elements (circles in Figure 1.3, lines in Figure 1.4) distort and determine what we see. Subconsciously we may be able to see the similarity in these figures, but on a conscious level we would "swear" that they were different. As I will say repeatedly throughout this work, everything—including perceptions of "reality"—is relative and contextual.

All of these figures are presented here merely to demonstrate that we can't always trust our perceptions—even when they are culturally neutral. What we see may very well depend on what surrounds it, or what it is near. But many of the most important of our perceptions—like our attitudes, values, and beliefs—are not culturally neutral. Rather they have been taught by the groups that are most important to us. Further, everything that has been shown here about visual perception could be replicated for all of the other senses as well. It is just easier to reproduce pictures than it is to reproduce sounds, tastes, or smells.

What is more, different cultures will not even see the same things we do. Go back to Figure 1.4. Research has indicated that some cultures have no difficulty in seeing that the horizontal lines are of equal length.[18] It is precisely these kinds of differences in perception that are so very difficult to deal with. How do I communicate accurately with someone who perceives differently than I do when it would never occur to me that that person could possibly perceive differently?

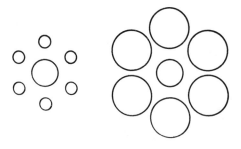

FIGURE 1.3 From *Human Behavior: An Inventory of Scientific Findings* by Bernard Berelson and Gary A. Steiner, copyright © 1964 by Harcourt Brace Jovanovich, Inc. Reprinted by permission of the publisher.

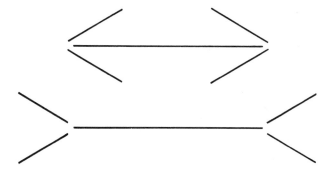

FIGURE 1.4 The Muller-Lyer illusion. From "Cross-Cultural Studies" by D. Price-Williams from *New Horizons in Psychology,* edited by Brian M. Foss (Pelican Books, 1966), p. 398, copyright © Penguin Books, 1966.

Learned Determinants of Perception

Far more important than either physical or environmental differences in determining an individual's perceptions of the external world are the *learned* factors involved in the reception, organization, and processing of sensory data.

Even identical twins born into and raised by the same family (and thus presumed to have the same physical and learned inheritance) will not have identical perceptions of the world. If one could accurately measure perceptions, there is no doubt that the degree to which twins share similarity of perceptions would be considerably higher than for most other individuals, but those perceptions would be far from identical. Certainly the younger the identical twins were at the time the test was given the more similar their perceptions would likely be, but even so, anyone who lives with twins knows how different they can be, from the earliest age. Looking in from the outside, someone who is not a part of the family may not notice those differences. Indeed, the outsider is much more likely to be struck by the similarity of the children than by the differences. But a parent or siblings, from the first weeks, have no difficulty telling them apart physically, and by the end of a few months are amazed at the personality differences. Why this is so, is difficult to explain. It's relatively easy to understand that as twins get older their experiences are increasingly dissimilar, but it is startling to see how what appear to be miniscule variations in their exposure to the outside world can produce such profound differences in even the youngest children. Perhaps one caught a cold and the other did not. Perhaps while the twins were resting outdoors a bird flew close to one and startled it but was unnoticed by the other. Perhaps a dog "nipped" one and not the other. Whatever the specifics there is no question that while their experiences may indeed be far more similar than for most people, they are never identical. And because those experiences are not identical, they simply will not view the world identically.

It would push the concept of "personal culture" beyond credibility to argue that two very young identical twins would have different personal cultures since presumably each would have been exposed to all and only the same group-related perceptions. However, it would not violate the concept to argue that as the twins got older and did things separately their personal cultures would diverge. After all, *all* children are slowly, gradually, but inevitably, socialized into the multitude of cultures of which they ultimately become a part. On the other hand, it would not be incorrect to argue that even at a very early age identical twins do not have identical perceptions.

If for physical and experiential reasons it is not possible for any two individuals to perceive the universe in an identical manner, neither is it possible for them to have absolutely no similarities of perception. In a sense there is a continuum of similarity of perception among individuals. One extreme approaches—but never reaches—zero; the other approaches—but never reaches—100 percent. Actually, degree of similarity of perception can probably best be expressed not as a point on a continuum but as a range of points. For example: A Catholic from a wealthy third-generation Boston family and one from an illiterate and impoverished village in Zaire may share not more than perhaps a 10-15 percent similarity of perception, *as Catholics,* but to that degree they are a part of the broad identity called Catholics. Teachers, considered as a broad group, may have a 15-20 percent similarity of perception. If we narrow the group to include only college teachers, the range of similarity of perception may increase to 20-25 percent. If we further specify that the group consists only of Irish-Catholic, American, middle-class, urban, white, male, heterosexual, college teachers of quantum physics, with Ph.D.s from the Massachusetts Institute of Technology, between the ages of 35 and 40, the range of similarity of perception might well increase to 75-80 percent.[19] Notice that while we have decreased the number of people who can be included in our group, we have increased the number of group identities the members share. By so doing, we have greatly increased the likelihood of easy communication among them and thus the likelihood of their sharing still greater similarities of perception in the future. (See premise 4, chapter 2.) It is no wonder that the smaller the group, the greater its cohesion is likely to be.

In order to illustrate how very different differences in perception of the same stimuli can be, a number of years ago I devised an exercise, which I have since run hundreds of times in many different societies. Allow me to describe it here in some detail to illustrate the enormous differences in perceptions of symbols that actually exist.

In this exercise I put four symbols on the board, one at a time, and ask the seminar or class participants to write on a piece of paper all of the meanings that come to their minds when they see the symbols. When they are done writing, I ask everyone in the room to tell me the meanings they attributed to the symbols. (See Figure 1.5.)

The answers I get vary enormously, depending upon the participants. There is strong indication that they would vary even more if I could do the exercise in remote villages with unschooled individuals in their own languages. As it is, except on three or four occasions when simultaneous translators were present, I have al-

FIGURE 1.5

ways done the exercise in English, usually with highly educated participants. This has automatically skewed the sample in the direction of *more* similarity of perception because all of the participants shared a certain similarity of perception as speakers of English and usually as highly educated professionals. (Normally the participants are graduate students in public and international affairs or midcareer civil servants.)

The two most common answers I get for the first symbol are "cross"—in the religious sense—and "plus"—in the mathematical sense. Now, since more than half of the participants I get are educated Christians, that is not really a surprising result. Also, since most come from the more developed parts of developing countries, the third most frequent response—"crossroads"—is also not surprising. The surprises, for me at least, usually come because of my own perceptual limitations. I am not really surprised by answers like "the letter *T*," "quadrants on a map," "the hands of a compass," "check mark" as in *correct,* or "a check mark" as in *incorrect,* the word *yes,* the word *no,* "Red Cross," and "the sign for Switzerland," although they are not answers I would have thought of myself. The first real surprises came for me when I did this exercise at a United Nations school in Costa Rica with a group of senior Central American civil servants from all six Central American Republics and a Spanish interpreter. Virtually every answer I got for that symbol suggested Latin Catholic romantic symbolism: "death and transfiguration," "life after death," "love," "sacrifice," "eternal life," "suffering," "God's son," "redemption," "crucifixion," "resurrection." These were just some of the meanings that were suggested to those people by that symbol. Not having been raised in a Latin Catholic culture, there was no way I could see those meanings in that symbol. From a communication point of view it doesn't matter how *I* was raised. What is important is that *they* were raised in that culture, and those were the meanings that symbol held for *them.*

The second real surprise for me with that symbol came when I did the exercise at the University of Malaya in Kuala Lumpur, Malaysia, with a group of second-year university students. Virtually every Malaysian of Chinese extraction (about half the students were of Chinese extraction) saw the symbol as the Chinese number ten because—as I discovered that day—that indeed is the way the Chinese write the number ten. Not having studied Chinese myself, there simply is no way I could possibly have seen the number ten in that symbol. On the other hand, there is almost no way in which a person born of Chinese parents, who has been taught to read and write Chinese as her first language, could *not* see the number ten in that symbol.[20]

This is just another example of why communication across cultural barriers is so very difficult. If the way in which *you* perceive a stimulus is completely outside *my* perceptual ken, how can I possibly begin to communicate with you?

At the point where all the participants have told me the meanings they saw in the first symbol, I usually ask them which one is correct. Obviously the answer is that all of them are correct—for them. *Symbols have no intrinsic meaning. Meaning resides not in the symbol but in our minds.* If you see this + as the number ten or as a symbol of resurrection or as a red cross, who am I to say that you are wrong? What I can say is that it is not the meaning I had in my mind when I devised the exercise. When I decided to use that symbol I saw it as one horizontal line and one vertical line crossing more or less at the midpoint. But that is only what was in *my* head at the time. It is no more correct or incorrect than any other meaning that people ascribe to it. Yet if two people are to communicate effectively, each has to know with some degree of accuracy what the symbols they use mean to the other. All language, after all, is symbolic. If I attribute different meanings to your words than you do (and most often I probably do), then there is no way we can communicate accurately. But that is precisely the point being made here. *No two humans can communicate 100 percent effectively because no two humans have learned to perceive identically.*

For the second symbol I have gotten responses that in some ways were even more revealing to me. In one group of participants there was a man from Egypt. When I drew this symbol on the board, he violently threw down his pencil on the desk and in an angry voice said, "I will not draw that symbol! I give my life to oppose it! I will not play games with that symbol!"

"But it is only two triangles superimposed upon each other; one pointing down, the other pointing up," I said, surprised not at his perception of the symbol as something representing the State of Israel but by the violence of his reaction.

"No," he said, even more angrily than before, "it stands for everything evil in this world! Death! Destruction! Murder! Torture! Violence! Hate! I will not play games with such a symbol!" Whereupon he rolled back one shirt sleeve and asked, "Do you see that scar?" pointing to a long, red scar about three inches above his right wrist. "I got that fighting murderous Zionism in Sinai in 1956." Then putting his wrist on his head he said, "I wear it like my halo of thorns! I will not play games with evil."

Now who am I to argue with his perception of that symbol? Obviously for him it really did mean all of those awful things, and nothing that I was going to say could change that perception. I recognized then, for the first time perhaps, at an emotional gut level, why it would be so difficult ever to resolve the Middle East situation.

The more I have thought about that Egyptian's reaction to that symbol, and compared it to other reactions I have gotten from different people with different life experiences, the more amazed I am that any communication at all ever takes place. When I have done this exercise with a group of predominantly Jewish, middle-class, American students from New York City I have gotten answers like "Manischewitz wine," "Mogen David products," "Jewish star," "star of David," "peace," "chicken soup," "high holy days," and many other meanings that only an American Jew could associate with that symbol. Now being a New Yorker myself, none of these meanings really surprised me—not even the chicken soup—though I hadn't thought of them when I designed the exercise. Sharing some degree of similarity of perception with that group, I could certainly understand why they would associate those meanings with that symbol.

The third symbol, I have always drawn carefully the way it appears here. While there is usually some diversity among the answers—depending upon the audience—anywhere from 60 to 100 percent will see it as somehow associated with Hitler, fascism, or Nazi Germany. The fact is that the symbol I put on the board is *not* a Nazi swastika. Hitler's swastika always points to the right, no matter how it is turned, and it is usually turned like this:

But as the saying goes, "Don't confuse me with facts. My mind is made up." It is stylized enough and reminiscent enough of the German swastika to elicit exactly the same depth of emotion—particularly from older Jews who lost relatives during the Nazi period—that a Nazi swastika would. The fact that it is really an ancient Aryan (Indian) symbol in no way changes the depth of one's perception of it as a Nazi swastika.

The fourth symbol is much more ambiguous than the first three and is open to more interpretation. Still, a great many people see it as a "squiggle" or a "signature" or a "corkscrew." More people from developing countries see it as a "river," a "snake," or a "puff of smoke" than do people from developed countries. I once did this exercise at a graduate school of nursing, and more than 60 percent of the participants in that group saw it specifically as an "interuterine device (IUD)" or simply as a "coil" or a "birth-control device." But if you've never seen an IUD, there just is no way you can know what you don't know.

The last part of that last sentence really is at the heart of this exercise and my lengthy discussion of it here. It is so important and so obvious that it is often overlooked. *We know what we perceive; we don't know what we don't perceive. Since there is no way that we can know what we don't perceive, we assume that we perceive "correctly"– even if we don't.* We tend to assume that almost everyone perceives what we perceive, and that we perceive everything (or almost everything) that everybody else perceives. Thus we engage people in discussion on a very wide range of topics assuming that the people with whom we are attempting to communicate share the same perceptions that we do. The two exceptions to this rule usually are people who look terribly foreign (or don't speak our language) and people who are specialists in fields about which we know nothing.

Beyond those exceptions, however, most of us assume that we know what the other person meant when he said something until we discover, by whatever circumstances or accident, that we do not. I automatically assume that someone else perceives what I perceive until proven otherwise. If I didn't do that even the simplest communication would be exhausting.

The more specific the symbol, the more agreement about its meaning we are likely to find. The more abstract the symbol, the greater the variety of meanings we are likely to find associated with it. A word like *table,* for example, is a symbol. But because it is specific the range of perceptions associated with it are likely to be fairly limited. One may see a wooden table or a formica table, a round one or a rectangular one. One might see a mathematical table, a statistical table, a water table, or a table of contents. But the range of choices is fairly limited. On the other hand, the range of choices one might—and does—associate with abstract concepts like "God," "justice," or "democracy" are truly mind boggling. There probably are as many different meanings associated with those abstract concepts as there are groups in the world.

Attitudes and Values

Attitudes: Daryl J. Bem says of attitudes:

> Attitudes are likes and dislikes. They are our affinities for and our aversions to situations, objects, persons, groups, or any other identifiable aspect of our environment, including abstract ideas and social policies. . . . our likes and dislikes have roots in our emotions, in our behavior, and in the social influences upon us.[21]

Not only does each of the groups into which we have been socialized teach us *its* judgment toward specific stimuli (this one is good, that one is bad; this one is beautiful, that one is ugly), even more important, it teaches us an *attitudinal framework* through which we can evaluate all *new* stimuli that reach our sensory receptors. These attitudinal frameworks become an integral part of both our censor screens and our decoding mechanism. Many of the groups of which we consider ourselves to be a part may teach conflicting attitudinal frames. Which we will adopt as our own will depend in large part on the way we rank the various group identities we hold. Often these conflicting frameworks cause no difficulty, however, because the context of each is usually different. For example, our religious identity may teach us that life is precious, and that all killing—even of an unborn fetus—is wrong. Yet in a different context, our national identity may teach us that we have to defend our country, right or wrong, and that to kill our country's enemies in time of war is one of the most noble deeds we can perform. Ironically, it is often the very same people who are most devout in their religious beliefs who are also the most fervent in their nationalist ardor.

The variety of judgments about the same stimuli is truly astounding. In the same city in India one might find men who, as a sign of deference to God, never cut their hair (Sikhs), while a few blocks away at a Buddhist monastery one can find men who shave their heads and faces completely—as their sign of deference to God. In some places one finds it perfectly acceptable for a man to publicly walk down the street holding hands with a male friend, while he might be arrested (or at least disparaged) for walking down the same street holding hands with a female. In some places a woman could be killed for sleeping with the brother of her husband. In others she may be married to all the brothers in a family simultaneously. In some places if a man were to sexually molest a prepubescent boy he could be jailed and very possibly killed by the other inmates, while in other places it is not even considered immoral *provided* the boy is prepubescent. The contrasts and differences are almost endless. Which set of attitudes we adopt and how we rank them will depend very heavily on the degree to which we identify with each of the groups to which we belong.

It occasionally happens that we are confronted with a stimulus (it could be a thing, an event, or an idea) to which we simply do not know how to react. At those times we will sometimes check with "significant" other people from the groups with which we identify to see how they evaluate that stimulus. Their response then gives us our clues as to how we should react.

Sometimes we form an attitude about a stimulus based on the framework that is already in place and then check our judgment of that stimulus with significant others from the groups that matter most to us (people whom we know and trust and whose judgments we respect—meaning that generally their attitudes toward stimuli either conform to our own or are such that we have no difficulty accepting them as our own) just to reinforce our original assessment of the stimulus. But most of the time we don't need to check. Most of the time the attitudinal frame our groups have supplied are sufficient so that we can make judgments about a whole range of issues or events with which we may never before have been confronted.

Values: Recall that *values* are used in this work to mean the desired events or situations we would like to see happen. These refer to our desires, wants, needs, or goals. Those terms are all very close in meaning, although there are shades of differences. *Needs,* for example, connotes a desire having a physiological base. One "needs" something in order to survive as opposed to just wanting it. I'll say more about that in a moment. Normally one speaks of people having needs, of groups or organizations having goals, and of very large groups like societies or countries having values. The reason that it may often be overlooked is, just as with individ-

GROUP I
(MARY)

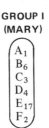

$$A_1$$
$$B_6$$
$$C_3$$
$$D_4$$
$$E_{17}$$
$$F_2$$

FIGURE 1.6

uals, groups and countries also have certain needs that must be met in order for those entities to survive. Be that as it may, every individual, group, or nation holds a number of values simultaneously. Just as with attitudes, some of the values an individual or group holds may be compatible but some may conflict with each other. Or an individual's values may conflict with the values of one or more of the groups to which he or she belongs. In fact, it is almost inevitable that they will. It may not be so much that the values themselves conflict—although that is certainly possible—but rather that the importance we attach to certain values may be different from the importance other individuals or groups attach to those same values. That is, each individual and group ranks the importance of those values (to themselves) differently. Each of the groups of which we are a part teaches us *their* ranking of values. Which ranking we accept, which we change, and which we reject outright is, I submit, a function of the degree to which we identify with each of those groups. That is why I argue that every individual is culturally unique.

Let us suppose that membership in group I implies acceptance of the hypothetical values listed in Figure 1.6. That does not mean that every member of group I will accept all of these values or will rank them in exactly that order. Indeed they will not. Membership in a group does imply acceptance of some of the basic group values, but it is clear that each member of the group will accept some of the group's values and reject others. Even among those group values that are accepted by all, each individual will rank the importance of those group values somewhat differently. Indeed some members of group I, because of overlapping membership in some other groups, will inevitably hold some values that are completely alien to other members of group I.

While person 1 of group I (let's call her Mary) might have ranked the predominant group values as shown, persons 2 and 3 of the same group (let's call them Margaret and Mildred) might have ranked them as shown in Figure 1.7. Each indi-

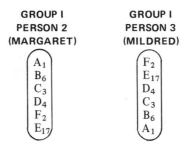

GROUP I	GROUP I
PERSON 2	PERSON 3
(MARGARET)	(MILDRED)

GROUP I PERSON 2 (MARGARET):
$$A_1$$
$$B_6$$
$$C_3$$
$$D_4$$
$$F_2$$
$$E_{17}$$

GROUP I PERSON 3 (MILDRED):
$$F_2$$
$$E_{17}$$
$$D_4$$
$$C_3$$
$$B_6$$
$$A_1$$

FIGURE 1.7

vidual is still holding all of the same group values but ranking them differently. The combinations possible—even for people holding all and only the same group values—are virtually endless.

Let's take some real-world examples. Being American implies acceptance of the value of American-style democracy, acceptance of the values of free speech and freedom of religion, toleration for groups other than our own, and acceptance of the essentially free-enterprise economic system, to mention just several of the predominant American values. Now, any American reading this might instantly take issue with the values I have chosen to list. Being just as American as I, they might rightly ask, Why didn't you include the right to bear arms, the Judeo-Christian ethic, the right to life, love of country, willingness to fight to preserve what we have, or any of a number of other values that other Americans hold? The answer is simply that I don't rank those values as highly as I do the values I listed. That doesn't make others, or me, any less American. It just makes us different.

But now complicate the picture still further by recognizing that no two humans are members of all and only the same groups. Thus, assuming membership in only twelve different identity groups (which is a vast underestimation of the number of groups of which all of us are simultaneously members), Mary's value structure might look something like Figure 1.8. Mary would be at the confluence of these twelve specific identity groups (remember that each group has a culture of its own) and presumably would rank the values of each of these groups in her own unique way. Another individual belonging to all and only the same groups as Mary—even if that were possible; and we have seen that it is not possible—would still be culturally different from Mary because of the probability that she—this

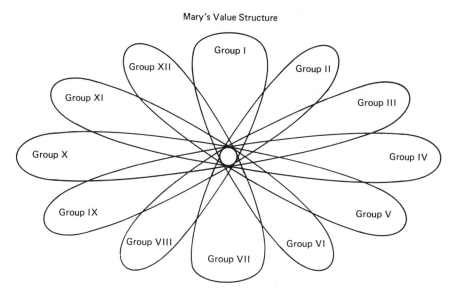

Mary's Value Structure

FIGURE 1.8

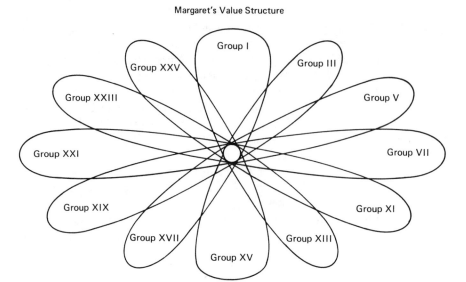

Margaret's Value Structure

FIGURE 1.9

other individual—would rank the values of each of those groups somewhat differently from the way Mary ranks them.

Margaret's value structure (also assuming membership in only twelve identity groups), even sharing membership in six of the same cultures as Mary, might look something like Figure 1.9.

I don't think the point has to be labored further. Of course every person is culturally unique. That is why every interpersonal communication is also an intercultural communication. Knowing that should allow us to recognize the differences for what they are and strive to find the cultural similarities—which just as certainly are going to be there, since each of us shares some similar group identities merely by virtue of being human—and start by building upon those. The more we explore another individual's value structure, the more we are likely to find that we share. From these we can learn how to learn about those other values we do not share.

Let's return to our discussion of values as such. Whatever we call them— needs, values, goals—the fact is that every individual and group has them. Some individuals and groups may have different values from other individuals and groups or they may have them in different proportions and/or they may rank them differently, but every human has values.

Some have argued that precisely because the human animal is, after all, just that—an animal—we must fulfill our most basic animal needs first. They would argue that either we eat, drink, sleep, and find shelter or we die. We either procreate or the species dies. Those are the basic animal needs to which we must first attend. But as a complex social animal, there are other needs to which we must also attend. Psychologists would argue that we *need* to feel safe and provide for the safety of those whom we care about; we *need* to give and receive affection; we *need* to have a feeling of self-esteem; and ultimately, if there is time and energy left over, and we have the chance to think about it, we have a *need* for self-actualization.

A. H. Maslow describes these as the hierarchy of needs.[22] That is, he argues that we must fulfill our most basic needs *first,* and only when those have been satisfied do we turn our attention to the fulfillment of the "higher order" needs. He goes on to say:

> In actual fact, most members of our society who are normal are partially satisfied in all of their basic needs and partially unsatisfied in all their basic needs at the same time. A more realistic description of the hierarchy would be in terms of decreasing percentages of satisfaction as we go up the hierarchy of prepotency. For instance, . . . it is as if the average citizen is satisfied perhaps 85% in his physiological needs, 70% in his safety needs, 60% in his love needs, 40% in his self-esteem needs and 10% in his self-actualization needs.[23]

Regardless of the percentages involved, Maslow would argue that we are always trying to fulfill all of those needs all of the time.

Now whether they are actually physiological needs or learned values does not have to overly trouble us here. I would argue that to the degree that they have a physical imperative associated with them they may indeed be needs as opposed to desires or wants or goals. Regardless of which they are, however, several things have to be said about them.

For one thing, it is clear that we try to fulfill several or all of them simultaneously. To the degree that those values are compatible that is not a problem. To the degree that one or more of those needs conflict, however, particularly if we rank them as equally important, that could be a problem. We could—and many of us do all the time—find ourselves trying to satisfy two totally conflicting values simultaneously and thus achieve neither. Elsewhere we will talk more about the importance of prioritizing our needs, goals, and values in order to be able to direct our behavior toward meeting them all. But there is no way we can meet all of them simultaneously even if they don't directly conflict.

Second, except in those extreme cases where the deprivation is all consuming, many—indeed most—of these needs or values are perceived only on a subconscious level. Consciously we may deny vehemently—even to ourselves—that we are lonely, yet our actions can indicate loudly to the trained observer that much of our behavior revolves around trying to assuage that loneliness. Most often we are simply unaware consciously of what our needs are or how pressing some of them are at different times. Yet we try communicating with others (who may be no more conscious of *their* value ranking than we are) and oftentimes come away not knowing why we found the exchange so unsatisfying.

Third, to some degree fulfilling one need can partially—but only partially—substitute for another. Filling up on water is not really a substitute for food, but it does stave off hunger to at least some degree. People who eat compulsively don't do so because they are perpetually hungry. They may do so because eating provides instant gratification and substitutes for other needs that are not being gratified. Meeting self-esteem needs may not substitute for love needs, but may be perceived by the individual as a means to an end.

Fourth, and probably most relevant to this discussion, whatever our needs or values, or how we rank them, what they are and how they are ranked are learned from the groups with which we identify. We are taught which values we *ought* to hold by each of our groups. What is more, we are also taught in what ways it is acceptable to go about satisfying those desires and in what ways it is not. Milton Rokeach says of this:

> Values are the cognitive representation not only of individual needs but also of societal and institutional demands. They are the joint results of sociological as well as psychological forces acting upon the individual. . . .[24]

But that is just the point. Each group teaches *its* "societal and institutional demands," and each group—i.e., each culture—makes different demands. That is precisely what makes intercultural communication so difficult. If we fervently value "the greatest good for the greatest number" of our fellow humans, how do we possibly communicate effectively with those who just as fervently value getting all they can for themselves and their families? If we value peace and nonviolence above all else, how do we communicate effectively with someone who believes that one has to take what one wants by whatever means? All of us believe that our values are the best ones to hold. If we didn't we would hold other values. Because no two groups value exactly the same things or rank their values with the same intensity it is inevitable that there will be basic value conflict between individuals from different groups. Yet somehow, if communication among individuals from different groups is ever to be effective, we must not only recognize which values we rank most highly but we must also recognize that "they" are likely to rank perhaps totally different values just as highly. The first step to effective intercultural communication, it seems to me, is to recognize just what those value differences are. We may not like the values "they" hold, but we must recognize that their values are as important to them as ours are to us. The second step—and it is perhaps the most difficult one in the intercultural-communication process—is to find some way to reach an accommodation between those conflicting values.

One final point before we leave the discussion of values. The reason I have taken up so much space discussing values is that *so much of human behavior is geared toward satisfying those needs, goals, and/or desires.* Thus we interpret situations and relations with other people and groups in terms of trying to satisfy those needs and values. Having needs and desires, we try to fulfill them. In chapter 4 I define *political behavior* as the attempt that all humans engage in to manipulate and/or structure their environment, people, and groups in order to achieve their own needs, goals, and/or values. The fact that most of those efforts are subconscious does not deny the fact that they motivate just about all of our behavior. They are crucial for understanding human behavior.

Virtually all of the values or needs scholars speak about are themselves components of power—i.e., the things that give the people or groups who have those values or needs the capability of influencing other people or groups who do not. That being true, it may well be that people seek these values not only for the "good" they do for the possessor of them (in and of themselves) but also because we may all instinctively know that they give us influence (power) over other people. If that assertion is correct, then those political scientists who have been arguing for years that the drive for power is the basic force motivating human behavior may well be correct. That is, it does not matter how we rank these values or whether we all have them all or only some of them. As long as we have any of them—and all of us, regardless of culture or personality have some—then to the degree that our behavior is geared toward trying to bring about some desired state or situation, we are engaged in political behavior—i.e., we are trying to exercise influence over either our environment or other people and groups. That is precisely why I argue that aside from being to some degree intercultural, all interpersonal, intergroup, and international relations are also to some degree "political." The study of political behavior very much enhances our understanding of the intercultural communication process. But what most political scientists seem to have overlooked until now is that the study of political behavior is very much informed by the study of intercultural communication.

In chapters 5, 7, and 8 we will look specifically at how those values are dealt with by individuals, groups, and states and at the intercultural communication implications at each level of analysis.

Belief Systems

Earlier I argued that a belief system is the totality of perceptions, attitudes, values, and identities. I believe that something more should be said about them before we move on.

In an earlier work on belief and disbelief systems, Milton Rokeach wrote:

> The *belief system* is conceived to represent all the beliefs, sets, expectancies, or hypotheses, conscious and unconscious, that a person at a given time accepts as true of the world he lives in. The *disbelief system* is composed of a series of subsystems rather than merely a single one, and contains all the disbeliefs, sets, expectancies, conscious and unconscious, that, to one degree or another, a person at a given time rejects as false.[25]

Not only is his concept of one belief system (and several contrary disbelief systems) held by all individuals important for this work, but what else he said in that book is also crucial to this work. For one thing, he differentiated between different kinds of beliefs: those that are most central to a person, those that are "intermediate," and those that are only "peripheral."

He says of beliefs in the "central region":

> Every person may be assumed to have formed early in life some set of beliefs about the world he lives in, the validity of which he does not question and, in the ordinary course of events, is not prepared to question. Such beliefs are unstated but basic.[26]

According to Rokeach these "primitive beliefs" have to do with the definition of a person's physical world, his or her social world, and feelings about self. These are the beliefs that are so basic that the individual believes that every other human also holds them. And precisely because these beliefs are so basic, they are probably least susceptible to change. This is the range of beliefs, of course, that make intercultural communication so very difficult. We take them so very much for granted that they are only rarely, if ever, consciously considered. Thus on a conscious level, at least, we are unaware that anyone could possibly have very different basic beliefs. If we are consciously made aware that other people hold different basic beliefs, we reject those beliefs as unworthy of serious consideration.

According to Rokeach, beliefs of the "intermediate region" are predicated on reference to some authority (authority being defined as "any source to whom we look for information about the universe, or to check information we already possess"[27]).

Rokeach feels that this range of beliefs is important because "it spotlights a possible intimate connection between the way we accept and reject people and the way we accept and reject ideas stemming from authority."[28] More will be said about this in a moment. First let us go on to describe his "peripheral region" of beliefs.

According to Rokeach peripheral beliefs—or more specific beliefs—are derived from intermediate beliefs. For example, beliefs about such things as birth control, the New Deal, and the theory of repression Rokeach would consider peripheral beliefs because they are derived from one's beliefs about the Catholic church, Franklin D. Roosevelt, and Sigmund Freud,[29] respectively. According to Rokeach's analysis, all of the beliefs that are neither primitive nor held because of identification with some authority but rather are derived from that identification are in the peripheral region. And, of course, these are the ones most subject to change.

Let us return to that notion of the degree to which authority is accepted, which Rokeach discussed in his intermediate region. According to him—and his and other people's empirical research seems to bear it out—the way one views authority determines in very large measure how one will view the world. That is, the more one interprets information coming from the outside world, independent of the authority of the source of that information, the more "open" Rokeach considers that person to be. The more one relies on authority to determine his or her attitude toward information, the more "closed" he or she is considered.

While Rokeach would argue that all people are driven to some degree by both "open" and "closed" perceptions, his empirical research indicates strongly that most people tend to fall more strongly into one category or the other. And his research shows that an individual's way of looking at the external world ("open" or "closed") very much determines not only what he will see but also what he will not.

If Rokeach is correct in his assertion—and his empirical evidence is certainly very convincing, despite the fact that his conclusions are virtually all from research in the United States—then that finding is extremely important for intercultural communication at all levels of analysis. What it implies is that an individual or group that is more "open minded" in their belief systems will be much more likely to try to understand another individual or group with a different belief system—and thus will be much better able to communicate with "them"—than would an individual or a group with a different belief system. In other words, projecting his theory into the intercultural-communication field, individuals from cultures that rely heavily on unquestioning acceptance of authority would be much less likely to be open to different ideas, attitudes, values, and belief systems than would individuals from more "open" cultures. If that is so, then what it implies is that communication between individuals from different "closed-minded" cultures (or between individuals who are themselves more "closed" than others in their culture) should be much more difficult than communication between "open-minded" individuals from different "open" cultures. Much more specifically, intercultural research on this hypothesis will have to be conducted before any firm conclusions can be reached, but the prospects are intriguing that it will help to better understand (and facilitate) intercultural communication.

REALITY, PERCEPTION, AND MISPERCEPTION

Earlier we argued that objective reality may exist but that humans can never "know" reality: rather, they have perceptions of reality. That is an important enough assertion to warrant further discussion.

Whether in philosophy, politics, religion, or history, one always comes across assertions that there is a knowable reality and that honest people just have to be willing to look at all the facts to know that reality. I'm afraid that I must challenge that notion directly. If the people who study the way we learn about the world are correct—and everything I will say in this work assumes that they are—then we learn about the world through our sensory receptors. Further, I believe I have demonstrated here that each individual perceives "reality" differently. Now this raises some serious problems. If people's perceptions are valid for them, then how can any accurate communication occur between individuals? Can't individuals be wrong about something? Clearly they can. How then do we get out of the intellectual corner we seem to have painted ourselves into?

First, let me deal with reality. I am not arguing here that reality does not exist. Indeed, I'm certain it does. There are mountains and people and wars and even ideas. Rather, I have been arguing that reality may be less important, in both determining and understanding human behavior, than are perceptions of reality. Since I cannot know reality directly but only through my sensory receptors, I tend to treat my perceptions of reality *as though they were reality.* That is, through a long series of trial-and-error tests I behave toward objects, people, events, and ideas as though they were what I perceive them to be.

As I write those words I pause to contemplate how to illustrate what I mean. I look up at my bookcase and see row after row of books. Books exist. They are reality. I can hold and touch them. Wouldn't anyone—no matter from where—perceive them to be books? Not necessarily. In the first place, not all books are shaped like these or are made of the same materials. When I show friends a book from ancient Ceylon that I have in my collection, written on dried banana leaves each about two inches wide by fourteen inches long and held together by string running through two holes in each leaf and two painted wooden end pieces, they have absolutely no idea what it is. Second, many people in nonliterate societies have never seen a book and would have no idea what one was even if they were shown one. Have you ever seen a very young child playing with a book? Babies have no idea what a book is or what to do with it until they have been taught by their parents how to deal with it.

Third, ask a physicist what a book is. He might tell you it is a book, but he might also tell you that each page is merely a collection of certain kinds of molecules held together by a force field, while a chemist might tell you that the individual pages are actually wood pulp with a certain rag content treated in certain ways, then rolled into long sheets, dried, and later printed on with certain dyes having such and such chemical content. Some people in the book-printing business, on the other hand, might see the binding, the quality of the paper, and the typeface. Some people collect books merely because they "look nice" as a decoration for a room.

Books are real enough, but each person who comes into contact with them will view them differently. The ideas contained in the books are also real—but they are much more abstract than the physical book itself and thus open to much greater variety of interpretation than the book is. The more abstract the reality, the greater the variety of interpretation one should expect.

What about people? Surely they exist, but what kind of person is anyone? Every term I show my classes a very old film starring Richard Conti called *The Eye of the Beholder.* In that film Conti plays a character named Michael Gerrard. The film asks the question, What kind of person is Gerrard? It then goes on to show several different people's perceptions of him. A waiter in a lounge sees him as a "ladies' man," a taxicab driver sees him as a "hood," his mother sees him as a "good boy" who works too hard, the landlord of the artist's studio he rents sees him as "a lunatic," and the cleaning woman in the building sees him as a "murderer." The movie replays what happened in a twenty-four-hour period from each of those different perspectives and then shows the audience how Michael Gerrard views himself and the events of that period from his perspective. What is very clear is that each person in the film—including Gerrard—attended to different bits of information in forming an opinion of what he was like and what happened that day. But even questions of "fact" change in each retelling. From Gerrard's perspective, he told the cab driver to "Please be quiet. I'm trying to concentrate." From the cabbie's telling of it, he said, "Shut up, Mac. I'm busy." Which is reality? I'm not certain that we could know unless there was a tape recorder to play it back as it happened. But even then we might not know. The words could have said, "Be quiet," but the tone could have said, "Shut up." Or the words could indeed have said, "Shut up." We don't always say what we intend to say.

In the chapter on intra- and interpersonal behavior I will talk at much greater length about individuals, but suffice it here to say that we never truly know ourselves fully, let alone others. Since others know us less well than we know ourselves, it is inevitable that their perceptions of us (or our perceptions of them) will be very different from their perceptions of themselves. But whereas abstract concepts are open to more interpretation than are concrete concepts, so too, complex creatures like people are probably open to much more interpretation than are simple creatures like fish or dogs.

Somewhere out there, there is reality. Trying to know what that reality is, however, is not simple. In every age everyone has his or her own perceptions of what that reality is. In medieval times people behaved toward the world as though it were flat. It wasn't, but never mind that. They thought it was and therefore tended not to travel too far for fear of falling off. Now people know it is round and therefore treat it differently. They know that they can get east by traveling west, and they do. They also know that they can get to the moon but aiming not at where it is when they start the trip but at where it will be when they get there.

If we all have different perceptions of reality, how can we differentiate what is more nearly "true" from what is "less true"? After all, there are such things as hallucinations, and we do recognize when someone has "lost touch with reality" and believes (and behaves) as though he were Jesus Christ or Napoleon. One could, after all, argue that he merely had a different perception of reality. I know that there are some mental health theorists who might very well take that point of view. Others would argue that it is only the "insane" who see reality and that all the rest of us who think we do and call ourselves "sane" are in fact deceived. Yet intuitively we know that those kinds of answers simply will not do. Neither, it seems to me, can we resort to a vote to determine what reality is. Copernicus and Galileo would both have been overwhelmingly outvoted. So too would Hellenists and Christians in early Rome and heathens and heretics during the Inquisition in medieval Europe.

It seems to me that the scientific solution of observing and noting what our perceptions of reality are, of formulating a hypothesis that helps us to explain what it is we think we observe and then of monitoring data to test that hypothesis, may be the most useful approach. No hypothesis ever holds true indefinitely. Rather, prevailing views of reality are retained so long as they are useful in helping to explain phenomena. As soon as we start finding data that "don't fit" that view, we begin to try to formulate a different hypothesis that might better help explain what it is we are looking at. The same thing happens in trying to explain things, events, people, and ideas.

Trying to determine what reality is takes a great deal of time and hard work.

This is particularly true of situations in which different individuals, groups, or nations have totally different perceptions about the same "reality," as they frequently do. But not all situations require that we test our perceptions of it. Indeed, very many probably do not. In most day-to-day situations in our life, nothing major is lost by trusting our perceptions of reality to be a fair assessment of what it really is—until we discover that we were wrong. When we do, then often no great harm has been done or will be done by changing our perceptions and searching for a new hypothesis that will better explain the event or phenomenon we want to know about. This principle says: "Assume our perceptions of reality are correct until proven otherwise." In other cases it is terribly important to come as close to reality as possible before making a decision about whether our perceptions are correct, as in a murder trial or an international event that could lead to war. I would argue that in those cases it is wisest to assume that our perceptions of reality are probably *incorrect*—or at least different from the perception of reality held by others—and hence to keep working to determine what reality is until we are convinced "beyond a reasonable doubt" that we know.

The other device we should be careful to try to preserve is a constant level of analysis. Are we looking at a total system or merely at a subset of a system? Because "he" tends to carry a knife, does that mean that everyone in one of the subsets to which he belongs is also likely to carry knives? And which subset is it that best helps to categorize and describe his behavior? Is it the subset based on his skin color, his age, his height, his socioeconomic class, his level of education, his intelligence, his sex, his sexual preference, his religious preference, his political preference, the food he eats, the movies he likes, the upbringing he has had, some "criminal personality," or his genes? Or is it some other subset that we have not yet thought of formulating?

Of course a book is a book at one level of analysis. But it is just as certainly a collectivity of molecules at another. Indeed it is precisely because of the existence of different levels of analysis that we must come to the conclusion that there is not just one but different "realities" out there, all of them, perhaps, equally valid. It may very well be the existence of these different realities on different levels of analysis, added to our differences of perception about reality—regardless of level—that makes for so much confusion.

If it is not possible for us to know reality directly, if we can know it only through our perceptions of it, and if each person's perceptions are inevitably different—and probably just as valid for him or her as mine are for me—then what are misperceptions? Doesn't the word itself imply that someone is "wrong" in the way he or she perceives reality? Not necessarily. That is one way to look at it, to be certain. But we could also argue that the word *misperceptions* most properly should be reserved for those situations when two (or several) individuals or groups are wrong about the way the other individuals or groups perceive an object, event, person, or idea. That is, it is not our, or their, perception of the event (or whatever) that is wrong but rather my perception of how they perceive the event that is wrong. In almost every conflict situation, for example, one group makes certain assumptions about why the other group is behaving the way it is. If those assumptions are incorrect—that is, if the other group is in fact not behaving the way it is because of the reasons the other group assumes, then that is a misperception. Not only why one group does what it does, but even what it does, may be misperceived.

If both you and I believe that the other is preparing to attack us, and neither of us is, that is a misperception. Further, if because I believe that you are about to attack I pick up a gun to defend myself, you are very likely to believe that your perceptions of me were correct and to point to my taking a gun as proof of my intention to attack you. Unfortunately this is precisely how most wars start. My reaching for a gun may indeed have been completely defensive, but can you take a chance in a situation like that? There is, after all, the chance—no matter how remote—that in fact I do intend to attack. Doesn't one have to do something to protect oneself? Of course. Since you can never know reality for certain, you have no alternative but to prepare for the worst. The only trouble is that as you prepare, I take that as further proof that it is you who are preparing to attack me.

The point is that people can be, and often are, wrong in the way they perceive situations, motives, or intentions. Whenever they are, we have to refer to that as a "misperception."

There are a great many things external to myself that I cannot know about for certain. But things about myself, in particular, I can know. When someone attributes actions or motives to me that are incorrect, that is a misperception and ought to be clarified as quickly as possible. Just because you and I perceive each other correctly will in no way assure that I will like you or that we won't have conflicts. But at least if misperceptions are clarified, we will know what it is we are disagreeing about and may be able to resolve our conflict peacefully. I submit, however, that in the overwhelming majority of cases of conflict situations, neither party really knows what it is precisely that they are fighting over because the misperceptions tend to obscure everything else.

Allow me to relate a true story about differing perceptions of reality to illustrate just how important such differences can be to successful intercultural communication.[30] Many years ago a successful American businessman by the name of Sam Green retired to the mountains of Guatemala, near Lake Attitlan. He had made his fortune doing business in Guatemala and had fallen in love with the land and its people. Every evening after sunset when the Indians in the region returned from the fields to their villages, he would ride out to their villages on his horse and sit for hours talking with them. He came to know and trust them very much, and they him. He had learned their language, their culture, and their reality world very well. They would tell him of their needs and their dreams. It seemed to him that many of the things these simple people wanted were the same things that people everywhere wanted: health, safety, food, security. He discovered that one of the problems they had in obtaining these basic things was lack of cash—sometimes very small quantities at that. To the peasants in those small villages a hundred dollars or a thousand dollars seemed like an inordinate amount of money—and given their reality world, it was. But he also learned that these Indians did have a little surplus cash, maybe only a penny or two per person, per day, but they did have some cash. Accordingly he hit upon the idea of loaning them the money to dig the well they needed, or buy the medicine, or whatever (never a lot of money—usually on the order of magnitude of a few hundred dollars). They, in return, promised to pay him back a penny, per day, per family, until the loan was repaid. Because these were a very honest people whose word was their bond, Sam Green was always repaid in full for every loan he made. Indeed, his efforts with the Indians were so successful that he established what came to be known as the Penny Foundation in Guatemala to institutionalize this practice.

One year Mr. Green returned to the United States for an extended period. Very shortly after he returned to Guatemala he was met by a representative of the Guatemalan government who wanted to know why it was that he—a foreigner—could get those Indians to pay back loans he made, but they, the government of Guatemala, could not. It seems that in his absence, one of the drinking wells in a village had gone dry, and the Indians had approached the government asking them if they would supply water. Since the village next to the one in question had a more than ample water supply, the government arranged to pipe the water from the over-supplied village to the dry village. The government thought that the villagers had agreed to pay back the government for this service, but when the government tried to collect, the villagers refused. Mr. Green said that he couldn't explain why that had happened until he spoke to the villagers in question. When he rode out to the village and asked what had happened, he was told that yes, the village well had run dry, but that now the government was trying to make them pay for the water they used—the government had imposed a water tax to recover the loan—and everyone knew that God gave water free. Mr. Green agreed that was so but pointed out to the villagers that while God gave water free, metal pipes were made by man, and they cost money. He asked if the villagers would mind paying the government back for the pipe it had bought and installed to bring the water to the village. Of course, the villagers had no problem at all agreeing to pay for the pipe, and thus the issue was resolved.

I think the story illustrates well my contention that for intercultural communication, perceptions of reality may be more important than trying to establish any intrinsic reality itself.

PROPOSITIONAL SUMMARY FOR CHAPTER 1

Culture: Culture is defined as a pattern of learned, group-related perceptions —including both verbal and nonverbal language, attitudes, values, belief systems, disbelief systems, and behaviors—that is accepted and expected by an identity group.

Group culture: Since, by definition, each identity group has its own pattern of perceptions and behavioral norms and its own language or code (understood most clearly by members of that group), each group may be said to have its own culture.

Perceptions: Perceptions are defined as the process by which an individual selects, evaluates, and organizes stimuli from the external environment. Those perceptions that are group-related are the ones that are sometimes used synonymously with the word *culture* in this work.

Attitudes: Attitudes are defined as likes and dislikes. They are our affinities for, and our aversions to, situations, objects, persons, groups, or any other identifiable aspect of our environment, including abstract ideas and social policies.

Value: A value is defined as an enduring belief that a specific mode of conduct or end-state of existence is personally or socially preferable to an opposite or converse mode of conduct or end-state of existence.

Value system: A value system is defined as an enduring organization of beliefs concerning preferable modes of conduct or end-states of existence along a continuum of relative importance. Since each individual and group ranks the importance of the values of the group differently, it is inevitable that some of the values an individual holds will be in conflict with the values of one or more of the other groups to which the individual belongs.

Belief system: A belief system represents all of the beliefs, sets, expectancies, or hypotheses, conscious and unconscious, that a person at a given time accepts as true of the world she or he lives in.

Disbelief system: A disbelief system is composed of a series of subsystems rather than merely one and contains all of the disbeliefs, sets, expectancies, conscious and unconscious, that to one degree or another, a person at a given time rejects as false.

Determinants of perception: Three sets of determinants of perception were analyzed: physical, environmental, and learned. It was argued that no two individuals can perceive identically because no two individuals have exactly the same physical sensory receptors. More important than physical differences among individuals are the learned differences among them. No two humans can have exactly the same life experiences—either group-related or individual—yet these learned differences account for the greatest variation in perception that individuals hold.

Reality: Reality exists, to be certain, but since our knowledge of the external world is learned, and since no two individuals perceive reality identically, it is argued that, for human behavior, perceptions of reality are more important than reality itself.

Misperceptions: The term "misperceptions" is used here to describe those situations when two (or several) individuals or groups are wrong about the way other individuals or groups perceive an object, event, person, or idea.

NOTES

[1] E. B. White, *The Second Tree from the Corner* (New York: Harper and Brothers, 1935), p. 173.

[2] This concept was presented first in an article entitled "Culture: A Perceptual Approach," published originally in *Vidya,* No. 3, Spring 1969, and more recently reproduced in Larry A. Samovar and Richard E. Porter, eds., *Intercultural Communication: A Reader,* 4th ed. (Belmont, CA: Wadsworth Publ. Co., 1985).

[3] From *Collected Papers on Metalinguistics,* quoted by Franklin Fearing in "An Examination of the Conceptions of Benjamin Whorf in the Light of Theories on Perception and Cognition," in Harry Hoijer, ed., *Language in Culture* (Chicago: University of Chicago Press, 1954), p. 48.

[4] Here I am using *language* in the broadest sense. It may include the jargon or symbols used by social scientists or mathematicians, for example, to express the concepts peculiar to their group, or it may include the myriad of nonverbal gestures sometimes referred to as body language.

[5] Ruth Benedict, *Patterns of Culture,* 1934; reprint (New York: Mentor Books, 1959), p. 18.

[6] C. T. Patrick Diamond, "Understanding Others: Kellyian Theory, Methodology and Applications," in *International Journal of Intercultural Relations,* 6 (1982), 401.

[7] In this work the terms *nation, state,* and *country* will be used interchangeably, even though some political scientists prefer to reserve the term *nation* for those countries that share one and only one ethnic, tribal, racial, and/or religious identity.

[8] Harry Hoijer, "The Sapir-Whorf Hypotheses," in Harry Hoijer, ed., *Language in Culture* (Chicago: University of Chicago Press, 1954), p. 94.

[9] Diamond, "Understanding Others," p. 403.

[10] Paraphrased in ibid., pp. 397, 396.

[11] Milton Rokeach, *The Nature of Human Values* (New York: Free Press, 1973), p. 5.

[12] Ibid., p. 7.

[13] Although drawn heavily from anthropological and social-psychological literature, this way of viewing culture is my own and can be used at every level of analysis—personal, group, or national.

[14] Since this is not a medical text, for the sake of readability, I prefer the imprecision of referring to the eyes simply as being the sensory receptors that handle visual perception and will do so in many similar instances throughout the work.

[15] Wilson Key, *Subliminal Seduction* (New York: Signet Books, American Library, 1974) and Joan S. Wilentz, *The Senses of Man* (New York: Thomas Y. Crowell, 1968).

[16] Richard W. Cottam and Ole R. Holsti are two scholars who come to mind. Cottam in particular, in personal communication to this author, argued the importance of temperament.

[17] Bernard Berelson and Gary A. Steiner, *Human Behavior: An Inventory of Scientific Findings* (New York: Harcourt, Brace & World, 1964), p. 104.

[18] Cited in D. Price-Williams, "Cross-Cultural Studies," from Brian M. Foss, ed., *New Horizons in Psychology* (New York: Penguin Books, 1966) and reprinted in Larry A. Samovar and Richard E. Porter, eds., *Intercultural Communication: A Reader,* 2nd ed. (Belmont, CA: Wadsworth Publishing Co., 1976), p. 34.

[19] All figures used in this example are completely hypothetical and are included merely to illustrate a concept. They are not based on any known research.

[20] An interesting variation occurred when I did that exercise in Pittsburgh some time ago. A Japanese student did *not* see the number 10, even though the Japanese write the number 10 the same way the Chinese do. Later when I asked him why, he said that it never occurred to him in the context of a Pittsburgh classroom that an American professor would know Japanese.

[21] Daryl J. Bem, *Beliefs, Attitudes, and Human Affairs* (Belmont, CA: Brooks/Cole Publishing Co., 1970), p. 14.

[22] See A. H. Maslow, "A Dynamic Theory of Human Motivation," in Charles R. Lawrence, ed., *Man, Culture and Society* (New York: Brooklyn College Press, 1962).

[23] Ibid., pp. 2–11.

[24] Milton Rokeach, *Nature of Human Values,* p. 20.

[25] Milton Rokeach, *The Open and Closed Mind: Investigations into the Nature of Belief Systems and Personality Systems* (New York: Basic Books, 1960), p. 33.

[26] Ibid., pp. 40–41.

[27] Ibid., p. 43.

[28] Ibid., pp. 45–46.

[29] Ibid., p. 47.

[30] Personal communication to the author by someone directly involved in the situation.

CHAPTER TWO
THE ROLE OF CULTURE
AND IDENTITY
IN COMMUNICATION

This analysis is based on a model I developed a number of years ago and have been refining ever since. Essentially it is a systematic set of premises[1] and hypotheses designed to help explain human behavior in general and intercultural communication in particular. Although these have been reproduced in many different places many times,[2] I present them here in greatly revised form because I believe they relate so specifically to problems of identity, behavior, and intercultural communication.

BASIC PREMISES

Any study of cultural, or identity groups[3] really has to start with the step before that and look at perceptual groups.

> *Premise 1. A perceptual group may be defined as a number of individuals who perceive some aspect of the external world more or less similarly, but who do not communicate this similarity of perception among themselves.*[4]

We established in the last chapter that not all people respond to the same stimulus identically, and that is true, but here we should look at the other side of that coin. That is, a number of people who have, or have had, some shared experience—whether it is having a baby, digging coal, or speaking a particular language—have a higher degree of similarity of perception about that experience than they do with people who did not or do not share that experience. Urbanites, ruralites, mothers, fathers, first children, second children, middle children, secretaries, bookkeepers, accountants, businesspeople, steelworkers, miners, carpenters, peasants, teachers, students, fat people, skinny people, tall people, short people, young people, old people, doctors, lawyers, Indian chiefs, rich men, poor men, beggarmen, thieves, sick people, healthy people, religious people, atheists, communists, capitalists, socialists, fascists, black folk, white folk, yellow, red, and tan folk, virgins, nonvirgins, curly haired, straight haired, and no-hair men, nymphomaniacs, and acrobats all share some degree of similarity of perceptions with others who do the same things they do, who value the things they value, or who are the way they are. But if they don't communicate with each other they don't know that others think or feel as they do. I will remain an "I" until somehow you and I communicate and discover that together we form a "we."

Let us take the example of the peasant. Peasants the world over have an extraordinarily high degree of similarity of perception.[5] Most tend to be fatalistic, religious, awed by natural phenomena, tradition bound (whatever that tradition happens to be), with a deep sense of suspicion of "outsiders." There are probably a great many additional perceptual and attitudinal traits that peasants have in common with each other, but my intention here is not to list all of their similarities of perception. Rather, I mean to establish the fact that those similarities do exist. Despite the wide range of similarities among them, notoriously peasants do not communicate with other peasants, except perhaps with those from the next village. Part of the reason, of course, is the fact that the world view of peasants is so limited that they probably do not know that others with very similar views to their own exist by the millions and tens of millions on other continents. For many peasants the world does not exist any farther than perhaps fifty miles from where they were born, and if it does exist, it does so in only some dimly thought through, abstract way. In addition, the peasant is almost by definition voiceless. It is true that sons of peasants increasingly are going off to the big city to get their education, but once they have gotten that education they cease being peasants. Rarely if ever do educated children of peasants return to the land of their forefathers. But if people do not communicate with one another, they don't know that there are others out there who feel much the same about many aspects of the world as they do. Unless they communicate they cannot become a group. Given that they do not communicate among themselves, how is it possible for them to share such a high degree of similarity of perception? Indeed in premise 3 below I will argue that the less communication occurs the less likely it is that there will be similarities of perception. The answer, it would seem, has to do with the rather universal relationship of the peasant to nature. Everywhere peasants are equally at the mercy of the vicissitudes of nature for sun, rain, food, shelter, and even life and death. My guess is that this universally perceived dependency on nature—or on the gods—produces a rather universal response.

Oscar Lewis, Michael Harrington, and others who have worked extensively with poor people in various parts of the world are able to refer to a *culture of poverty*.[6] What they mean by the term is the high degree of similarity of world outlook, attitudes, and belief systems poor people seem to share, again, perhaps, because of the universality of their experience—in this case extreme poverty. Like the peasant, a poor person from Mexico City probably doesn't even know that Calcutta exists, let alone that there are poor people there who share a very similar world view. Yet despite the differences in language, religion, food preference, and the like, if poor people could communicate, they would probably be amazed to discover how very similarly they perceive the world.

Just because certain people don't know that there are others out there who think the way they do—about something—doesn't mean that they comprise an unimportant category of people. In fact it may be the most important category. Underlying every identity group is a perceptual group.

> *Premise 2. A number of people who perceive some aspect of the external world more or less similarly and recognize and communicate this similarity of perception form an identity group.*

The key words here are *recognize* and *communicate*. Sometimes I recognize that I share a similarity of perception with someone else merely by looking at that person. Recognition is, after all, a form of communication.

Individuals who share some similarity of perception but do not (or are not able to) communicate about the similarity of perception are not a group. A group—a sense that we are not alone—cannot form until two or more individuals communicate the fact that they share a common identity or view of something. Once they do communicate that similarity, verbally or nonverbally, they have become an identity group.

Knowing who "we" are is a learned process. That is, while it is true that one may just be born into a particular family, or have skin of a particular color, or what have you, that by itself is not what establishes identity. What establishes the identity is the learning that occurs in the process of being socialized into the group that tells us that one particular characteristic or another distinguishes "us" from "them." We have to learn that he or she is "one of us," but that this other person is not. What's more, subtly, ever so subtly, from the moment of birth we learn how "we" do things. Most often we learn just by the way we are held or spoken to or fed or by listening to adults talk. No one ever sits down and says to us, "Ok, now I am going to hold you just this way and I want you to remember that because when you grow up and have babies that is the way you will have to hold your children if you want them to grow up to be one of us." No. It's all far more subtle than that. Learning who we are and "how *we* do things" and how *we* see the world occurs in much the same manner as learning our first language. We just hear words over and over again and gradually—very gradually—over the course of time we come to identify those words with particular meanings. In the same way we also learn the attitudes, values, and belief systems our parents and other group "elders" teach us. Children don't begin to learn to differentiate skin color or hair texture or size and shape of nose or those other little differences that adults find so very important until well after they are old enough to talk. But learn them they do. Identity-group learning occurs whenever we experience something that others in our identity group have experienced.

Think of a number of people working at the same kind of task or job. It doesn't matter whether the job is raising young children, studying chemistry, or working at a particular kind of occupation. In the course of doing that work, experiences are being shared by all of the people doing the kind of task that is unique to that work. No other collectivity of individuals doing other kinds of tasks will share exactly the same experiences. In the course of becoming "specialists" in the accomplishment of those tasks, they will all learn to use the same kinds of tools. A shorthand language will be learned, which will be understood by other people doing the same kind of task but not understood by people doing different kinds of tasks. Acronyms will develop rather quickly. A way of thinking about how to accomplish the task will be developed, as will common expectations and "acceptable" patterns of behavior. The more everyone involved in accomplishing a certain task shares these similarities of perception, the easier it is for those people to communicate—thus the more efficiently the task can be accomplished.

Those examples were all task or job oriented, but there are many, many similarities of perception which develop around other things. Think, for example, of people from the same ethnic background. Again certain ways of thinking about the world are shared, a taste for certain kinds of foods, a preference for a certain kind of dress develops. Certain folk heroes are esteemed by one group and are unknown to others. Do you know how long it takes to cook chitterlings?[7] Do you know who Crispus Attucks was? If you are a black American the overwhelming probability is that you know. If you are not, the overwhelming probability is that you do not know. What about Garibaldi? Or Asoka? If you are Italian or Indian you know.

Similarly, adherents of religious, political, or other ideologies also form identity groups. Catholicism as practiced in Latin America is certainly markedly different from the variety practiced in Dublin or Chicago. Despite those differences, however, two religious Catholics, wherever they are from, can usually communicate *about religious matters* with a much higher degree of similarity of perception and identity than could, say, a Catholic and a Baptist both from Chicago. Or consider the Trotskyites in Bolivia or Sri Lanka. Why those two countries—and only those two—should have fairly large and well-established old Trotskyite parties is one of those mysteries that someone may some day try to explain. They are literally half a world apart geographically and in many other ways, but when it comes to their world political views, the degree of similarity of perceptions of the members of those parties is astounding.

It should be noted that it is not only important whether a specific group views itself as different; it is also important whether the society in which the group lives *accepts* its members as "one of us" or views them as alien. Thus, for example, while the Jews in Nazi Germany may have viewed themselves—or may have wanted to view themselves—primarily as Germans, their society viewed them, at best, as a particular kind of Germans (German-Jews) and, at worst, as not German at all. Faced with that circumstance, regardless of personal preference, most German-Jews had no choice but to see themselves as members of a group separate from other Germans.

Let me take a moment here to discuss further this question of the relationship to identity of how others see us as opposed to how we see ourselves. Some groups are highly inclusive, and others are highly exclusive. White America tends to be highly exclusive. If you have even 1/64 black ancestry you are considered by American society as "black." Now it makes absolutely no sense from any point of logic that someone who is 63/64 "white" should be considered "black" by society. But there is nothing logical about group identity. The prevailing white sentiment is that anyone with "even a drop of black blood" is black, and most whites will treat that person accordingly, regardless of how white his or her physical features may be.[8] If society treats one as though he were black, there is no way the individual can come to think of himself as anything but black.

> *Premise 3. Other things being equal, the higher the degree of similarity of perception that exists among a number of individuals, the easier communication among them is likely to be, and the more communication among them is likely to occur. Conversely, where there is little or no communication among individuals there tends to be a decrease in similarity of perception, which in turn tends to make further communication more difficult.*

This premise postulates a spiraling of communication or noncommunication. Stated simply, it argues that the easier communication is, the more we tend to communicate. The more we communicate, the more we share our perceptions with others. The more we share our perceptions with others, the easier still communication becomes. And so it spirals, with increased communication tending to lead to greater sharing of perceptions, and with greater sharing of perceptions tending to lead to greater ease of communication, and greater ease of communication tending to lead to still further increased communication. The problem with intercultural or intergroup communication is the spiraling in the opposite direction. That is, the very similarity of perceptions and sharing of common values, attitudes, beliefs, and languages that makes communication within a group so much easier makes communication between different groups that much harder. Less communication tends to lead to *less* sharing of perceptions (or greater dissimilarity of perception), and with less similarity of perception, communication tends to become more difficult. The more difficult communication becomes, the less people tend to communicate. Actually this is more than merely a premise. There is some hard empirical evidence to support it.[9]

One is almost forced to believe that this process is precisely how the proliferation of different cultures came into being in the first place. Somewhere back in history living conditions probably became too crowded for all the people who lived on the mountain, so they probably sent out a colony of their own kind, who started living in the valley. Because environmental conditions in the valley were different from conditions on the mountain, people had to do things somewhat differently in the valley. And because it was probably difficult for people from the valley to get back to the top of the mountain to visit friends and relatives there, they probably did so very infrequently. As time and generations passed there were probably fewer inclinations to "go back to the old country" because there wasn't anyone there any longer whom the people in the valley knew. So people in the valley would communicate almost exclusively with other people in the valley while people on the mountain would communicate almost exclusively with other people on the mountain. As the years and decades and centuries passed, someone from the valley venturing to the mountain would almost certainly find that "they don't do things on the mountain the way we do them back home." What is more, our adventurous traveler would probably find that the people on the mountain couldn't understand him when he spoke and that he couldn't understand them. And so it has gone for centuries as "people from the mountains" on every continent have ventured into their valleys setting up new homes and new cultures, ever increasing the differences among humankind. At least that was the way it was until the communication and transportation revolutions of the nineteenth and twentieth centuries, which now make it increasingly easy and necessary for valley and mountain people to communicate with each other.

Premise 4. As the number and importance of identity groups that individuals share rise, the more likely they are to have a higher degree of group identity. That is, the more overlapping of important identity groups that an individual shares with other individuals, the more important that particular group of people is likely to be to him or her.

The more group identities we share with someone—and the more important they are—the less intercultural (and therefore the less difficult) communication is likely to be. The fewer group identities we share—or the less important they are to us—the more intercultural (and therefore the more difficult) a communication is likely to be.

If I share membership in twenty different perceptual groups with one person and share membership in only five with another person, clearly the range of subjects about which I will be able to communicate easily will be greater with the first person than with the second, provided that the importance I assign to each of these identities is constant (which they rarely are. See premise 7.) Similarly, if there are a group of people with whom I share fifteen or twenty different identities, not only will communication tend to be much easier in that group than it would be in a group with whom I shared fewer identities, but there is a strong probability that I would have a higher sense of loyalty to the former group than I would to the latter. The people with whom we feel the greatest comfort (and those we trust most) tend to be those with whom we share the largest number of identities.

From all that has been said thus far, it should be clear that the more groups we share in common with people, the easier communication with them is likely to be. Conversely, the fewer group perceptions or identities we share with people, the more difficult are communications with them likely to be. The reasons should be obvious. The more group perceptions we share with people, the greater will be the range of subjects on which we can communicate easily. Sharing the same values and perceptions on a wide range of issues will make it less necessary to constantly probe to try to find out which of their beliefs or attitudes or values are simply outside of our perceptual ken. In addition, the more groups we share in common, the more cultural languages we will share, thus making communication (including feedback) that much easier.

Having said that, however, let me be very explicit: It is much more intercultural for me to try to communicate with, say, a steelworker in a different neighborhood of Pittsburgh than it is for me to communicate with another college professor in, say, Malaysia. Despite differences of race and nationality, my Malaysian counterpart and I share a very high degree of similarity of perception because of our education level (some of us would even have studied with the same professors), social class, professional identification, and the like. To be sure, there are some group identities I share with the steelworker—being Americans, Democrats, fathers, men—but even there, my attitude toward women, for example, is probably much closer to my Malaysian college professor's counterpart than it is to the American steelworker's.

Obviously it is not just the number of group identities one shares with another but also the importance of those group perceptions in molding one's most basic attitudes, values, and beliefs that determines just how intercultural any communication will be. Of course, how difficult communication will be will depend in large part on the subject under discussion. Little as I may know about baseball, it would be much less intercultural for me to discuss the standing of the Pittsburgh Pirates with a steelworker than it would be for me to try to discuss that topic with a Malaysian college professor. On the other hand, if Plato is what I want to discuss, I'd better look for someone with a college education to discuss him with.

In most societies the family enjoys the highest degree of group identity and loyalty. One reason this is so is that the members of the family group are also concurrently members of so many other perceptual groups. Thus, with rare exceptions, all adult members of a family speak the same language, are from the same locality, are of the same ethnic group or tribe, are of the same religious persuasion, have approximately the same educational level, are of the same socioeconomic class, are very likely to be employed in the same occupation grouping, and so on.

What is more, particularly in more traditional societies, the family or clan is the group that members are taught to trust most. That perception is reinforced by positive, supportive behavior from other family members, and thus all the messages coming to the individual support the notion that the family is, and should be, the group in which there is the greatest ease of communication and to which one owes his or her highest loyalty. (More will be said about this in premise 7.)

In the more mobile societies of urban industrial areas, this sense of loyalty to family begins to break down. I would argue that this happens in part because family members share fewer and fewer common perceptions and identities. It is not unthinkable in more urban societies for the children to be better educated than the parents; to marry someone of a different religion, ethnic group, or even race; to live in a different city; and to be part of a different class. In some countries it is not even that unusual for the children to prefer to speak English or French as their first language at home, instead of the mother tongue that their parents speak. No wonder that the intensity of family identity breaks down. But what replaces it when it does break down? I submit that in large degree it is replaced by those friends with whom we share many group perceptions and identities.

Think for a moment of the five people you would consider your "closest" friends. Define *close* here as the ease with which you can communicate with them on a wide variety of subjects. Now think of all the group identities you share in common with them. (You may well find that you share some identities with one or two of those people and different identities with others. That's fine.)

If you are like most people, you have probably left out the most obvious identities—the ones that are so obvious that one doesn't even think of them—like race, class status, educational background, age, political preference (not necessarily party affiliation), and religious predilection (again not necessarily membership in the same religious organizations—although that is possible). There is a reason for this—it is not an accident. Similarities of perception and group identities are often such subtle phenomena that we are simply unaware of them until (a) we come across others with whom we do not share those similarities of outlook, values, world view, and so on, and/or (b) until someone violates a group norm we so take for granted that we don't even think of it as a group norm. Sharing of group attitudes, values, and beliefs is a very subtle process. Most often that sharing remains below the level of consciousness. There is something about each of us—whoever we are—that tends to make us feel comfortable with "one of our own." Of course, this is not true in every case, but it is true in so many more cases than it is not as to go almost unnoticed.

One further note: We have already established that no two individuals can perceive identically. But suppose they could. Would any communication between them be necessary? I would argue that it would. In the first place, as we shall see in the communication chapter, feedback is an integral part of the communication process. I would not know that the other person's perceptions were identical to my own unless there was a great deal of feedback on a wide range of topics. Communication would be easy to be sure (like the transfer of energy without any friction), but it would have to occur. Second, there is a strong probability that I would communicate *more* with someone whose perceptions were identical to mine precisely because of the ease of communication and because I would be assured that the subjects that interest me most would also be the subjects that interest that other person most.

David Hoopes has argued that "communication is a process by which human dissimilarities are negotiated."[10] I agree with that statement, but I would argue that communication is also a process by which human similarities are shared. Thus I could carry on an enormously satisfying conversation with that other person who shared 100 percent identical perceptions, all of the time having my own perceptions, attitudes, values, and beliefs reinforced with no loss of energy. What a satisfying fantasy! What is more I wouldn't even have to feel guilty about talking to myself.

Premise 5. Any "we" (identity group) comes into much sharper focus when juxtaposed against any "they" (a different identity group).

Cultural values and identities are so all pervasive and subconscious that we simply take them for granted, only rarely, if ever, being aware of them on a conscious level. The moment *we* are juxtaposed against some other group we have no choice but to become conscious of that identity. This is particularly so if that other group is perceived by us to be hostile or threatening.

Most of the time most of us whose major identities are associated with majority groups are only dimly aware of some of our most important identities. That they are important in molding our attitudes, values, and behaviors there can be no question, yet for the most part most of us associate with other people who are so like us (indeed that is precisely why those identities are so important—they are constantly being reinforced) that we tend not to be conscious of them at all. We just take them for granted. Think of the white, male, middle-class American who spends most of his time associating at work and at play with other white, male, middle-class Americans. Rarely would he become conscious of the importance of those four identities to his behavior. Yet we know that each of them profoundly influences how he thinks and behaves. But let him just set foot into a predominantly black or Chinese neighborhood or onto an American Indian reservation, and instantly he becomes very conscious indeed of the color of his skin. Or let him have to deal with a group of very upper-class white Americans, or a group of very lower-class white Americans, and instantly he will become extremely conscious of his class identity. Now admittedly, the longer one stays in those "other" groups, the less conscious he is likely to become of the difference between himself and the others. But that is precisely because the way they talk, the way they think, and the way they act will eventually become less strange and more predictable. The same holds true for virtually any identity one can mention. As long as we surround ourselves with others who share the same identities as we do—and most of us do exactly that—we operate more comfortably in our environment. Because it is more predictable and because it is so familiar there we don't have to make a great many things explicit, and because it is so easy we tend to think about it very little. As soon as we step out of that familiar environment, however, everything has got to be made explicit, and it takes a great deal more psychic energy just to get the simplest tasks accomplished.

As with the examples in the previous chapter on the relationship of stimulus to surroundings, when everyone else is just like us, we tend to "fade into" our surroundings and not notice ourselves. But surround us by "them" and suddenly we stand out sharply. What is more, context is all important in determining who we perceive ourselves to be at any given moment. Regardless of ethnic background, Americans overseas are likely to see themselves as—and be seen by others to be—Americans. At home, however, their American identity fades (becomes less salient), and their identity as Polish-Americans, Irish-Americans, or any other of the hyphenated identities we all hold becomes more important in describing themselves.

The more threatening "they" are, the more sharply the differences are seen. For minority groups—whatever the minority—this is precisely the problem. They can try to surround themselves with "their own kind," but it may not be easy. Like it or not, they are usually forced to deal with the dominant majority. This situation is particularly so with the smaller minority groups. Most often their perception is that the majority is hostile toward them; thus (a) they are constantly reminded of their minority identity, and (b) they are being forced to exert that greater amount of psychic energy (required in dealing with "them") more often than majority people are forced to, simply by virtue of the numbers involved. This of itself is both anxiety producing and tiring.

Have you ever wondered why most big cities have so many ethnic and racial neighborhoods? I submit that is precisely because we all prefer to be with the people who are like us. Sometimes it is quite conscious. When the immigrants were pouring into the big industrial cities in the northeast United States in the later nineteenth century, they were drawn to those neighborhoods where people from the old country (in some cases even people from the same village or region in the old country) had settled before them. The things that drew them were shops where they could buy familiar foods, other people with whom they could converse in the mother tongue, churches where they could worship in a familiar setting, and perhaps most important, they were drawn to the place where there were a lot of other people like themselves—people who shared their values and attitudes—so that for a part of each day they could feel comfortable. For too many hours of each day "we" felt very conscious of what made us different. In the evening we wanted to "relax" and feel "at home."

I would submit that any "they" group is slightly threatening just because they are different. The more hostile they are, however, the more intensely we are likely to recognize and try to defend our identity.

Premise 6. If we want to communicate effectively with one of "them" it is important to get to know their perceptions, attitudes, and values as well as their cultural language. The more like them we become, the easier communication with "them" will become. But it may make communication with "us" more difficult.

As I argued before, since we are all human animals, no two individuals share zero percent similarity of perception, and thus we should be able to communicate at least on the most rudimentary human-animal level. I start from the axiom that no human communication is impossible. It is just more difficult with those with whom we share the fewest group identities. The more we get to know them, however, the easier communication becomes. In part that is because the better we know them, the more we get to understand their attitudes, values, and beliefs. We may not accept those perceptions as our own, but at least we will understand what they believe, and eventually we will learn how to communicate with them more effectively.

Throughout this work I have argued, thus far, that if we want to communicate effectively with "them," it is important for us to learn their cultural language. We can do that most effectively by living among them and getting to know them well. One of the problems with that is that the longer I live among them and learn their attitudes, values, and beliefs, the possibility exists that I will become more like them. At least, the more I speak their cultural language (which I must if I want to communicate with them), adopt their style of dress, mannerisms, and so on, the easier it will be for me to communicate with them, to be sure, but the less my own group is likely to continue to view me as one of "us."

This is a dilemma for anyone who has to work with "them." If I want to communicate with them effectively, I have to put my message into language they can understand. In order to do that, I have to learn their attitudes and values and their cultural language so that I can translate my message into terms they can understand and accept.

That is precisely the kind of people John and Ruth Useem describe when they write about "third-culture people."[11] By that they mean people who are originally from one societal group who have lived, studied, or worked in another society so long that they are no longer like other people from their native society. On the other hand, neither are they totally like the people in the society they have lived in. Rather they are a blend of both and become in the Useems' terms, "third culture."

Theoretically these people should be in an excellent position to act as a bridge between the two societies because they speak the verbal and cultural languages of each. Thus they could translate messages from one group to the other. The problem is, however, that in the process of learning the other society's language and attitudes, they run the risk of being perceived by their original culture as no longer "one of us," but rather as being more like them. Further, their new group is not likely to accept these people as one of us either. Thus they tend to become a group unto themselves.

Think of the person from the black ghetto who wants to have an impact on the white middle-class establishment in order to make things better for his group. Certainly that is a major intercultural communication. One of the only ways he can do that is to learn the white middle-class-establishment culture. The black person who does and does that well may indeed succeed in getting his message translated into terms the white establishment can understand and accept, but in the process he runs a definite risk of being perceived by his own group as having sold out. Every black kid who originally came from "the street" but went to college faces this problem with his or her former peers.

The same holds true for the foreign-affairs officer who is sent abroad. In order to be effective she must learn not only the spoken language of the foreign country but the cultural language as well. The longer she is there, the more open to learning about them she is, and the more effective she could become in translating messages from our government to their government in language that they could understand and accept. The only problem is that if she is very successful in learning about the other culture, she runs the risk of being perceived by us as having "gone native" and runs the risk of being recalled. Indeed, no matter how successful any foreign-service officer is at communicating across cultural barriers, most governments will send him or her on another assignment after four years precisely because of their fear that if the foreign-service officers stay in one country too long, they will begin valuing *their* culture and *their* beliefs over ours.

The point should not be overstressed, since most of us have more problems learning "enough" about them, than we do about learning "too much." Still, it can be a problem one should be aware of.

Premise 7. Every individual must inevitably be a member of a myriad of different perceptual and identity groups simultaneously. However, one shares a higher degree of similarity of perception and a higher degree of group identity with some groups than with others. Consciously or otherwise (usually subconsciously) one always rank orders these identities. Not only is each individual's rank order unique but that order varies as the context (environment) varies.

All of the identities we hold have some impact on our behavior. The more important the identity, the more it influences are attitudes, values, and beliefs, and the more it will influence our behavior, consciously or otherwise. Although the ranking of these identities can and does change with time and circumstance, to understand human behavior at any given moment it is important to know which identities are primary and which are only secondary or tertiary in that particular circumstance.

Getting to know our group identities is very complex. That is because we are members of so many different groups simultaneously. Still we are not a member of an infinite number. By identifying the groups of which we *are* members, we also identify some of the groups of which we are not members. If I am a man, I am not a woman. If I am middle-aged, I am neither young nor old. If I am an urban person, then I am not rural. If I am a parent, then I am not childless. If I am educated, then I am not uneducated. If I received a certain kind of education at a certain institution of higher education, that means that I did not receive any number of other kinds of education at any one of the perhaps thousands of other institutions that I did not attend. If I do one or two or even three different things in order to make a living, I am not doing any of the thousands of different things that other people do in order to earn their living. If I am middle-class, then I am neither poor nor rich. If I am white, then I am not one of four or five other shades I might be. If I am an American, then I am not a citizen of the hundred and eighty-odd other countries of the world. If I am of one religious persuasion, then I am not a part of several hundred other religions that exist in the world. If I speak English as my mother tongue (no matter how many other languages I may have learned later), then I do not speak any other of the thousands of other languages that people speak as *their* mother tongues.

If I really wanted to do a thorough job listing all of the identities of which I am a part—and of those of which I am not a part—then I should keep going at this, listing as many categories as I can possibly think of. Having done that, I should then try to rank how important each of those groups (of which I do form a part) has been in molding my perceptions. Almost all I have listed here are *extremely* important. I have not listed on these pages any identities that are of secondary or tertiary importance in molding my perceptions, and certainly there are hundreds of those. But a list like this helps me identify who I am. By ranking the identities—in specific contexts—I begin to see just how important each has been—or continues to be—in shaping my attitudes and values in those contexts. I may have great difficulty in ranking some of them, but that may be because I cannot think of them in the abstract but rather only in concrete situations. I know, for example, that my identity as a teacher is extremely important to me. I also know myself well enough to know that if there were ever to be a conflict between my responsibilities as a teacher and my responsibilities as a parent, the latter would certainly take precedence. That tells me something about how I rank each of those identities, and how they affect my behavior.

In premise 4 we discussed the fact that the more identity groups people share in common, the more loyalty they are likely to show to those people. While that is undoubtedly true, it did not deal directly with the question of *intensity* of identification. There is no doubt that we do not identify equally with all groups. Some are clearly more important to us than others. For some people religious or ideological identification can be all consuming. For other people it may be family, class, profession, ethnic group, race, or nation that is all consuming. For some people it may be level or type of education that is most important for their world view. Each one of us has some identities that are clearly more important for our behavior than others.

Richard Cottam has argued, not without some merit, that primary identities should be considered those for which an individual would sacrifice most of his time, most of his money, and if need be, his life. He has argued that secondary identities are those for which the individual would sacrifice only some of his time and money. For a tertiary identity, argues Cottam, the individual would be willing to sacrifice only some of his time and perhaps a little money.[12]

Whether those are the "yardsticks" that ought to be applied to measure the importance of particular identities or not, the point is well taken. People are often willing to kill and to die if they perceive a threat to the group that they define as being primary to themselves at any given moment. Thus for centuries identities like loyalty to a particular monarch, religion, ethnicity (often associated with language), and/or race (however defined) were (and in some cases still are) the primary identities for which many people have willingly died. More recently, identities like nationalism and ideology have become the primary identities over which people fight. For over one hundred years Europeans killed each other over Protestant versus Catholic identities, yet only a few centuries later Catholic Germans and Catholic Frenchmen were quite willing to kill each other in the name of their "higher" loyalty to nationalism.

Now, nationalism itself is a relatively new identity. It actually started with the American and French Revolutions and spread over most of the rest of the world in the nineteenth and twentieth centuries. For many people it is the most important identity they hold. What makes its hold over people so very strong is precisely the fact that it often combines language, ethnicity, religion, and long-shared historic memory as one people attached to a particular piece of land. Given what I talked about in premise 4 (when people share a number of important groups, it reinforces identity) it is no wonder that nationalism has become such a powerful primary identity. In the early twentieth century, particularly, it was thought that ideologies like democracy and communism would overtake nationalism as the primary loyalty to which people gave their allegiance, but during World War I the United States was talking about making the world safe for democracy while being aligned (for a short time) with czarist Russia against imperial Germany. And in the late twentieth century, while communism is specifically supposed to transcend nationalist loyalties, the two communist giants, Russia and China—for primarily nationalistic reasons—seemed, for twenty-five years, much more likely to go at each other than against their supposed common enemy, capitalism.

One final note about these primary identities: while it is the large group that more or less subconsciously decides which identity will take precedence in any historical period or context, there have always been individuals who will not go along with the group decision as to which identity should be ranked higher. Thus in every time period and in every context, some individuals have dissented from their group definition of primary identification and instead followed the dictates of their own personal identity ranking.

Clearly, only a few identities are primary, and rarely is one called upon to die for them. Most of the time we take these primary identities completely for granted and think very little about how they affect our daily lives. Indeed being an American or Christian or white or middle class may very much affect the day-to-day behavior of most of the people who live in the United States, but as I argued earlier, they are usually consciously unaware of those identities until juxtaposed against some threatening "they." Most identities are not conscious, despite the effect they have on our behavior. We simply take for granted the multiple identities we hold and go about our daily business of being professionals, students, parents, children, spouses, or whatever without giving any conscious thought to how those identities affect our behavior and our ability to communicate with others.

Indeed, one of the human problems with the study of identities is the fact that we are nearly always unaware of just how important they are in molding our behavior. As I said before, if we surround ourselves with "our own kind," we may very well not be aware that we are behaving and thinking the way we do because of the way we see ourselves. In a sense this is the exact reverse of recognizing our identity when juxtaposed against "them." In the absence of a clearly identifiable "them," we tend to take for granted that everybody thinks and behaves the way we do. We simply are not aware that our own groups are constantly conditioning us to think and behave the way they do. So very much of this conditioning and socialization is so completely below our level of consciousness that we are unaware that it is going on until it is brought to our attention, usually when we juxtapose our values or behaviors against "theirs."

The other major problem involved with the study of the effects of identity on behavior is context. At work—whatever we do—most of us dress, walk, behave, and generally communicate like the workers we are. With our parents we behave as we believe children should; with our spouses or lovers we behave like spouses or lovers; with our children we behave like parents; with friends we behave like friends; and with acquaintances we behave like acquaintances. Each of these contexts determines not only how we will behave, but also how we will communicate. Remember that almost all of this is completely subconscious. Still, clearly, context determines which identity will take precedence and thus which will most influence our behavior. But context changes from moment to moment. In the same room can be our boss, our secretary, our parents, siblings, spouse, and children, and our communication with—and behavior toward—each will be different. What is more, we never get our behaviors mixed up. More will be said about this question of role-related behavior later in this chapter.

This whole question of context determining identity—and therefore behavior—cannot be overstated. Under what conditions will an international businessman behave like a businessman first and only secondarily as a national of his country? In what contexts does the head of an American religious voluntary agency operating overseas behave as a representative of her church, her organization, or her country? In what contexts did Henry Kissinger's identity as secretary of state take precedence over his identity as a German-Jewish-American? In what contexts did his other identities take precedence? One might have predicted (without knowing the man) before he became secretary of state that he would be overly favorable to Israel because of his ethnic heritage. Yet that proved not to be the case. When he was dealing with diplomats the world over, who had been his former students at Harvard, did he deal with them primarily as fellow diplomats or as their former professor?

I submit that while context is important in determining identity and therefore behavior, there is probably a "blending" that occurs on many occasions (of the type described by the Useems). The role of secretary of state may demand certain kinds of behavior—in broad outline—but the way those behaviors are played out will depend very heavily on the unique blend of identities of the occupant of the office and his personality.

The list of identities people construct for themselves—and the relative ranking of each of those identities (even in identical contexts) is never identical for any two human beings. Precisely because each human's experience in life has been different, his or her perceptions (and therefore identities) will be different. And that, more than anything else, explains why each of the four billion inhabitants of this planet is unique.

We do know that the identity that takes precedence in any given situation will dominate and determine a person's perception of the situation, which will further strengthen that identity—in very circular fashion. Perceptions do affect attitudes and values, which do contribute to and mold identities, which do affect behavior, which in turn does affect our perceptions, attitudes, values, and identities. This is the circle of causality that was discussed in the previous chapter.

What we do *not* know is (a) precisely which affects which and in what ways; (b) how to accurately measure the relative ranking (importance) of either perceptions or identities at any given moment (they are so highly situation related that they change from moment to moment); and (c) which is easier to modify.

Premise 8. It is not only possible but necessary to distinguish between personal, group, and national cultures.

By personal cultures I mean the unique, learned, group-related perceptions (including verbal and nonverbal language, or codes) stored in the memory of each individual's data-storage bank plus the highly individual ranking we all make of all of the attitudes, values, beliefs, disbeliefs, and norms of behavior of all of the groups with which each of us identifies. Since no person is likely to be a member of all, and only, the same identity groups as anyone else or is likely to rank all of his or her identities identically with anyone else's, the overwhelming probability is that no two individuals can be "culturally identical"—i.e., no two individuals are likely to perceive and rank their attitudes, values, beliefs, or disbeliefs identically. Further, since each person's experience in life is, and must be, different, so perforce, each person must be considered culturally unique. That is why it is not only possible but necessary to speak of each interpersonal communication as also an intercultural communication.

Regardless of how strongly any of us identifies with any particular group, there will always be some aspect of that group's cultural attitudes, values, or beliefs from which we will deviate ever so slightly—at a minimum. Indeed, if we were to take the time and make the effort, all of us could construct an entire list of characteristics that distinguish us as individuals from the broad cultural groups of which we form a part. None of us is merely the product of the groups to which we belong. Nor are any of us members of all, and only, the same group cultures. That is precisely what makes each of us humans unique. And while that makes for a more rich, varied, and interesting world, it also makes generalizing about people, and learning about intercultural communication, that much more hazardous and difficult. But while we may all be unique, that uniqueness does know bounds, and those boundaries are usually those that have been prescribed by one or more of the groups with which we identify.

By group culture I mean the symbiotic relationship that exists between a group as a whole and the individuals who comprise the group. A group, as such, does not have a data-storage bank in which to record its historic memory outside of the data-storage banks of each of the individuals who comprise the group. Nevertheless, that "collective memory" of the group (dispersed as it may be) cannot be overlooked. Every group *does* have a culture of its own. Every group *does* teach its members its own perceptions, attitudes, values, and so on. That is why at the outset we made that premise the most basic one of this entire work.

Aside from collective memory, by group culture I refer here also to the aggregate ranking of attitudes, values, beliefs, and disbeliefs held by members of the group. There is little doubt that the perceptions of the dominant members of the group (however defined) usually count more heavily in the collective memory of the group than do the perceptions of the more peripheral members, but the predominant cultures of the rank-and-file membership of the group cannot be overlooked. One can think of innumerable cases (ranging from small social clubs, through formal organizations like labor unions, to whole countries) where the "dominant members" have been overthrown precisely because their value systems came to diverge so significantly from the value systems of most of the other members of the group.

A nation is nothing more than a particular kind of group, as we shall see elsewhere. However, since every nation is made up of many different identity groups, and since no nation contains within its boundaries all, and only, the same groups as any other nation, and since no nation occupies exactly the same environment as any other nation or has had exactly the same history as any other nation, every nation may be said to have a culture unique to itself. That would seem to imply that every international communication is also an intercultural communication, and that is correct in most situations. But because some people rank certain of their group identities (and group cultural values) more highly than they do their national identity in certain situations, sometimes *inter*national communications are *less* intercultural than are some *intra*national communications. More about that in later chapters. Here the intriguing questions for scholars to determine are, In which situations are specific group cultures more important in determining an individual's behavior? and, In which situations are national cultures more important? Actually this is no different from asking, Which group identity will take precedence in which contexts?

> *Premise 9. It is inevitable that individuals, groups, and nations will have internalized elements of several different, even conflicting, value systems simultaneously. They are able to survive and function under this condition primarily because:*
>
> *a. They are able to identify in different degrees—and at different levels of consciousness—with each of the value systems;*
>
> *b. Most simultaneously held group identities only rarely come into direct conscious conflict; and*
>
> *c. When two equally ranked identities do come into direct conflict, the individual, group, or nation will attempt to find some third identity that can accommodate, neutralize, rationalize, and/or synthesize those conflicting value systems.*

This premise is very closely related to the theory of cognitive dissonance developed by Leon Festinger.[13] The major difference is that Festinger uses the term *cognition* to mean more or less the same things I mean when I talk about attitudes, values, and belief systems.

Festinger argues that "two elements are dissonant if, for one reason or another, they do not fit together."[14] Further, "If two elements are dissonant with one another, the magnitude of the dissonance will be a function of the importance of the elements."[15]

His basic contention is that the individual will find conflicts in simultaneously held value systems psychologically very disturbing and will strive to reduce those conflicts. He says:

> The presence of dissonance gives rise to pressure to reduce or eliminate the dissonance. The strength of the pressures to reduce the dissonance is a function of the magnitude of the dissonance. In other words, dissonance acts in the same way as a state of drive or need or tension. The presence of dissonance leads to action to reduce it just as, for example, the presence of hunger leads to action to reduce the hunger.[16]

While this is very much of an encapsulation of Festinger's theory, it is the portion that is most relevant to this premise.

Now I have been arguing throughout this chapter that each of the groups with which individuals identify teaches its members their own cultural values. That being so, it follows that some groups to which the same individual belongs may teach totally different and/or conflicting values. Indeed, it is almost inevitable that this should be so. An individual is able to survive this conflict and function for three reasons.

First, we do not identify to the same degree (or with the same level of intensity) with each of the groups of which we form a part. (See premise 7.) The fact that one is an American, for example (primary identity), is much more important in molding our attitudes, values, and behaviors than would be one's identity as, say, a lover of Italian sports cars (tertiary identity). An enormous portion of the things one liked and desired and did for most of the hours of every day would be markedly affected and colored by one's identity as an American. On the other hand, that same person's identity as an Italian-sports-car lover would only affect his attitudes, values, and behaviors concerning one kind of car he wanted to drive. If the two identities came into severe conflict (as they did for a few years during World War II), it would be relatively easy for the American to give up driving (or at least buying) his Italian car for the duration of the conflict. (During World War I a great many American classical music lovers refused to listen to German composers, for example.) Or one may be an avid sports fan and spend much of his free time either participating in or watching sporting events. But even the most avid sports fan would not let that affect his going to work every day. Admittedly, he might take off a day now and then when there was a big game he wanted to attend, but I suspect that for most people, their primary identity as "breadwinner" would take precedence and prevent them from doing that too often.

Second, one can survive and function while holding two or more conflicting value systems—even if they are very nearly equally ranked—because they probably do not come into direct conflict very often. On some broad level of generalization one's identity as, say, a university professor may be equally ranked with his identity as a father, but context often dictates which set of values will take precedence. Most of the time the two simply do not come into direct conflict. When he is in the university he thinks and acts as a professor. At home, on the other hand, he is most probably a father. The sets of attitudes and values that are associated with each identity would be totally inappropriate in the other context. (Unfortunately we all know people who do rank their professional identities more highly and find that they have little time for their children. They may tell themselves that they are being better fathers or mothers because they are "successful," but I would argue that that is a rationalization for their attaching more importance to their professional identity. Such a case, however, is not the type I am discussing in this example.)

Now, it can happen, of course, that two *equally ranked* identities can come into conflict. That leads us to our third reason people survive and function, which is really just a way of coping. If our university professor was a divorced female parent with custody of her children and did rank her professional identity and mother identity completely equally, she would be hard pressed to decide what to do if one of her children were sick and needed her at the same time that she was supposed to be at the university teaching a class. If the individual ranked either of those identities more highly, there would be no conflict. She would teach her course or be with her child without a moment's hesitation because the unequal ranking would make clear what she "ought" to do. But if she did rank them equally then indeed she would have a problem. One of the ways one usually gets around that problem of equal ranking of identities in conflict is to find some third identity to get him or her out of the conflict situation. For example, in the case just discussed, she might decide that her identity as a humanitarian required her to be with someone who was sick. Or she might decide that her role as "breadwinner" for the family demanded that she not risk her job by being absent. Either way she would probably seek some third identity that would relieve her of the conflict. Most of the time the decisions made are totally subconscious.

In the psychological literature under the heading of "psychosomatic illness" there is a classic example of what can happen when a person values two conflicting value systems equally and simply cannot bring himself to rank one over the other, or cannot find that third identity that will enable him to escape from the conflict. The example cited is of a young Englishman at the start of World War I who apparently *equally* valued his identity as an Englishman and as a pacifist. Had he been able to value his identity as an Englishman more highly, he would have had no trouble going off to war to defend his country. Conversely, had he valued his identity as a pacifist more, he would have had no trouble going to jail for his beliefs. But because he did value both equally, he simply could not decide to act on behalf of one or the other. People in such a state can be said to be ambivalent. As with most people who are ambivalent—who cannot make a conscious decision—he allowed himself to be battered by circumstances. When he was conscripted he could not bring himself to refuse to serve. Instead he probably told himself that even though in the army, he would not carry a gun. When they told him he had to carry a gun, he probably told himself he would not use it. This type of rationalizing and refusing to make a conscious decision in favor of one identity or the other continued until it could continue no longer. The moment ultimately arrived when he was handed a gun, told that if the Germans started to advance he was to fire, and unfortunately for him, the Germans did start to advance. To have fired the gun at that point would have been to allow his English identity to take precedence over his pacifist identity and to actually kill someone. Not to have fired the gun would have been to allow his pacifist identity to take precedence but at the cost of being a traitor to his buddies and to his country.

Because he could not choose on a conscious level between these two identities, his body chose for him at a subconscious level. At precisely that moment he went physically blind! He was sent back to a hospital in England where he was subjected to every physical test known. A healthy pupil involuntarily contracts and expands with a corresponding increase or decrease in light intensity. His did neither. Accordingly it was determined that he indeed had gone physically blind. Then on November 11, 1918, when the church bells all over England tolled the end of the war, the conflict that had produced his blindness was removed and he immediately regained his eyesight.

This is perhaps one of the most extreme examples in the literature of what can happen when someone is unable to choose between identities, but it is probably only different in degree to what happens to others in similar situations. We "get sick" or "faint" or find some other physical excuse not to have to choose.

Before we leave the discussion of this premise, let us look at another example, this time on a political level. In empirical research I conducted in Sri Lanka (then called Ceylon) more than twenty years ago I discovered that among the political elite there were three distinct identity groups: the "Westernized," the "traditional," and a third middle group, which I labeled the "emerging elite."[17]

The Westernized political elite spoke, read, and wrote in English as their preferred language; had either studied in the U.K. or in Ceylon's equivalent of Eaton and Harrow; preferred to wear Western-style clothes; and if given the opportunity, would have remade Ceylon into a tropical replica of Britain. The traditional political elite spoke, read, and wrote in Sinhalese as *their* preferred language; had studied largely in rural, traditional schools; wore traditional Ceylonese dress most of the time; and if given the opportunity, would have remade Ceylon in the image of the ancient Sinhalese kingdoms. The emerging elite, on the other hand, were what Harold D. Lasswell and Daniel Lerner described as "double-value-oriented."[18] They spoke, read, and wrote in *both* English and Sinhalese; they went to schools where they learned *both* Western and ancient Sinhalese history, culture, and values; they wore *both* Western and traditional dress; and given their choice, they would have created a society that was economically and technologically as modern as

Britain but culturally as distinctively Sinhalese as the ancient Sinhalese kingdoms. This third group did value both identities equally and was trying desperately to synthesize both of those conflicting cultural values. At the time I wrote that book I was not certain whether their efforts at synthesis would succeed or whether ambivalence would win out. Twenty years later it is still not clear. This forces one to believe that perhaps they really were more ambivalent than anyone would have hoped. Apparently they have just not yet forged that third identity that would allow them to develop economically but in a distinctive Sinhalese fashion.

Premise 10. The environment in which a communication occurs can be a major factor in determining how effective one can be in intercultural communication.

The context of an encounter is quite important for how I am going to feel in an intercultural communication. If the context of the encounter is my environment, where I am surrounded by people who are very similar to myself culturally, most of my attitudes and values will constantly be reinforced. I may find a visitor in my midst who has different perceptions, attitudes, and values to be "quaint," "amusing," or "interesting," but I am not likely to feel terribly threatened by her world view. She will be the one who is "different." If our meeting is merely casual, there is virtually no threat whatever. If I am going to have to work with her, that may be a little bit more difficult, but I can always console myself with the knowledge that given enough time she will "learn how we do things here." It is *she* who will have to learn our perceptions, attitudes, and values.

When the encounter is in the other person's environment, however, it is a totally different story. It is *I* who will have to do the learning. The entire burden of trying to figure out those sometimes very strange attitudes and values—to say nothing of language—falls on me. What is more, in my own environment—precisely because I do have a relatively accurate approximation of the attitudes and values of most of the people with whom I must work (or if I don't, it is not too difficult for me to find out, since I know what to look for and what to ask)—I feel a sense of efficacy. I know how to get things done; therefore, if you will, I have a sense of power. When in a totally foreign environment, however, not only does the burden of all the learning fall upon me but my very sense of identity—of who I am and the rightness of what I value—is challenged. Not only is living and working in a foreign environment tiring, it is threatening precisely because it involves a challenge to that identity. Since I do not share the attitudes and values—indeed since I may not even be certain what they are—it is much more difficult to get anything done. Hence there is also a challenge to my efficacy, and I may very well experience a sense of powerlessness. What is more, if there is no one there to reinforce my previously held values and attitudes, I may come to doubt their soundness myself.

We speak of some people "going native" in a foreign environment. What that means, of course, is an abandonment of one's own attitudes and values and the acceptance of theirs. I would submit that this is much less likely to happen if we are in that foreign environment with other members of our own groups whom we know and trust and with whom we identify. The reason that is so, of course, is that each of those people can reinforce the "correctness" of their own ranking of attitudes and values. When alone in a foreign environment—particularly when we are young and have not been thoroughly socialized into our own groups—there is much more likelihood of going native.

It is not working just in a foreign country that can be difficult. Trying to work in any city other than our own can be surprisingly more difficult than one might expect. In my own city I know how to get from here to there. I don't have to look at maps or constantly ask directions. I know what sections of town are safe and which are not, and I don't inadvertently wander into the "wrong part of town." Even the pace—how rapidly people move—changes from city to city, as do the norms for the time one is supposed to arrive at certain kinds of social functions. Also the way people are expected to dress at different professional and social functions varies from city to city within the same country. All of this must be learned by newcomers, and it can't help but impede their productivity and effectiveness—at least at first—if for no other reason than the time and effort that is required.

I would even go one step further and argue that one's effectiveness may be somewhat impaired by trying to do business in someone else's office. If I go to his office it may very well be he who sits behind *his* desk, who calls upon *his* secretary to take notes, who can choose to divert his attention from me by answering *his* phone when it rings. The situation is, of course, reversed when he comes to my office. That is why it is not uncommon, when neither party in a negotiation is willing to give even the slightest advantage to the other party, that meetings are sometimes arranged "on neutral turf," where neither party is any more "at home" than the other. This is, of course, quite common in all union/management negotiations, as it is in negotiations among nations. Often the only way one party will agree to meet on the other's turf is if the next meeting will be on the other party's turf.

All of this is presented here merely to highlight the importance of environment to the effectiveness of any intercultural communication.

> *Premise 11. Because biologic and environmental factors are ever changing, perceptions, attitudes, values, and identities are ever changing. Consequently, new perceptual and identity groups are constantly being formed, and existing groups are constantly in a state of flux.*

The biologic process is inextricable: we are young, teenagers, young adults, middle-aged, and old. Those growth and decay factors alone inevitably must account for constant changes in our identity. Yet those physical factors, as we have seen, account for only a fraction of our perceptions. Just think for a moment of the ever-widening circles of new experiences and associations attendant upon physical growth. In the first years of our life particularly, but often considerably longer, we are surrounded by the protective cocoon of family. Only rarely is the shell penetrated by an outsider, and when it is, most often the family acts as a shield between us and the intruder. Hence it is not at all surprising that it is the family identity that is the most basic and primary for most humans. As we learn to walk and talk our world widens, first to the houses and other children next door, and then to those at the end of the street. The next big step comes when we are allowed to cross the street (with not too much traffic) by ourselves. Suddenly the physical expanse of our world has doubled—along with all of the different people in it. Next comes school. If crossing a street opened the world, going to school is equivalent to exploring the planets. No matter how restricted the neighborhood served by the school, inevitably there will be children there from a vast array of cultural milieux. Suddenly we meet children of different economic classes, ethnic backgrounds, religions, and races. And the process continues. The further on we go in school, the more diverse the backgrounds of our classmates become. Not only are we associating with people from even more different kinds of groups but we are coming across even more different experiences and ways of viewing the world. At first most of them seem terribly strange. After a while they seem less so. Just think of all the groups we may have become a part of in the process. We have learned to read, and that event alone exposes us to centuries of thought. Yet even that is only a part of the academic experience. Beyond the academic there are sports, music, dance, and drama.

Still the process continues. Somewhere along the line we discover the wonders of the opposite sex and for most, eventually, that incredible institution called marriage. Suddenly we are a family ourselves, and wonder of wonders, parents. Then we watch what we were too young to remember, as our children go out and discover their own worlds. We can't help but compare how different our children's world is from our own. "We didn't have that when we were young." "The world was different back when I was growing up." Yet it is amazing: for all the differences we see, how very similar all children are.

Every culture changes, some more slowly than others. We are a part of so many different cultures in the course of our life it is inevitable that some of the groups with which we identify will change more rapidly than others. Some will disappear entirely. Yet others are constantly emerging. It may be true that the more things change the more they remain the same, but change they do.

PROPOSITIONAL SUMMARY FOR CHAPTER 2

Perceptual group: A perceptual group is a number of individuals who perceive some aspect of the external world more or less similarly but do not communicate this similarity of perception among themselves. Technically they are not really a group if they do not communicate among themselves. As soon as they do communicate about their shared perceptions they become an identity group.

Identity group: An identity group is a number of people who perceive some aspect of the external world more or less similarly and recognize and communicate this similarity of perception.

Spiraling of communication: Other things being equal, the higher the degree of similarity of perception that exists among a number of individuals, the easier communication among them is likely to be, and the more communication among them is likely to occur. Conversely, where there is little or no communication among individuals there tends to be a decrease in similarity of perception, which in turn tends to make further communication more difficult.

Sharing of identities: As the number and importance of identity groups that individuals share rises, the more likely they are to have a higher degree of group identity. That is, the more overlapping of important identity groups that an individual shares with other individuals, the more important the particular group of people is likely to be to him or her.

Recognition of identity: Any "we" (identity group) comes into much sharper focus when juxtaposed against any "they" (a different identity group). The moment "we" are juxtaposed against some other groups, we have no choice but to become conscious of that identity. This is particularly so if that other group is perceived by us to be hostile or threatening.

Getting to know "their" perceptions: If we want to communicate effectively with one of "them" it is important to get to know their perceptions, attitudes, and values, as well as their cultural language. The more like them we become the easier communication with "them" will become. But it may make communication with "us" more difficult.

Ranking of identities: Every individual must inevitably be a member of a myriad of different perceptual and identity groups simultaneously. However, one shares a higher degree of similarity of perception and a higher degree of group identity with some groups than with others. Consciously or otherwise (usually subconsciously) one always rank orders these identities. Not only is each individual's rank order unique but that order varies as the context (environment) varies.

Personal, group, and national cultures: It is not only possible but necessary to distinguish among personal, group, and national cultures. Personal cultures are those unique learned, group-related perceptions stored in the memory bank of each individual. Since no person is likely to be a member of all, and only, the same identity groups as anyone else, or is likely to rank all of his or her identities identically with anyone else, the overwhelming probability is that no two individuals can be "culturally identical"—i.e., no two individuals are likely to perceive and rank their attitudes, values, beliefs, or disbeliefs identically.

Group cultures are those symbiotic relationships that exist between a group as a whole and the individuals who comprise the group. Every group does have a culture of its own. Every group does teach its members its own perceptions, attitudes, values, and so on.

A nation is nothing more than a particular kind of group. Since every nation is made up of many different identity groups, and since no nation contains within its boundaries all, and only, the same groups as any other nation, and since no nation occupies exactly the same environment as any other nation or has had exactly the same history as any other nation, every nation may be said to have a culture unique to itself.

When values conflict: It is inevitable that individuals, groups, and nations will have internalized elements of several different, even conflicting, value systems simultaneously. They are able to survive and function under this condition primarily because

   a. They are able to identify in different degrees—and at different levels of consciousness—with each of the value systems;
   b. Most simultaneously held group identities only rarely come into direct conscious conflict; and
   c. When two equally ranked identities do come into direct conflict, the individual group or nation will attempt to find some third identity that can accommodate, neutralize, rationalize, and/or synthesize those conflicting value systems.

Communication environments: The environment in which a communication occurs can be a major factor in determining how effective one can be in an intercultural communication.

Cultural change is inevitable: Because biologic and environmental factors are ever changing, perceptions, attitudes, values, and identities are ever changing. Consequently, new perceptual and identity groups are constantly being formed and existing groups are constantly in a state of flux.

NOTES

[1] These premises draw heavily on the work of cultural anthropologists, sociologists, psychologists, communication theorists, and linguists. In particular, the model is strongly influenced by the concept of "perceptual constancies." See Franklin P. Kilpatrick, ed., *Explorations in Transactional Psychology* (New York: New York University Press, 1961). While I believe that the approach is more important than the specific components, the premises are presented in order to make the model as explicit as possible.

[2] See Marshall R. Singer, *Weak States in a World of Powers: The Dynamics of International Relationships* (New York: Free Press, 1972), pp. 10–13; and "Culture: A Perceptual Approach," in *Vidya,* No. 3 (Spring).

[3] Because I argue that every identity group has a cultural ensemble somewhat different from every other identity group, I will use the terms *cultural groups* or *cultures* interchangeably with the term *identity groups.*

[4] There are those social scientists who would argue that no collectivity of people who do not communicate can legitimately be called a group, and thus the term *perceptual group* may be a misnomer. Strictly speaking, that is true. For the sake of precision we should call those

individuals who do not communicate their similarity of perception a *perceptual collectivity*. This is one of those cases, however, where I prefer some imprecision in order to avoid cumbersome jargon.

⁵ For one of the classic works on the subject see Robert Redfield, *Peasant Society and Culture: An Anthropological Approach to Civilization* (Chicago: University of Chicago Press, 1956).

⁶ Oscar Lewis, *Five Families: Mexican Case Studies in the Culture of Poverty* (New York: New American Library, 1959); and Michael Harrington, *The Other America: Poverty in the United States* (New York: Macmillan, 1962).

⁷ Chitterlings are a food widely eaten by American blacks, particularly by poorer blacks in the southern part of the U.S. The reference here is to something called the chitterling test, which was developed in the late 1960s to demonstrate to middle-class white Americans the enormous cultural bias that is built into so-called intelligence tests. Few if any whites could answer any of the questions on the chitterling test, yet few poor black Americans would miss more than a few answers. It demonstrated very effectively how very much each group takes for granted that "everyone knows," when in fact that "everyone" is most often only "everyone in our group."

⁸ For a fascinating fictionalized account of what this meant in Southern American society a few decades ago—and the sentiment would be only somewhat less today—read Sinclair Lewis, *Kingsblood Royal* (New York: Random House, 1947).

⁹ See, for example, Karl Deutsch, *Nationalism and Social Communication: An Inquiry into the Foundations of Nationality* (Cambridge: Technology Press of MIT, and New York: John Wiley & Sons, 1953).

¹⁰ Personal communication.

¹¹ John Useem and Ruth Hill Useem, "American Educated Indians and Americans in India: A Comparison of the Two Modernizing Roles," *Journal of Social Issues* 24 (1968), 143–58.

¹² Richard W. Cottam, personal communication.

¹³ Leon Festinger, *A Theory of Cognitive Dissonance* (Stanford, Calif.: Stanford University Press, 1957).

¹⁴ Ibid., p. 12.

¹⁵ Ibid., p. 16.

¹⁶ Ibid., p. 18.

¹⁷ Marshall R. Singer, *The Emerging Elite: A Study of Political Leadership in Ceylon* (Cambridge: MIT Press, 1964).

¹⁸ See the Introduction to *The Emerging Elite,* pp. ix–xiii.

CHAPTER THREE
THE COMMUNICATION PROCESS

"One cannot *not* communicate." I know of no more basic statement about the communication process than that. It comes from an article by Watzlawick, Beavin, and Jackson published originally in 1967 and reprinted in 1973. The paragraph from which the statement comes says:

> . . . there is a property of behavior that could hardly be more basic and is, therefore, often overlooked: Behavior has no opposite. In other words, there is no such thing as non-behavior or, to put it even more simply: one cannot *not* behave. Now, if it is accepted that all behavior in an interactional situation has message value, i.e., is communication, it follows that no matter how one may try, one cannot *not* communicate. Activity or inactivity, words or silence all have message value: they influence others and these others in turn, cannot *not* respond to these communications and are thus themselves communicating. It should be clearly understood that the mere absence of talking or of taking notice of each other is no exception to what has just been asserted.[1]

But just because we cannot avoid behaving or communicating doesn't mean that the people with whom we try to communicate will necessarily understand what it is we are trying to communicate. Allow me to illustrate with two personal anecdotes.

Many years ago while traveling in India, after having spent a year studying in Sri Lanka, an incident occurred that I think illustrates the complexity of all inter-cultural communication. It is important for the reader to know that in Sri Lanka people don't shake their heads to signal yes and no the way they do virtually every-where else. In most of the world one indicates yes nonverbally by nodding the head up and down, vertically. A horizontal motion of the head from left to right in most places normally means no. In Sri Lanka that is not the case.[2] If one wants to signal yes or OK nonverbally, one slowly moves his or her head horizontally from left to right and right to left. Indicating no also involves moving the head horizontally, but it is done more rapidly. Having spent a year in Ceylon, I had adopted the Cey-lonese pattern without being aware that I had done so. (Few of us are consciously aware of how many of the local mannerisms we pick up when we have lived in a place for a while.) Anyway, upon arriving at Banares, India, I wanted to rent a rowboat to take a trip down the holy Ganges River. Since my knowledge of Hindi (the local language) was limited to *Nimasti* ("hello") and *ek, doe, teen* ("one," "two," "three"), I knew that my communication with the boat owner would have to be primarily in sign language. I had done pretty well at it until we came to the question of price. With some difficulty I finally conveyed to him that I wanted to know "how much?" He held up three fingers and said, "Teen rupee." In English I responded, "OK" and without realizing it simultaneously shook my head slowly from side to side, Ceylonese fashion. He responded by holding up two fingers and said, "Doe rupee." Instantly I realized what had happened and reverted to my American way of nodding my head up and down to indicate that I accepted his offer.

OK. But that was in India between people who clearly were not from the same culture. Now move closer to home. Haven't all of us, at one time or another made some gesture to someone we knew well (and who we assumed was "one of us") taking it for granted that our meaning would be understood as we intended it to be understood, only to discover that the exact reverse was read into the ges-ture? For example, in my own case, being of Eastern European ethnic heritage I learned to hug men whom I know and like when I greet them. I do that often. But when I tried to hug a colleague I had come to know and like who was of Anglo-Saxon heritage, I'm afraid that he thought I was part of a group of men about which he had heard and clearly did not like.

As I have argued all along in this work, the reason that kind of misunder-standing happens at home among people who are "part of our group" is that they are not part of all of the groups to which we belong, and we are not part of all the groups with which they identify.

What those little incidents have taught me is that if one wants to communi-cate more accurately with another human being, one had better try to recognize and get to know both the verbal and nonverbal languages of as many as possible of the groups to which the other person belongs.

What I'd like to do in this chapter is to systematically go through all of the steps in the communication process—as I see them—and point out to the reader the complications added to that process by trying to accurately communicate with people from cultures other than our own.

Before we do that, however, we ought to have a very clear idea about the purpose of communication.

THE PURPOSE OF COMMUNICATION

The human animal is perhaps the most social of all animals. He or she must interact with other humans merely to survive. The earliest interaction that occurs is between a newborn infant and its mother. The child has needs that have to be met in order for it to survive. In order for the child to have its needs attended to, it must let those needs be known. As we grow older our needs become more complex, but still if we are to have them attended to by others, we have to let those others know what those needs are.

Virtually all human communications are attempts to achieve goals. The goal may be as simple as wanting to buy two tickets to the theater, or as complex as trying to prevent a thermonuclear holocaust. Regardless of the complexity of the message, consciously or subconsciously the sender is always trying to achieve a purpose by sending the message.

The purpose of studying intercultural communication is to make it more effective. The reason it is important to communicate effectively is so as to be certain that the message the other person receives is as close as possible to the way it was intended when it was sent. The more accurately the receiver gets the message, the less likelihood there is for conflict (over the wrong things) and misunderstanding, and the more likelihood there is of the sender's achieving his or her purpose.

Let me be very specific about my bias on this matter; I do not believe that "better communication" is a panacea. At every level of analysis conflict has persisted and probably always will. I am convinced that to the degree that interpersonal, intergroup, or international communication can be facilitated (a) there is likely to be less misperception and fear of others and (b) at least the actors can be more certain, if they are in conflict, that they both agree on what the conflict is about.

It is a basic tenet of this work that communication is a process. As such it is continually operating, through feedback, with the environment and with everyone and everything in that environment. It is an ongoing process that never ceases, until we die. It is applicable regardless of the level of analysis. The same process operates whether one considers intra- or interpersonal communication, intra- or intergroup communication, or intra- or international communication. Of course, the specifics of how that process operates changes as one changes the actors and settings, but the process remains constant.

George Barnett and Lawrence Kincaid say:

> Communication is . . . a process of convergence in which two or more participants share information in order to reach a better mutual understanding of each other and the world in which they live.[3]

While I wouldn't say that is the only reason people communicate, I would agree that every time people do communicate, they come away from the exchange knowing a little better what the other person is like or understanding better what the other person was trying to say than they would have had, had a convergence not occurred.

"Culture is directly and indirectly the product of communication," says Brent Ruben. It is because of communication that it is possible to transmit the ideas of one time and place to another and from one generation to another. "In effect, then, there is a reciprocally causal and mutually defining relationship between human communication and culture; culture is the product of communication, and human communication processes and outcomes are the result of culture."[4]

Aristotle characterized the communication process as being concerned with "who says what to whom with what effect." Not at all a bad beginning for the first known attempt to deal with the communication process in a scientific manner. Indeed it was so good that it has survived for almost twenty-five hundred years. Harold Lasswell modified that original question by adding the phrase, "in what channel" in 1948.[5]

As we shall see, human communications are so complex that they can never be 100 percent accurate. That is, no one can ever convey to another human *exactly* the idea that one intended. At best, one can come close. At worst, one is forced to give up the attempt. (Or perhaps, still worse, one thinks that he or she has communicated accurately only to discover later—or never to discover at all—that in fact, one has not communicated accurately at all.)

From what was said in the chapters on perception and identity, it is quite clear that no two humans can share *exactly* the same perceptions or identities—regardless of how similar they may be. Therefore, as we have seen, every interpersonal communication is to some extent also an intercultural communication. The more similar the cultural backgrounds, the easier communication should be. The more different the cultural backgrounds, the more difficult communication is likely to be. The more different the individuals are, the harder they are likely to have to work to communicate effectively. That is simply a reality of life that one cannot escape.

I paint a very bleak picture of the difficulties inherent in *all* human communication, not, however, to discourage the reader from ever trying. Quite the contrary. Experience has shown that as long as we recognize all of the difficulties involved, we will not automatically assume that we are communicating well but, on the contrary, will make a more conscious and concerted effort to communicate accurately and thereby: 1. Probably communicate better, 2. Probably not become easily frustrated at the amount of effort required in accurate communication, and 3. Be more selective in our choices of where it is important for us to make that effort and where it is not. Further, by recognizing all of the steps involved in the process we will be better able to attempt to control and correct those steps that we can affect, in order to improve our communication skills. Yes, communication is difficult, but by understanding why it is difficult and at what steps breakdowns are most likely to occur, we enhance enormously our ability to communicate more effectively. Since there is virtually no human endeavor one can imagine that does not require effective communication, the whole range of human interaction—at the interpersonal, intergroup, and international levels—can be improved by better understanding and coping with the communication process.

THE COMMUNICATION PROCESS DISSECTED

Among specialists in the field of intercultural communication there seems to be general agreement that intercultural communication is merely a subset of the broader field of communication generally. Indeed at a recent conference of inter-cultural specialists of the Speech Communication Association there seems to have been agreement that

1. Intercultural communication is an extension of the study of communication phenomena generally.
2. The uniqueness of intercultural communication as a field of study lies in its focus on the cultural factors that impede communication among or between persons or groups of different cultures.
3. Major theoretic perspectives that underlie the study of human communica-tion can provide fruitful directions to guide the study and the practice of intercultural communication.[6]

While I believe all that is true, I'd like to turn the last point around and argue that since all human communication is at least to some degree intercultural, the study of intercultural communication can provide fruitful direction to guide the study of human communication. Forgive me if this sounds arrogant, but I am absolutely convinced that many people in the general field of human communication simply have not been perceiving the problem from the most useful perspective, and once they do, great strides in the study of human communication will be made.

   If one is to improve communication at any level of analysis, it is important to understand clearly how the communication process operates. Accordingly I present here my own model of the communication process. Models are ways of thinking about problems or processes that exist in the real world. They are neither right nor wrong. Some are just more useful than others. There are in the commu-nication field a great many that are in use. The conference of the Speech Commu-nication Association to which I referred earlier identified eight such models (or theories)[7] that intercultural-communication scholars are currently using:

1. Codes and code systems
2. Constructivism
3. Different philosophical perspectives (non-Western)
4. Mathematical modeling
5. Relationship development
6. Rhetorical theory

7. Rules perspective
8. Systems theory[8]

While my own model draws to some degree on codes and code systems (1), constructivism (2), relationship development (5), rules perspective (7), and systems theory (8), it draws most heavily upon the work done by Claude Shannon, Norbert Wiener, Colin Cherry, and Karl Deutsch, from which much of the systems theory has also drawn.[9]

I present my model here (Figure 3.1) with numbers and letters added so that the reader can follow it as I discuss each step in the process in some detail. After we have discussed each of the steps in my model, I will complicate things still further by introducing Dean Barnlund's model of the communication process. In no way does his model contradict anything that I will say here, but it does add a refinement and a sense of the ongoing nature of the process, which my model alone may not adequately capture.

Senders and Receivers (1)

Since I am interested primarily in human communication,[10] I take the individual as my basic unit of analysis. He or she is both the sender and receiver of communications *at all times.* People are always sending *and* receiving messages simultaneously. There is no way they cannot. At the very same time you are reading these words you are reacting: consciously or subconsciously, verbally or nonverbally. Thus, you are sending off messages all of the time that you are receiving them. Conversely, in a face-to-face conversation, even as I talk, I am picking up not only the messages you may be sending but also thousands of other bits of information from the environment. Whether, or how, I convert those bits of information into messages that I can understand will be discussed shortly. Here it is simply important to note that neither our sensory receptors nor our transmitters ever cease to function until we die.

Not too long ago a book on communication theory appeared arguing that "most of us spend up to 80 percent of our waking hours engaged in some form of communication. . . ."[11] I think it is safe to say that most people working in the field of communication today would agree that is not true. All of us are engaged in communication 100 percent of the time, twenty-four hours of every day. That communication may not necessarily be conscious or be with another person, but we send off and simultaneously receive messages all of the time. Merely walking down a crowded street requires the taking in and sending out of an incredibly large number of messages simply to avoid bumping into other people. We all do that all the time in our own cultures, only rarely having an accident. The reason we can accomplish it is that we and the other people walking in the street are all simultaneously sending off and receiving messages. We have learned so well how to send and receive these messages that none of us are consciously aware of how we do it. But we are sending and receiving them just the same.

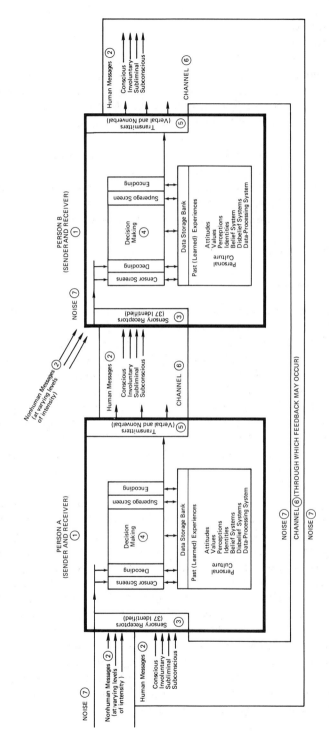

FIGURE 3.1 The communication process. Adapted from an earlier version that appeared in Singer, *Weak States in a World of Powers*, p. 17.

Dean Barnlund and others have criticized the use of the terms *senders* and *receivers* because they fear that people will read them to mean a kind of one-way relationship. Someone sends and someone else receives. Of course that is not the case. Communication is an ongoing process. Barnlund has said:

> New conceptual opportunities may arise if functional terms, such as sending and receiving—or better, encoding and decoding—are substituted for the former labels. It is clear, then, that these are operations and that, as such, they may assume a variety of patterns: symbolizing and interpreting may go on in a single person when he is alone; meanings may develop in two or more communicants simultaneously; messages, in the absence of either a source or receiver, may generate effects; meanings continue to flourish or deteriorate long after they are initiated, and so on. . . . Communication seems more accurately described as a circular process in which the words "sender" and "receiver," when they have to be used at all, serve only to fix the point of view of the analyst who uses them.[12]

I have chosen to retain the use of those terms, however, because I think it is important for us to be able to discuss the sending and receiving of messages. In doing so, however, I ask the reader never to forget that communication is an ongoing, two-way process all of the time.

In the previous chapters I stressed what makes each individual unique. However, we cannot lose sight of the fact that as long as both senders and receivers are human, they share many traits in common. Not the least of those common traits is that we all have the same number and kind of sensory receptors and transmitters. While each may operate ever so slightly differently for each of us—and some of us may not even have the use of one or more of them—all of us do have receptors and transmitters. Further, individual differences aside, they all operate in essentially the same ways. Having said that, however, we must not lose sight of the fact that each individual is unique, both physically and experientially. Therefore, inevitably there will be differences between individuals. The more different sender and receiver are, the harder one has to work to overcome those differences.

Messages (2)

Message is a communication term used in the strict sense to mean any stimulus that can be perceived by the nerve endings in any of our sensory receptors. Each discrete "bit" of data that fires even one or two nerve endings in any of our receptors can be viewed as a message. More commonly we think of a message as being a pattern of perhaps hundreds or thousands of discrete bits of data that make up an intelligible whole, but depending on the circumstances, the individual bits of data themselves can be viewed as being messages. The stimuli by themselves have no meaning. People attribute meaning to the stimuli, thereby transforming them into messages. Because no two individuals can attribute exactly the same meaning to the same message, no two individuals can communicate 100 percent effectively.

Each of us attends to messages—stimuli—twenty-four hours of every day. Although for most of those hours we are attending to stimuli from nonhuman and internal sources, they are stimuli nonetheless. The door closing in the next apartment, the wind blowing the trees, the light coming in the window, our stomach informing us that we need food—in short, anything that can be picked up by our sensory receptors—are messages. Even when we sleep, we are receiving stimuli from the internal and external environments and unconsciously reacting to them. If the room gets too cold or too warm, while remaining asleep we adjust the blankets accordingly. If a particular topic is being discussed in the next room, the topic may find its way into our dreams. And if the message is loud enough (a car backfiring, perhaps), intense enough (perhaps a *very* full bladder), or important enough (the baby crying), we might wake from our sleep to attend to the message. Indeed, in the course of every hour of every day from the moment of birth, a human is bombarded with hundreds of thousands of discrete bits of information—stimuli of one sort or another that reach our sensory receptors.

Obviously we cannot attend to all of those messages equally because (a) if we did, there would be no way that we could concentrate on any specific message; and (b) we have not been trained by past experience to recognize the meaning of *all* of the different messages that bombard us.

Nonhuman messages   Unquestionably, the greatest number of messages we receive every moment of the day are from nonhuman sources. Aside from seeing with your eyes the words on these pages, simultaneously the millions and millions of nerve endings on the surface of your skin have been reacting to the temperature in the place where you are sitting as you read this. Your ears are reacting to noises being made by movement around you. Your nose is picking up the variety of odors that may be present in your surroundings. You may not have been conscious of any of those "messages" until I mentioned them, but they have been there all along. More will be said in a moment about how we cope with all of those millions of bits of data we receive simultaneously. Here it is important for us just to recognize all of the many sources of stimuli (messages) that surround us, even when we are alone in a quiet room.

For example, every place has an odor peculiar to itself. The room in which you are sitting as you read this is giving off odors different from those in any other room. A hospital smells different from a dentist's office. A room smells different from a meadow. A meadow in the tropics smells different from one in colder climates. Odors are often low-intensity messages, and if we work around the same smells all of the time, we become oblivious to their existence. But they are there. Go to an unfamiliar place, and one is often struck by the strange smells—until one has been there long enough not to think them strange any longer.

Messages are also being sent by everything in one's environment, merely by virtue of the fact that they are there. When we become used to them, however, we are aware of them only on a subconscious level. Take them away suddenly, and we may become consciously aware of their absence.

Before this chapter is completed we hope to have made the reader aware of the bewildering number of messages—nonhuman and human—that each individual must choose to either attend to or ignore. Sometimes, of course, no matter how hard individuals may try to ignore certain nonhuman messages (so that they may concentrate on other things), it is impossible to do so. The heat or cold in the room may be so intense that it is simply impossible to think about anything else. The level of noise outside can be very high, but so long as it is fairly constant it is possible to adjust our screening devices to overcome it. But when it is unpredictable—sometimes very loud, sometimes very quiet—it becomes difficult to ignore. We can read where the light source is dim, just so long as those nonhuman messages are consistent. But if the light gets bright one moment and dim the next, in unpredictable fashion, reading becomes impossible.

Human messages: Verbal and nonverbal The human animal is a complex creature indeed. We are continuously sending out a multitude of messages simultaneously. Some of the messages we send are conscious, but many many more are involuntary, subliminal, and/or subconscious.

For the moment grant me that humans transmit perhaps dozens of messages simultaneously with all parts of their body. The problem then becomes, To which message does one attend? Think for a moment of the young child who verbally sends the message, "I don't have to go to the bathroom," while nonverbally she has her legs crossed and is turning red in the face. To which message does the parent attend? As the child grows, her ability to control and/or mask involuntary or subconscious messages increases enormously, thus making it often very much more difficult to decode precisely what it is that the person is trying to communicate. The child in this example, of course, is trying to ignore the very loud message she is receiving from her body in order that she may continue to attend to whatever it was that she was doing. It is only when the internal message becomes so "loud" (intense really) that the child can no longer ignore it—or the parent intervenes—that the child will finally attend to her bodily needs.

Indeed, all available evidence indicates that no one is 100 percent successful at camouflaging most messages. Yet everyone is communicating so many different messages at the same time (even if one is not trying to mask them) that it is difficult in the extreme to know to which messages one should attend. When you are talking with just one other person, are you just listening to what he is saying? Or are you also noticing the way he is saying it? The way he is dressed? The way he is standing? The deodorant he is using—or not using? The way he combs his hair? The look in his eyes? The list could go on and on. The fact is that you attend to *all* of those messages simultaneously—on at least some level of consciousness.

The process is complicated still further when the sender is trying to keep certain messages hidden—as we all do at least some of the time. One of the major problems with trying to camouflage or hide certain thoughts is that they may be received by the other person as a totally different message from the one being hidden. Thus because one cannot, or will not, articulate clearly and openly what the message is that she or he is trying to hide, the receiver often picks up some little hint of something, and attributes meaning to that hint that could have nothing at all to do with what the sender was thinking.

Why it is that a person feels that some messages must be camouflaged or not sent at all will be dealt with elsewhere. For now it is important for us to recognize that all of us receive a multitude of human messages simultaneously—from each person with whom we come into contact. The receiver may not understand what the messages that he is receiving mean, but almost certainly he will pick up something.

This gets considerably more complicated when the person with whom we are trying to communicate belongs to a culture that is quite alien to us. She will be sending off a host of conscious and subconscious messages—and we will be sending a different host of messages to her—but neither of us may be able to "pick up" those messages because we don't understand the codes. Worse, perhaps, we may think we are picking up one message when in fact the message being sent is a different one. (Recall the shaking of the head mentioned at the beginning of this chapter.)

Subliminal Messages (Almost Always Nonverbal)

There was a time when some scholars would have said that if a stimulus was not perceived consciously it was not perceived. More recent research, however, has recognized the importance of "subliminal perception" (literally, beneath the threshold or *limen* of awareness),[13] although there is some dispute as to the importance of these messages to human behavior.[14] Aside from the work of Wilson Key, who takes a very strong stand on the importance of subliminal messages to behavior, the work of the people in what is known as neuro-linguistic programming as well as my own work in intercultural communication leads me to believe that subliminal messages may be much more important for human behavior and particularly for intercultural communication than are conscious perceptions.

Let me report on one research project, which illustrates how very involuntary and subliminal messages can be: Ask a male homosexual what it is he looks for in order to be able to identify another homosexual. Certainly gays can spot each other far more easily than heterosexual males can spot them. When asked, however, the homosexual will respond that he doesn't know how he knows, he just does. Sometimes a homosexual will tell you that he can tell by looking into another person's eyes. Now that is a very interesting response given what we now know *scientifically* about involuntary reactions of the pupil of the eye. Berelson and Steiner report on a study done by E. H. Hess in which admittedly homosexual men, heterosexual men, and heterosexual women were asked to look at a series of pictures while some fancy optical machinery measured the dilation and contraction of the pupils of their eyes. What they found was that when the subjects were shown pictures of nude men (presumably well built), the pupils of the eyes of homosexual men and of the women tended to dilate measurably, while the pupils of the eyes of the heterosexual men remained unchanged. When pictures were shown of nude women (also presumably well built), on the other hand, the pupils of the heterosexual men dilated measurably (interestingly, so did the pupils of the heterosexual women but not to the same degree as did the heterosexual men), while the pupils of the homosexual men actually contracted measurably.[15]

There is simply no way that anyone could be *consciously* aware of several millimeters' dilation or contraction of the pupils of the eye. Yet for centuries poets and lovers have "known" that it is possible to read affection or attraction in someone's eyes. The scientists have finally devised a way to measure what others have known for centuries! Can anyone honestly believe that eye-pupil movement is the only previously undetected signal people send off? Indeed most nonverbal behavior is so much below the level of consciousness that it may be impossible to measure precisely because it is as yet impossible for us to know it exists.

Additional research on involuntary nonverbal messages, which until now went totally undetected, is being done by a group of people who call themselves neuro-linguistic programmers and call their work neuro-linguistic programming (NLP). It stems from work done in hypnosis and therapy, and while I believe that the claims made by this group may be highly exaggerated, their findings cannot be ignored by scholars or practitioners in the field of intercultural communication.[16]

The neuro-linguistic programming scholars argue that *physiologically* all people favor certain sensory receptors over others, both as a way of taking in data from the outside world and as a way of accessing data once they are stored internally. They believe that by observing very subtle body movements one can determine the sensory mode being used at the moment and also the preferred mode. They claim that all people—regardless of culture—will exhibit the same body movements. The reason is that it relates directly to right- and left-lobe domination of the brain, and brain lobe dominance is not culture related.[17] That is, people who are right-handed—indicating left-lobe dominance—will more or less always move their eyes up and to their left when they are trying to visually remember something. Their eyes will involuntarily move up and to their right when they are trying to visually construct an image. Left-handed people will do the reverse. According to the NLP people, not only do our eyes involuntarily move in certain predictable and different directions when we access visual, audio, and kinesthetic experiences, but also our breathing is different, and our posture and muscle tone change. What is more, these changes in breathing and muscle tension cause changes in our voice tempo and in the tonal quality of our voices.[18] Now, if these scholars are correct in their findings—and there is every reason to believe they are—then all of us have been involuntarily sending out messages about how we process information all of the time, without knowing we were doing it.

Further, the authors claim that each of us has a very strong preference for one sensory mode over others. That is, some people will tend to *see* things, while others will *hear* those same things, while still others will *feel* them. Although some tasks require certain responses, we each nonetheless convert the accomplishment of those tasks to our preferred behavioral style. Thus, for example, while some people can spell a word by visually remembering how it looks, others will spell it by sounding it out to themselves.

Interestingly, the NLP people claim that some tasks are better accomplished by certain sensory strategies than by others. They point to the fact that the better spellers all use visual recollection to achieve their goal. Still, each of us seems to favor one sensory mode of behavior over others. What's more, if we listen carefully, we will hear people tell us about their sensory preference. Some people will tell us they "see" what someone else is trying to say, while others will "feel" that someone else is either right or wrong, and still a third type will tend to "hear" what they are saying.[19]

The body of NLP work is much more complex than I have been able to present here, and I urge my readers to become acquainted with it, if they are not now. What is truly fascinating about it from the perspective of intercultural communication is that until I became familiar with their work, it would never have occurred to me to group people by the sensory receptors they prefer to use to access the world, yet that is precisely what the NLP people argue all of us do all of the time without realizing we do it. What is more, we do it almost completely involuntarily—although they do claim that with practice we could control those preferences and shift them at will. Now that is important because they argue that we relate more easily to someone who organizes sensory data the way we do. In other words, if we want to be more effective communicators we need to teach ourselves to communicate in a number of different sensory styles, learn to observe other people's preferred styles more closely, and then communicate with them in the style they prefer. That is, they would argue, people who keep telling you that they "see where you are coming from," whose eyes go up to either the left or right when you ask them a question, whose shoulders are tense and breathing shallow and high in the chest are visual people. If you can respond to them in their own sensory language, the NLP people argue, then the person with whom you are trying to communicate will relate to you as "one of us" on a subconscious level, and that will make you a much more effective communicator. The content of your message will be much more readily accepted. Notice, the NLP people are not at all addressing themselves to message content. Rather, they address themselves to the way messages are communicated. The subliminal sensory code, if you will. Interestingly enough, once you have read the NLP literature you may find yourself constantly attending to those subliminal messages that you hadn't even known people sent.

While I do believe that their claims about what this type of communication can accomplish seem highly exaggerated, in no way do I doubt that they are on to something very important in communication in general and for intercultural communication in particular. For regardless of which other cultures someone may be a part of, if we can tune in to that person's involuntary sensory-preference style of communicating, we may be building just one more bridge to effective communication.

The significance of subliminal perceptions to intercultural communication is immensely important primarily because (a) so many stimuli are probably subliminal and (b) they are below the level of conscious awareness so we don't consciously know they are there—and thus they are very difficult to deal with.

Let us stay with just these two points before moving on. Wilson Key argues that the overwhelming majority of the stimuli that bombard our sensory receptors are subliminal. The evidence he presents is very persuasive. Even more persuasive, however, is the logic of his argument.

Key says:

> Data provided from studies in neurology and psychology strongly support the conclusion that all senses (including those yet undiscovered) operate on at least two perceptual levels. Information is collected at what might be called a cognitive or conscious level, a level where each human is consciously aware of what is going on. Information is also collected simultaneously and continuously at a subliminal level, a level at which there is no conscious apparent awareness of data entering the brain.[20]

Further on, Key makes what is perhaps the most important assertion of his study:

> . . . the conscious mind merely adapts itself to the basic program established in the unconscious; *no significant belief or attitude held by any individual is . . . made on the basis of consciously perceived data.*[21]

In effect, what Key is saying is that the attitudinal and value frames through which all sensory data are processed may themselves be established on the basis of unconscious or subliminal data. If he is correct in that assertion—and I believe that he is—then it becomes particularly difficult to get people to establish different perceptual frames, precisely because they do not know—consciously—what caused them to establish those frames in the first place. The importance of that assertion to this study will become even more apparent as we get further into this work.

Sensory Receptors (3)

Since the time of Aristotle we have believed that humans have five basic senses and the sensory receptors that enable us to use those senses: sight (eyes), sound (ears), smell (nose), taste (tongue), and touch (hands). Modern research indicates that there are many more. For example, we have an internal kinesthetic sensory mechanism that allows us to determine which way is up (at least we can in the earth's gravitational zone) even if all other sensory receptors are nonfunctional.

Wilson Key argues that there are over thirty known senses and that more are being discovered all the time. He says of them:

> . . . all these senses are inputting data simultaneously and constantly into the brain. A bias—temporarily favoring sight, or hearing, or whatever—may occur as a person changes concentration from, say, a newspaper to a radio broadcast, but none of the senses ever stops operating.[22]

The notion that each of our senses operates independently of each other is a Western concept. Eastern thought and tradition teach that all of the senses are integrated, each affecting the others. Thus for an Asian meal, not only are the appearance, texture, and smells of the food thought to be important to the way food tastes but the total dining environment—decoration of the room, sound level, temperature of the room, emotional climate—is thought to influence the flavor of the food.[23] Of course, when we think about it, we realize how true that is.

It sometimes happens that through disease or accident one or more of our sensory receptors is damaged and becomes inoperative. When that does happen there is an extraordinary human tendency to compensate by relying even more on other sensory receptors or on the same kind of receptors in different parts of the body. For a blind person, hearing and smell and touch become much more important and refined receptors of sensation than they are for those of us who have vision. For the person who loses the ability to feel sensation in certain parts of the body, other parts seem to compensate. None of us are really aware of how acute each of our sensory receptors actually is or can be until we are forced to rely more upon certain ones than we would in ordinary circumstances.

Physiologically not all of us are born with equally acute sensory receptors. That is, in some individuals some receptors are undoubtedly more acute than in others. Some of us have very acute vision, others have a stronger sense of hearing, and so on. Probably because of that physiological bias in favor of certain receptors than others, we tend to "favor" our stronger receptors. That is, we learn to rely more upon them. What is more, although there are almost certainly some experiential factors involved, we recognize that some people have "an ear for music," as we say, while others are "tone deaf." Some have "an eye for color or form," while others seem to be oblivious to visual stimuli. Allow me here to report a story that a colleague reported to me almost twenty years ago.

The colleague and his family had occasion to visit Mexico City for the first time. They were put up at a hotel in the heart of the downtown district. As they got into their room, their older teenaged son, who was studying to be an artist, ran to the window and said, "Wow! Look at the spectacular view of the city we have from here." Moments later their younger son (who had been out of the room until then), who plays several musical instruments, ran to the same window and said, "Dad, just listen to the sounds of the city we can hear from here."[24]

Of course this relates directly to the work of NLP. But the fact is that some cultures do favor certain receptors over others. The example cited above may help explain why "art culture" people are different from "music culture" people. Similar examples could be found for other visual cultures (such as dancers, hairdressers, or fashion designers) as opposed to cultures in which words and/or ideas are more important (as for example with poets, lawyers, or philosophers). All of those examples, however, *may* depend more on conditioning than on physical acuity of the sensory receptor. But then again it may not. Edward Stewart has argued that certain colors may actually be seen differently by different cultures.[25] He has argued, for example, that the reason tropical cultures emphasize "hot" or "warm" reds and oranges in their art work may be that they actually see those colors quite differently from the way Nordic peoples do. Conversely, the "cool" or "cold" blues, which are so prevalent in Northern art, may not be perceptible in the same way to people from tropical cultures.[26]

Decision Making (4)

For every single bit of data picked up by our sensory receptors a decision has to be made by us with regard to it. Is it to enter our consciousness, remain subconscious, or be totally ignored? Is it to be merely stored or acted upon immediately? If it is to be acted upon, how? There are a number of processes at work in each of those decisions, and while for the sake of analysis we shall discuss them one at a time, it should be remembered that they are all operating simultaneously and at incredibly rapid rates of speed.

Censor screens   Obviously, we cannot attend equally to all stimuli to which we are exposed. For one thing, not all stimuli reach the sensory receptors at the same level of intensity. That is, some sounds are louder than others, some images are clearer than others. All things being equal, the louder sounds and the clearer images—the more intense stimuli—would probably be transmitted to the brain by the sensory receptors before the less intense stimuli. But all things are not always equal. Some stimuli are so important or so salient to us that regardless of intensity, we are likely to pick them out first. Conversely, some stimuli are so repugnant to us or difficult for us to handle that regardless of intensity, we are likely to pick them out last, if at all. As Berelson and Steiner explain:

> Of all possible stimuli—i.e., all bits of energy capable of firing receptors at any given moment—only a small portion become part of actual experience; and that portion is not a random sample of what is objectively available. . . . The observer, of course, plays an active part in determining what will be allowed to stimulate the receptors at all: we look at some things, ignore others, and look *away* from still others ("selective exposure"). Beyond that, only a fraction of those stimuli that have gained effective entry to a receptor ever reach awareness ("selective awareness").[27]

The first range of decisions the brain has to deal with are what appears at first blush to be a simple ordering device: What do I focus attention on, and in order to do that, what do I block out? It is just not possible to attend to all stimuli equally: some stimuli get more attention, others get less. Nothing gets our "undivided attention." As you drive your car home from school you make the decision to "focus your attention" on the other cars on the road, pedestrians crossing the streets, stop signs and lights, and driving conditions in general. Thus driving home *may* be receiving your primary attention at that moment. But that does not mean that you are totally unaware of the sounds of the music coming from your car radio, the temperature in the car, the vibrations the car may be making, familiar people who may be on the sidewalk as you pass, the ache in your bones, or your awareness that you have to be home by a certain time in order to attend more fully to something else that you must do. It just means that driving is what you are focusing most of your attention on at that moment. If it were not for this ability to temporarily "screen out" some or even most stimuli, it simply would not be possible for us to focus our attention on anything. And as we know from the study of computers, we can deal with even the most complex problems, requiring perhaps millions of discrete decisions, just as long as we can handle them one at a time, in proper order.

Although this censor screen does permit us to focus our primary conscious attention on one activity at a time, consciously sending most other inputs to subconscious storage for the time being, it does more than that. The censor screen is not something we were born with. *What we are born with is the ability to construct such a screen.* Just how that screen is to be constructed, which stimuli it is to let through, and which it is to block out is *both* a physical and a learned phenomenon. It is physical in the sense that some of us are born with certain of our sensory receptors being favored over others. It is learned in the sense that each of our group cultures has taught us what we ought to see and what we should expect to see. Thus in the process of being socialized into some groups and not others, we have learned what we should consider important, and thus should attend to, and what is not important, and is therefore to be relatively ignored. If we have not learned certain things (such as a particular alphabet), stimuli relating to those things will be perceived merely as nonsense symbols or will be disregarded entirely.

Joseph deRivera says of the selection of stimuli in the process of communication:

> Any stimulus is initially amorphous; it is not a psychological stimulus until the person attends to some aspect of it. In order to act, the observer selects an aspect of the stimulus which he can distinguish and thinks important. He determines the aspect of the stimulus to which he responds.
> . . . both the perceptual and attentive processes are usually completely intertwined, so that both determine how a person constructs his world. A person cannot be said to attend to a stimulus unless he perceives it, and yet every perception involves a selective attention.[28]

Berelson and Steiner report that there are probably three major factors that determine which stimuli are selected, ignored, or missed:

> . . . the nature of the stimuli involved; previous experience or learning as it affects the observer's expectations (what he is prepared or "set" to see); and the motives in play at the time, by which we mean his needs, desires, wishes, interests, and so on—in short, what the observer wants or needs to see and not see. Each of these factors can act to heighten or to decrease the probability of perceiving, and each can act on both exposure and awareness.[29]

The existence of identities—and of the belief and disbelief systems that are associated with those identities—may be crucial to what is admitted and what is excluded. If I were a devout Hindu, I would be much more likely to admit messages pertaining to Hinduism and all of the associated beliefs that I held (like the unquestioned belief in reincarnation, with all that implies) and to screen out other identities and other belief systems that I did not hold. The same process would be true regardless of which identities were most important to me. Someone who works in the women's clothing industry sees a woman and is immediately conscious of what she is wearing. A dermatologist might well notice her skin. A shoe salesperson will probably notice her shoes, while a "lecher" will see only her body. Two women from the same town—one a Republican, one a Democrat—read the same morning newspaper. The Republican reads everything the Republican candidate had to say the day before both because it is relevant to her and because it is automatically worth knowing about. Even if she were to notice that the paper also contained a speech by the Democratic candidate she probably wouldn't bother to read it because she knows full well that the Democrat would *not* have anything of value to say. Even if our newspaper-reading Republican were to read the Democrat's speech, what she would find was reinforcement of her preconceived belief that the candidate was a fool. Clearly, the higher I rank certain identities, the more likely I am to attend to their messages before I attend to other messages relating to other identities that I rank lower. The opposite side of the coin, so to speak, of selective attention is selective inattention. We consciously or subconsciously *do not attend* to those stimuli to which our culture has not trained us to attend.

As we have seen, learning occurs in the group one happens to be born into or that one happens to come into significant contact with. Each group teaches somewhat different responses to the same stimuli. Learned responses become part of the culture of the group. Since each group teaches its own culture, two people from entirely different groups observing the same stimuli could respond so differently in some cases that one might wonder whether, in fact, the stimuli were the same ones to which they were responding.

The censor screen helps us see what we expect to see or want to see. It also helps us to avoid what we don't expect or don't want to see. More than thirty years ago G. W. Allport and L. Postman conducted an experiment that graphically illustrated the effect of stereotyping on perceptions.[30] In the experiment a large number of Americans were shown a photograph of what appeared to be a scene in a subway car. In the scene two men are standing, one black and well dressed and the other white and wearing working clothes. The white man in the picture is holding an open razor of the type men once used to shave with. Each person was asked to describe the picture to someone who could not see it. The second person would then describe to a third person what had been described to him or her. The third person, in turn, would describe it to a fourth, and so on through six or seven people. In over half the cases reported by Allport and Postman, the razor changed hands from the white to the black man, and the black man became the one who was poorly dressed. Indeed, in some cases the black man was reported to be "brandishing" the razor or "threatening" the white man with it. As Otto Klineberg points out, "This does not mean that half the subjects reacted in such a fashion, since one shift in a rumor chain might be reproduced by all who followed. It does mean that in 50 percent of the *groups* this phenomenon was observed."[31] In the study the distortion was avoided in only two groups: among blacks, for what were assumed to be obvious reasons, and among young children, who had not yet learned the stereotype. However, when this experiment was repeated approximately twenty years later at an all-black high school in New York City, as much distortion occurred among black students as had been reported among whites in the original study.[32] One possible explanation may be that black students participating in the experiment had subconsciously accepted the predominant white stereotype of the blacks.

These experiments illustrate two principles involved in any communication process. Most obviously, and what is most pertinent for any discussion of intergroup communication, they show the transmutation of sensory data to conform to expectations. But they also illustrate that in any process of communication the more steps a message must go through from its original source to its intended recipient, the more distortion is likely to occur. I have not seen a recent update of the Allport and Postman study, but I suspect that the most significant change among whites in the intervening years would be that now they would report blacks carrying knives—not razors.

The point is that whites tend not to see the ninety-nine blacks who are well dressed or are not carrying knives. Instead, if we read about or see one black with a knife, not only do we attend to it, but it also reinforces our preconceived belief that "blacks carry knives." All of us elect to attend to some stimuli and elect to screen out millions of other stimuli that we are not prepared to see or do not want to see. We must do that simply to be able to function. If we did not, the cacophony of the millions of discrete stimuli to which we are exposed would be so overwhelming that we could not cope. But we should also be aware, that while doing this allows us to focus our attention and to get things accomplished, it also distorts reality enormously. For each of us reality becomes not what is really "out there" but rather only those relatively few bits of "reality" that our censor screens have admitted into our consciousness. The remainder go unattended or at best get stored in our subconscious.

Decoding "One if by land, two if by sea." The fellow on the other side simply had to know not only what to look for but also what the signal meant if any communication was to take place. That is true of all communications. Unless both the sender and the receiver of the message understand the same meanings of the code or the language used, little communication, or none, will occur—or worse, miscommunication will occur instead.

If I stand by the shore and watch the waves break on the beach, all I see are waves breaking on the beach. But if a trained oceanographer stands on the same beach and watches the same waves break, she or he can tell a great deal about the tides, storms out at sea, and a great deal more. That is because she or he knows what to look for and I don't. She or he knows the codes.

If I write the word *стол*, anyone who knows how to read Russian will know immediately what it means. But to anyone who does not know that code it might just as well be a nonsense syllable. When I write the English *rappel* or *belay,* people who have engaged in rock climbing—but only they—will know what I mean. To be sure, people who do crossword puzzles, play Scrabble, or are simply very well versed in the English language may know the dictionary meaning of those words, but only those who climb and descend regularly and share the same love of heights and adventure can really know their meaning.

L. E. Sarbaugh and Nobleza Asuncion-Lande define a code as "a culturally defined, rule-governed system of shared arbitrary symbols used to transmit (and elicit) meaning." They argue that meanings are *not* transmitted; symbols are. Those symbols serve as stimuli to elicit meaning in the person receiving the stimuli. "Included within the concept of code are language, paralinguistic phenomena, nonverbal phenomena, silence, language choice, multilingual behavior, interruptions, turn-taking and organization of talk."[33] This is a definition with which I agree completely.

As Sheila Ramsey and others have reminded us on many occasions, one of the reasons it is possible for us to decode messages as well as we do is that communication does not occur in a vacuum. Rather, there is always a context in which communication takes place. What is more, regardless of the broad national differences among people, the people communicating in a given situation probably have at least some group identities in common. Ramsey writes:

> Pragmatically interactions do not occur between "a Latin American" and "an American" within a contextual vacuum. Rather, each belongs to a very specific group; each is a particular sex, age, status, and role relationship. Actors are more or less acquainted with each other, they have particular feelings about each other, they engage in one of numerous social or task discussions, they do so in a particular place, and they are bound by culturally determined display rules.[34]

The point is that each of the groups of which we are a part will have taught us its own special language, attitudes, values, and ways of perceiving the world—in short, the group codes—and only if we know those codes well can we understand messages relating to that group identity. What is more, each of the codes we have learned is stored in our "data-storage bank." Thus as soon as any of our sensory receptors picks up a stimulus, it is immediately checked through the literally trillions of bits of data stored in our data-storage bank to determine if we know what it means. If we have ever learned the code we will be able to decode the stimulus, at least on a subconscious, if not a conscious, level. We do not forget codes once they have been learned; we simply lose the ability to call them into conscious memory unless they were very well learned initially and/or are periodically reinforced at the conscious level. People will tell you that when they were young they spoke a certain language but that they have since forgotten it. Yet under hypnosis it turns out that they can often be induced to speak the language they consciously do not remember.

Part of the decoding process is learning how to listen and watch. In the United States the presumption is that if you want to communicate with someone else, the burden of figuring out how to do so effectively rests with you. After all, it is you who wants to communicate, not the receiver of your message. In Japan and some other parts of Asia the exact reverse is the case.[35] In those cultures the burden of understanding the communication rests on the receiver of the message. It is his or her responsibility to figure out what it is the sender is trying to communicate. In part this difference in perspective may be the result of cultural perspectives within the respective societies. In the United States we tend to think we are being ignored or misunderstood if people don't ask questions. In Japan, which has a much more hierarchical society, it would be a sign of disrespect (and ignorance) to ask questions.

Both extremes are, I think, just that—extreme. Being an American social scientist I can't help but believe that indeed the burden for being understood rests with the communicator. I also recognize the value and importance of learning how to listen in any communication process. For one thing, the whole point of feedback is to try to interpret what images are in the other person's head. If we don't listen carefully when they speak we will never be able to calibrate our message so that the other person can understand and possibly accept it.

Learning how to watch is probably considerably more important than learning how to listen. Messages that can be observed with the eyes are particularly important in decoding subconscious messages that the sender may be transmitting. This is particularly true in the light of the recent work of the neuro-linguistic programs reported earlier. The kind of clothes a person wears has already been touched upon. What about the way he walks, sits, or uses his hands? How far or close does he stand when he talks to you? Does he position himself perpendicular to you or parallel? Does he look you in the eye when he speaks? Does he bite his nails? What are his other nervous habits? These and perhaps thousands of questions like these about a person's nonverbal behavior help us to get much greater insight into other people than verbal communication alone would convey.[36] The trouble is, we have to learn what these nonverbal messages mean to the people sending them. Certainly not all of these nonverbal messages mean the same thing in every culture, and it is very difficult to observe these nonverbal behavior patterns in cultures foreign to our own since we don't really know what the norms of nonverbal behavior are. But by watching we can begin to find out.

Albert Mehrabian says:

> Both within and between cultures . . . there is some degree of consistency in the use of subtle behaviors to convey a certain state, relation, or feeling (encoding), and in the ability to infer another's state, relation, or attitude from such behaviors (decoding). Although the exact degree of this consistency cannot be established readily because it differs for different people, situations, and types of behaviors it is, nevertheless, legitimate to consider such behaviors *communicative*.[37]

Edward T. Hall in his path-breaking book, *The Silent Language*,[38] describes and analyzes how both time and distance are used differently by people in different cultures. In Latin America time is a much less important value than it is in the United States. In North America "time is money." The Latin American is relatively nonchalant in making and keeping appointments. Being two hours late for an appointment in large parts of Latin America might well be the accepted norm in those societies. There is no insult intended to a visitor when kept waiting that long for a business meeting or to a host when a guest is that late for dinner. To an American, of course, being that late is taken as a message assumed to mean disregard or disrespect for the other person.

Similarly, most of us are unaware that we all surround ourselves with an imaginary wall behind which we enclose our "personal space." We become very uncomfortable when anyone violates that space except under prescribed circumstances. For example, our own children and lovers can violate that space without our being aware of it. Dentists, barbers, and the person we happen to be wrestling with can also, but only under set rules.

In each culture the distance of that wall from ourselves varies. In every culture it seems, the more personal the topic, the closer the approved distance; the more impersonal, the farther the distance. Despite that, however, in all categories of subject matter Latin Americans, Arabs, and certain other groups are more comfortable communicating closer to each other than are North Americans. Hall estimates that for "neutral" personal subject matter Americans are most comfortable with twenty to thirty-six inches separating them from the other party.[39] Latin Americans and Arabs simply are not happy communicating about personal matters that far apart. For them about fourteen to eighteen inches is a much more comfortable distance. Thus without being at all aware of their behavior, in a conversation between a North American and a Latin American, the Latin is likely to keep moving closer, trying to find a comfortable distance for communication (from his perspective) while the North American keeps retreating, trying to establish what for him or her is the more comfortable distance.

Studies reveal that there are some basic differences between black and white Americans regarding distance, positioning, and eye contact. The black American male seems more comfortable at a closer distance than does the white American male, but whereas the white American will tend to stand parallel to the person to whom he is talking, enabling him to look the other person directly in the eye, the American black tends to position himself perpendicular to the person with whom he is communicating and thus tends to avoid eye contact. These same studies reveal that in general, blacks (both male and female) tend to avoid eye contact much more than do whites.[40] One can begin to see how important this can be in intercultural communication between, say, a white teacher and a black student. Out of cultural habit and preference, the black student listens best by not looking directly at the speaker but rather at some neutral object like the ceiling or out the window. White teachers, unaware of this cultural difference, tend to assume, since white students only avoid eye contact when they are *not* paying attention, that black students must not be paying attention most of the time.

On the same subject of eye contact, it was reported to me by several Nigerian students that in northern Nigeria (where most of the population is traditional Muslim) it is a sign of disrespect to look directly into the eyes of a superior. Thus when northern Nigerians come to this country to study, their efforts to display respect for their teachers by avoiding eye contact may be interpreted as lack of attention. Conversely, when Americans (both white and black) go to northern Nigeria, whites more than blacks, but both groups more than Nigerians, try to look their superiors directly in the eye as a mark of their attention and respect, only to be perceived as being disrespectful and discourteous.[41]

In a more recent book called *Beyond Culture,* Edward Hall reports on work being done in the field of synchronized body motion.

> People in interaction either move together (in whole or in part) or they don't and in failing to do so are disruptive to others around them. Basically, people in interactions move together in a kind of dance, but they are not aware of their synchronous movement and they do it without music or conscious orchestration. Being "in sync" is itself a form of communication. The body's messages (in or out of awareness), whether read technically or not, seldom lie, and come much closer to what the person's true but sometimes unconscious feelings are than does the spoken word.[42]

The work being done in the field is truly remarkable. The problem is that the evidence is overwhelming that each group teaches a different pattern of body movement and synchronization. What is fascinating, however, is the evidence that as people begin to learn how to react to each other, over time they get "into sync" with each other. Hall quotes William Condon, who has done a great deal of work in this field:

> . . . it no longer makes sense to view human behavior as " . . . isolated entities sending discrete messages" to each other. Rather it would be more profitable to view the "bond" between humans as the result of participation within shared organizational forms. This means humans are tied to each other by hierarchies of rhythms that are culture-specific and expressed through language and body movement.[43]

Once again, the important thing to remember about the codes—whether verbal or nonverbal—that each of the groups of which we are a part teaches is that they make communication much, much easier for people who are a part of the group—who know the codes—and very, very difficult for those who do not know them.

Data-storage bank   There is no question that the data-storage bank that all of us carry around in our heads is the world's most complex, sophisticated, and fastest information-storage-and-retrieval system. Our most sophisticated manufactured computers, as amazing as they are, simply cannot begin to compete with our brains. To be certain, they can do computations much faster than we possibly could "in our heads," but they have nowhere near the storage capability nor as efficient retrieval systems as ours. Nor of course are they yet capable of reasoning or of feeling emotion.

Stored in our data-storage bank are:

1. All of the past experiences we have ever had, as well as the attitudes toward those experiences that we held at the time of the initial experience and the attitudes we have developed since;

2. The complete belief systems (and disbelief systems), attitudes, values, and modes of perception that each of the groups of which we form a part has ever taught us; (currently in the communication literature, this idea is being referred to as rules theory[44]);

3. A knowledge of all our needs, drives, desires, and urges—in short, information about everything contained in our id;

4. The memory of what behavior patterns are expected of us in each conceivable situation—our superego—and also the memory of the rewards that each group of which we are a part bestows for behaving in those prescribed ways, as well as the punishment they are likely to distribute for violation of those patterns;

5. A collection of all the learned images of ourselves, the multiplicity of identities we hold about ourselves, our groups, and others—our ego;

6. That peculiar combination of inherited and learned traits called personality or temperament, which makes us each unique;

7. A learned series of probabilities as to the likelihood that any particular action will produce a specific effect; and perhaps most important of all;

8. Something equivalent to a learned computer program (unique for each of us), which tells us what data to select from the universe of bits of data "out there," as well as a program to help us process the data once they are selected.

In sum, our data-storage banks contain not only information about everything we have ever learned or felt but also information about how to go about learning what we do not yet know.

Clearly, no two people in the world can possibly have the same information, attitudes, and values stored in their data-storage banks. That is why every communication is—and must be—to some degree intercultural. Indeed, the very best that can be hoped for is that two individuals can have some more or less similar codes and values. Obviously, the more similar the data in their storage banks, the easier communication between them is likely to be. The more different the data, the more difficult communication is likely to be.

Just as a chain is only as strong as its weakest link, so too a communication is as accurate as its most inaccurate step. *The major problem in any communication process is the dissimilarity of data stored in the data-storage bank.* Thus it is probably the storage of data that is more responsible for miscommunication or lack of communication than any other step in the entire process. That is why the last two chapters were devoted to helping us understand the kinds of things that get stored in our data-storage bank and how these things then determine so much of what we see and how we behave.

Superego screen   In order to describe what I mean by superego screen, allow me to present what Karl Deutsch once called "a child's guide to Sigmund Freud."[45] Freud argued that thought processes consist of three parts. The *id* consists of those animal drives and urges, which all of us have, that crave instant gratification—food, water, safety, power, affection, and sex; what we really want and want now! (The sexual urges Freud called *libidinal urges*—coming from our libido. What made Freud so unacceptable to his Victorian contemporaries was his insistence that all people have these—including the sex drive—even as infants.) As we are socialized into the group norms, we learn how to suppress (either repress or sublimate) those urges for the sake of group cohesion. No group could survive if each member sought instant gratification of all of his or her urges regardless of the needs or wishes of other members of the group. These constraints on our behavior Freud called the *superego*—what we *ought* to do or want. Caught between what we really want, and what we have been taught we *ought* to want and how we *ought* to get it, the individual develops a compromise image of himself—the *ego*—which attempts a balancing of the inner drives and outer constraints. We speak of someone having a "strong ego" who has a clear picture of what he wants and needs and knows how to deal with superego constraints on those needs in order to achieve his objectives. Conversely, someone with a "weak ego" is someone who is so intimidated by society's "oughts" that he is unable to admit to himself, let alone others, that he really does have needs and desires of his own. To the degree that such a person does admit to himself that he has these needs, he may then feel terribly guilty for having them.

Clearly, as animals, regardless of who we are, or where we were born, most of us will have similar animal needs, although for any number of different reasons— some physical, some learned—some needs will be stronger in some of us than in others. Just as clearly, each society or group has developed its own set of behaviorally acceptable norms for dealing with those needs. Thus the compromise individual ego of each person has to be different. This is no small matter in facilitating communication between people socialized by the same group norms. It becomes a gigantic barrier to communication between people socialized into different sets of norms or "oughts."

Most groups have done their work of socialization so well that most of us—at least on the conscious level—have learned to deny to ourselves that we even have urges that we are not supposed to have. The urges are there, of course, but they are there at the subconscious level. We know that they are there because they can be articulated under hypnosis or in dreams or in therapy. And because they are there, despite all of our conscious efforts not to communicate to others that they are, invariably they inadvertently get sent out to others as messages. Most often our superego is strong enough to prevent them from being consciously expressed, but my own suspicion is that they "leak out" at least on a subliminal level despite our best efforts to contain them. To prevent the expression of these instinctive urges, every human constructs for himself or herself what I call a superego screen. By that I mean a filter we impose between the instinctive animal reactions we have to certain stimuli and the actual reactions we allow ourselves to have. I call it a superego screen precisely because it contains all of the information we have learned from our identity groups about what reactions to stimuli are expected and accepted. It helps us translate those inner urges into external communications that will be acceptable to the groups that are important to us.

For the sake of a sexist argument, let us say you are a happily married man and you see a female acquaintance standing in the street. (For those readers who don't like the male-chauvinist connotations, say it is a male acquaintance; it doesn't matter. The process is the same.) There is the stimulus. Your censor screen has blocked out in one degree or another all of the other stimuli on the street and focused your attention primarily on her and only secondarily on the tall man standing with her. Information in your data-storage bank tells you that you find her attractive (your past experiences tell you what features you have learned to associate with attractiveness). Libidinal urges within your data-storage bank tell you that you really would like to have sexual contact with her, perhaps of a very specific variety. At the same time, you have been sufficiently socialized as a married man to believe that it is improper to have sexual relations outside of marriage. Further, past experience also tells you that (a) the man standing with her could well be her boyfriend and might not take at all kindly to your making sexual advances toward her and (b) because he is considerably taller than you he is probably considerably stronger (we will discuss perceptions of power relationships in the next chapter). Thus because all communication decisions you make must first pass through your superego screen before they are translated into action, the reaction you might like to make to that particular stimulus will not be the reaction you will ultimately make.

A middle-class black hearing a racial slur in an exclusively white setting may actually want to react by punching the person who made the remark, but the superego screen filters that reaction and the message that comes out is likely to be much more moderate. A "closet" homosexual hearing a joke about a "queer" may also want to hit the person who told the joke, but because he may not want to reveal his true identity, he may laugh along with everyone else. Anyone sufficiently angered by something someone else may have done or said may momentarily feel capable of murder, but—when the superego screen is functioning as it is supposed to—instead, a much more socially acceptable response is substituted.

So it is with every stimulus we perceive. No matter how we might like to react, on the basis of past experiences, impulses, needs, or what have you, all of our reactions are tempered by the filter of the superego screen to make our reactions more socially acceptable than they would otherwise be.

Encoding Having decided what response would be appropriate to a particular stimulus in a particular circumstance, we still have to decide how to encode the messages we want to send. Accordingly, we must check our data-storage bank for information about the intended recipient of the message. The more we know about the intended recipient of our message, the easier it is for us to choose a code in which to send our message. That is, if I know that the intended recipient of my message understands English, English will be an appropriate code for me to use in sending the message. But if I know that the person with whom I am trying to communicate does not understand English, and I don't know any of the languages she does understand, then I have no choice but to encode my message in some non-verbal language. The problem is, of course, that if I don't know her verbal language, the probability is not terribly high that she will understand my nonverbal language either.

We needn't refer merely to linguistic codes here. The same holds true for all other group identities. If I want someone to understand my message, I simply must translate it into a cultural language she or he understands and accepts. Regardless of the message we want to send, if we want it to be acted upon favorably, we had better know the cultural values of the people with whom we want to communicate and how to encode our message in terms that they can understand.

Transmitters (5)

By this time it should be quite clear that we send messages with our entire bodies. Each part of our body is capable of transmitting messages. What is more, it should also be clear that we send out many messages simultaneously. Our voice, our eyes, our face, our heads, our hands, our skin, our muscles—indeed our entire bodies—are all transmitters of messages. To the degree that we can use all, or most, of our transmitters to communicate the *same* message simultaneously, we will certainly be more effective in getting our message across. The reason is that redundancy is an important part of effective communication. The more of the other person's sensory receptors we can stimulate with the same message, the more likely that person is to understand the message the way we meant it to be understood. The problem is, however, that there are only a very few times when we succeed in concentrating our thoughts so completely that even our subconscious is geared to sending the same message. Remember that at all times—even while we are trying to concentrate on sending the same message—we are also receiving messages, and some of those messages we receive will undoubtedly distract us from concentrating on the message we are trying to send. Indeed, we simply can never concentrate 100 percent on sending the same message precisely because part of our brain is always reserved for dealing with involuntary internal bodily communications and functions, while another part is reserved for monitoring all of our sensory receptors. Given all of that, however, the more we can concentrate on sending the same message with as many of our transmitters as we can mobilize, the more effective our communication is likely to be.

Conscious messages Let us start with the messages an individual consciously decides to send. We can use our voice box to send verbal messages. Not only can we control the content of the message but we can also control the tone to achieve our purpose. I can say, "No," or I can say, "No!" My tone of voice can add the emphasis that an exclamation mark conveys in writing.

As for nonverbal messages, whole books have been written about how we express ourselves with our bodies.[46] The clothes we choose to wear in different situations,[47] whether men shave or do not shave the hair on their faces, the way they comb their hair and how long or short they choose to keep it, the kind, color, and amount of makeup a woman chooses to wear, even how highly polished a man keeps his shoes, all transmit messages to other people about how we choose to be perceived. The reasons we choose to dress as we dress or groom as we groom are usually subconscious, of course, but the decisions we make with regard to these things are often conscious.

We can write our messages, play them on musical instruments, or send them via smoke signals. The range and magnitude of ways in which we can send conscious messages is enormous. Probably the major limitations on how we send conscious messages are the constraints of the situation (whether the intended receiver understands the languages we know), the distances involved, the number of people to whom the message is being sent, their attitudes toward us, the context in which the message is being sent, and the limits of our imagination.

The trouble is that very often, even on the conscious level, we are sending not just one message but several simultaneously. Probably that is because our mind operates far more rapidly than our ability to communicate. So that while we are saying one thing with our voice (sending one message) to one person we may be saying something else (sending different messages) to that same person by our body movement and still something else (different messages) to someone else standing nearby. Put aside the other transmitters for a moment and consider just the verbal messages. Here again, the words may be saying one thing but the tone of voice or the speed with which the words are delivered may be saying something entirely different. Often when we really don't mean the words we are saying we try to compensate by overly reinforcing the deceptive message by concentrating on our deception, thus not "acting natural" and thereby defeating our intention to deceive. It is very hard to consciously "act natural" because most of the time we are really being natural we are not at all conscious of the way in which we are sending messages. It is a little like walking. Once we have learned how to do it, we do it without thinking about what we are doing. When we try to be consciously aware of how we are walking we become very clumsy and "unnatural" in our movements.

Involuntary messages Just as in walking, once we have learned to communicate, many of the messages we send are sent by involuntary reactions. Someone says something funny and "we can't help" but laugh. We see something we don't like and our whole body shudders. Note that both these examples deal with learned involuntary responses to stimuli. They are messages in that they say to others how we are responding. Because they are learned it means that everyone may learn somewhat different responses, and we must be very careful when we interpret these that we are doing so correctly. Because we respond involuntarily in a certain way to a certain stimulus does not mean that everyone has been taught to respond in the same way. Some of us tend to think of crying on the death of a loved one as being an involuntary response. Others of us have grown up in cultures that teach that one is never to display extreme emotion publicly. Tens of millions of people watched on television as Jacqueline Kennedy (who had been raised in the latter tradition) controlled her emotions at President Kennedy's funeral. The message she probably thought she was sending to the world was, "Look how well I can control my true feelings. I have learned well the proper way to behave in public." Those watching her who were raised in that same tradition probably recognized fairly accurately the message she was sending. For those raised in a culture that expects tears and wailing as involuntary reactions to death, on the other hand, Mrs. Kennedy was perceived as being either cold, heartless, or worse. Both crying and laughing may be involuntary responses to stimuli, but we *learn,* through the groups into which we have been socialized, which is appropriate in which situation.

We really cannot control involuntary responses to stimuli, but please note that which stimulus produces which involuntary response is learned. Sweating and perhaps shaking in situations where we are nervous may be involuntary messages we send, but the stimuli that make us nervous are learned. The same for blushing when we are embarrassed or turning pale when we are frightened. Often we would dearly love to be able to control those responses so as not to let other people know how we feel, but most often they elude our conscious efforts at control.

The examples I have used are merely that: examples. For several reasons, I have made no effort to construct an exhaustive list of involuntary messages we are capable of sending. One reason is that they are not the same for all people, even in the same culture groups. Another is that different cultures teach different involuntary responses to stimuli. Recall the example of the shaking of the head used at the beginning of this chapter. For the Sri Lankans, it is just as involuntary to shake their heads from side to side as it is for people from the West to nod their heads. Still another reason for not attempting a list of involuntary messages that people send is that not all of them are known. Wilson Key reports, for example, that just as with many other animals, the human animal gives off an odor when we are sexually aroused.[48] What other involuntary messages we send that we do not yet know about remains to be discovered.

Subconscious messages   Because of the work done by Sigmund Freud and those who have followed him I doubt that anyone today would seriously question either the existence of our subconscious minds or the fact that we send many messages without being conscious of the fact that we are sending them. Every once in a while thoughts that we are having on the subconscious level intrude into our consciousness. The famous "Freudian slip" (when we say aloud what we were thinking on the subconscious level) forces us to recognize this. Indeed, there is little doubt today that the greatest bulk of our thinking processes occurs on the subconscious level. It also seems pretty clear today that it is a good thing for us that it does. It would just be too difficult for us to cope consciously with the vast number of thought processes that seem to be going on inside our brains simultaneously.

But if those thought processes are going on in the brain, it seems fairly clear that some indication of those thoughts will be communicated by us, somehow. Whether the person will be able to receive correctly what is being transmitted is another question entirely. But we will probably be communicating something.

Not every message we send is sent with enough intensity for the receiver to pick it up at the conscious level. Most often the message being sent—whatever it is—is just too weak (in terms of intensity of stimuli) to be consciously perceptible. Subliminally, however, there is no doubt such messages are being sent and received.

Although I do not have "hard" empirical evidence, I am fairly certain that most subconscious messages are transmitted subliminally. It would seem to me to be logical that this should be so. In the first place I am not certain that we are sufficiently practiced to be able to control subconscious messages. It seems to me that it may be somewhat analogous to the use of certain muscles of our body. They are there, and they function at an involuntary or subconscious level all the time. But before we can gain conscious control over their use we are required to put in a great deal of effort training ourselves in control over them. The number and location of those muscles is extraordinary. Most of us at one time or another have engaged in an activity that is outside our normal range of physical behavior, and if we do it long enough, the muscles involved can hurt the next day, whereupon we are likely to say, "I used muscles I didn't know I had till now." More to the point, however, we have many transmitter muscles of which we are totally unaware. Indeed, the NLP people have shown how obvious these involuntary subconscious messages become, once we know what to look for. I am certain that we use them all the time, but we have no idea—on a conscious level—that we do. Precisely because we are unaware of them at the conscious level, my suspicion is that the vast majority of messages we send are sent subliminally.

Channels of Communication (6)

Every message in every communication must be sent over a channel. Without a channel there is no way for a message to travel. In the case of one individual talking to another, the channel is the air through which the sound travels. In the case of a broadcast the channel is the airways. In a written communication the channel might be the postal system. If in the first case the sender whispers and the intended recipient is too far away to hear the message, no communication has occurred. If in the second case the intended recipient does not have a radio or does not have it turned on or tuned in to the correct frequency at the time of transmission, no communication has occurred. If in the third case the address is wrong and the letter never gets delivered, again no communication has occurred. One of the major problems in the communication process—but often one of the easiest to overcome—is the lack of sufficient channels of communication. The so-called hotline between Moscow and Washington was set up precisely so that there would be a direct channel of communication between the leader of the Soviet Union and the president of the United States over which messages could travel, if those gentlemen chose to use it. That, of course, is a different problem. We can set up all of the channels of communication we want, but if the people the channels were intended to serve choose not to use them, no communication will take place. Still, having the channel there is one of the first steps to effective communication. Once the channel exists there is, at least, the possibility that the parties will use it. Without that channel the certainty is that no communication will occur. Since certain groups may have a cultural preference for one type of channel over another, it is likely that our message would be attended to more seriously if we knew their cultural perference and transmitted our message over their preferred channel.

Another point that should be made is that if it is important that there be open communication between two persons or two places at all times, it is probably wise to be certain that there exists a number of different channels, so that in the event one channel gets blocked (for whatever reason) or does not work temporarily, another channel will be available. For example, trying to get a message through on a telephone will be no good if a storm has knocked down all of the telephone lines, but if there is a direct radio link, messages can still get through.

In the previous section I argued that all of us use many transmitters to send the same message simultaneously, which is good because it helps to get the message across as the sender intended it to be received. That works best in face-to-face communication, of course, because all of the channels are available for each of the messages to travel through, so that the receiver's sensory receptors can be stimulated by all of the messages being sent. One of the reasons telephone communication is so unsatisfactory is precisely that although the sender is transmitting nonverbal messages along with the verbal, the only channel being utilized to transmit the message is the channel to convey the verbal message. Hence, the other messages are being lost, so to speak, and the full communication is not being picked up by the receiver for lack of sufficient channels.

But even if the channels between sender and receiver are adequate to the messages being sent, there are still difficulties to be overcome.

Noise

In every communication system there is what the communication specialist calls noise. Noise is anything that interferes with the transmission of the message. It might be a baby crying and drowning out the voice of the sender in a face-to-face conversation or the gum the speaker was chewing at the time he was talking, or a beautiful sight that caught the eye of the intended recipient and distracted her attention just at the moment the message was being sent. Or it might be some nonverbal body movement that is perfectly acceptable in one's own culture but offensive in another. In the example, where the airways are the channel, the noise might be the electrical storm that interferes with the airwaves or the jamming of certain frequencies that many governments practice or the irritating accent of the speaker that causes the recipient to pay more attention to the speech pattern of the speaker than to the message. In the example of written communications, noise could be the poor handwriting that makes the message illegible, or the rain that smears the address and makes the letter undeliverable, or the psychological state of the recipient at the time of receiving the letter that prompts him to throw it away unopened.

Sometimes there is something in our minds that is so important or so all consuming that we are simply not able to concentrate on anything else except that subject. That, too, constitutes noise with regard to communication on all other topics.

Although a problem, noise is one of the easiest problems in the communication process to overcome, provided we take it into account and then compensate for it. If the heating system or the traffic outside or anything else is making noise, we simply have to speak louder to overcome the noise level. If our message was interrupted by any one of the "noises" mentioned thus far in this section, all we have to do is be aware of the problem and we can take steps to rectify it.

Not all problems of noise in the system can be overcome completely, however. Sometimes differences in attitudes or values or other cultural differences constitute noise in a communication system. In the example of the open zipper used earlier, the violation of a cultural norm created noise. The lack of trust that often exists between individuals, groups, or nations can constitute noise in the communication process. Someone from group "us" may not be able to "hear" what someone from group "them" is saying, not because the intensity of the message is too low or because of lack of linguistic or other codes but rather because the mistrust between them is so great that virtually nothing a "them" said would be received by "us" as it was intended. That constitutes noise. Often the mistrust between the parties is so great that no direct communication can occur. In those cases the only way to establish any communication is through some "neutral third party," whom both trust, through which at least some communication can occur. In those kinds of situations there can probably be no direct communication until at least some modicum of trust can be established so that the level of "noise" in the system is reduced.

In short, not all noise can be dealt with by increasing the intensity of the message or by removing the cause of the noise. Nevertheless, noise is one problem in the communication process that is *relatively* easy to overcome, some of the time.

ROLE OF FEEDBACK IN COMMUNICATION

Perhaps the most important method for overcoming the deficiencies of the communication process is feedback—the return to the sender of data about the results of his or her communication effort. Feedback is built directly into some communication systems, particularly that of face-to-face communications. If the receiver of a message in a face-to-face communication does not understand some portion of the message being sent, she or he can immediately convey that lack of understanding to the original sender, who can then attempt to correct the deficiency. This is precisely why face-to-face communication can be so effective. But we are constantly getting feedback from the environment as well. Earlier in this chapter I said I wanted to add Dean Barnlund's model of the communication process as a refinement of my own. Here is the place to do that. The reason that I feel that Barnlund's model is important is that feedback from both the environment and the individuals are such an integral part of his model. Also it conveys better than my own, I think, the continuous nature of the communication process.[49]

Barnlund starts with a hypothetical case of a single person (Mr. A) sitting alone in a doctor's office. There are three sets of cases Mr. A can and does attend to simultaneously: what he calls public cues, private cues, and nonverbal behavioral cues. Mr. A assigns meaning to these cues (decodes them). He also transforms (encodes) these stimuli to which he attends into "neuro-muscular sets," which in turn are available to others in the form of verbal and nonverbal cues.

The public and private cues themselves can be any stimulus, verbal or nonverbal, to which Mr. A can attend. To be a "public cue" these stimuli must be "part of, or available to, the perceptual field of all potential communicants." Private cues are stimuli that are not automatically available to anyone else (for example, the fact that there is a pain in his stomach, or the memory that he has an appointment in an hour that he must keep). Whether public or private, both types of cues in Barnlund's model must have been created prior to the event under analysis and must remain outside the control of the persons under observation.

Nonverbal behavior cues are the behaviors of Mr. A himself—seeing his own reflection in a mirror, straightening his tie, or changing his position in the chair. They differ from public and private cues in that they are initiated or controlled by Mr. A himself whether consciously or unconsciously. To all of these cues Mr. A can and does assign positive, negative, or neutral values based on his prior conditioning. But he does not attend to all of them simultaneously. Rather, he selects from the plethora available as his attention or gaze shifts from some to others. Barnlund points out that given the opportunity, the individual will probably attend to those stimuli he has assigned positive meanings and values to rather than attend to meanings he has assigned negative values to.

From Barnlund's description, the reader should get a sense of the richness and complexity of *intra*personal communication alone. Remember, no other individual has yet been introduced into the model. All of this communication and steady flow of feedback is occurring from within the individual and between the individual and the environment.

As soon as another individual is introduced into the model (Mr. B in Barnlund's model), the picture gets infinitely more complicated. In the first place, the other individual has the option to attend (or not to attend) to all of the public environmental cues that Mr. A was exposed to. He will assign different meanings to many of those cues than Mr. A did, to be sure, but the same public stimuli are there for anyone to attribute meanings to. He will also bring with him his own set of private cues to which Mr. A will have no more access than Mr. B has access to Mr. A's private cues. More important for the study of intercultural communication, however, each will try to attend to the verbal and nonverbal behavior cues of the other, attributing meaning to each of the cues based on his own past experience, attitudes, and values rather than on the other person's, which of course are not known to him. What is more (and this is the reason I have included this in the feedback section rather than elsewhere), each person will begin to regulate the cues he provides for the other, each may recognize (Barnlund says "will recognize") the possible meanings the other may attach to his actions, and perhaps even more important, each will attempt to interpret his own acts as if he were the other. Barnlund says that "these two features, the deliberate choice and control of cues and the projection of interpretation constitute the criteria for identifying interpersonal messages."[50]

While there may be problems with Barnlund's model, I like it because it conveys the sense that the communication process is an ongoing continuous process rather than a series of discrete events and also because it represents the incredible complexity of that process. Add to that how much more difficult it becomes (1) when the two individuals in the exchange do not share a great many cultures in common (and therefore will attribute different meaning to the same cues) and (2) when more than two people are involved.

Let's leave Barnlund's model now and take a look at an exercise that Harold Levitt devised many years ago to demonstrate the necessity for feedback in communication.[51] In that exercise a volunteer is given a sheet of paper with six or seven rectangles drawn on it. The drawing is the message, and the volunteer is asked to communicate that message to a group of people who will attempt to draw it from his or her instructions as precisely as possible. The exercise is done twice: once without any feedback and the second time with feedback. Almost invariably without feedback no more than 20 percent of the people (and usually considerably less) are able to approach correct representation in their drawing of the placement of the rectangles on the page. With feedback—that is, with participants asking as many questions as they feel are necessary in order to draw it correctly—between 50 and 90 percent are able to make a very close approximation of the correct placement of the rectangles. The exercise with feedback usually takes *at least* twice as long as the same exercise without it, but the results in terms of precision of communication are obviously worth the extra time.

One of the more interesting things about the experiment is that when the sender estimates, immediately after she has attempted to communicate without feedback, how many in her audience got the message more or less accurately, she almost always overestimates the number she believes to have received her message. Invariably she thinks she has communicated quite well. Similarly, if the audience is asked immediately after they have completed the exercise without feedback how well they think they have drawn the rectangles, they too overestimate their degree of success. Many more people think they have done the drawing accurately than actually have. Now, if no feedback were built into the system, both sender and receiver would believe they had communicated quite well, even though they had not. Only when the exercise is repeated, introducing feedback, do both sender and receiver begin to estimate realistically how well or poorly they are communicating.

An even more interesting aspect of this exercise is that it is one of the only examples I know where one can actually compare visually the message as it was sent and the message as it was received. In recent years I have taken the drawings done in my classes without feedback and put them up on the wall on one side of the room, separating into two columns those by students who said they had done the drawing correctly and those by students who said they had done it incorrectly. On the other side of the room I have put on the wall all of the drawings that were done with feedback, dividing them in the same way. Through this procedure some startling facts became obvious:

1. The overall contrast in the degree of correctness between those drawings done with feedback and those done without becomes immediately apparent.

2. The variety of opinions on how correct *correct* really is also becomes apparent. Invariably there are some drawings by students who said they had done them incorrectly that are far more correct than other drawings by those who said they had done them correctly. Similarly, there are always some drawings in the "correct" section that are far more incorrect than many of the drawings hanging in the "incorrect" section.

For me this is a striking example of how badly we generally communicate most of the time, even when the message is culturally neutral and far from threatening. If we can't communicate accurately how to draw approximately six rectangles on a page among educated adults who are more or less culturally homogeneous, how can we ever hope to communicate accurately with someone with totally different perceptions, attitudes, values, and belief systems?

Rectangles drawn on a page in a particular arrangement is a relatively unambiguous message. The more ambiguous or abstract the message becomes, the less accurately it is likely to be communicated. If culturally similar people have difficulty communicating among themselves how to draw rectangles, how can people who are culturally heterogeneous possibly communicate about subjects like democracy, justice, equality, or social change?

More than anything else, what repeated use of this exercise (in any number of different cultural settings) has taught me is that when I ask people if they understand what I have said and they nod their heads yes, all I can be sure of is that the muscles that connect their heads to their necks are in good working order.

What depresses me most about the implications of this exercise is that most of the time we tend to attempt to communicate without feedback or at least without adequate feedback. There are a number of reasons why this is so:

1. Communicating with feedback often takes *at least* twice as long (sometimes much longer), and none of us has the time to use feedback in every communication we attempt.

2. The process of giving feedback, aside from being time consuming, is exhausting. When I ask the people who have volunteered to do the exercise how they feel when it is over, "tired," "drained," or "exhausted" are the words I hear most often. None of us has the physical or psychological energy that would be required to communicate with adequate feedback all the time.

3. Most of us, I'm afraid, would rather *not* have the feedback on how well or

poorly we have communicated. We would all, I think, rather just assume that we have communicated well and let it go at that.

4. Mass-communication systems—such as the mass media: television, radio, newspapers, and magazines—simply do not have direct feedback built into their systems. They can tell if their number of viewers, listeners, or readers drops, but there is little or no direct way that they can know how their audience has perceived the material they have put out. When you consider that most people learn about events around the world—of vital importance to their well-being—almost exclusively via the mass media, one is forced to pause and wonder how accurately they can possibly be getting the message.

Having said all of this, however, I must add a positive note. Difficult as the communication process may be, the fact is that all of us communicate all of the time. We may not do it as well as we could, but we do it. What's more we do it at times with people who share few of the perceptions we hold. In other words, difficult and complex though the process may be, we do it all the time, so we know it is not impossible. Understanding these complexities should not paralyze us; rather, knowing how complex the process is, we will approach it somewhat more realistically than we have previously. Just doing that should automatically make us better intercultural communicators.

PROPOSITIONAL SUMMARY FOR CHAPTER 3

The purpose of communication: Virtually all human communications are attempts to achieve goals. The goals may be as simple as wanting to buy two tickets to the theater or as complex as trying to prevent a thermonuclear holocaust. Regardless of the complexity of the message, consciously or unconsciously the sender is always trying to achieve a purpose by sending the message.

Communication is a process: As a process, communication is continually going on, through feedback, with the environment and everything in that environment. It is a process that never ceases until we die.

The same communication process operates at all levels of analysis: The same process operates whether one considers intra- or interpersonal communication, intra- or intergroup communication, or intra- or international communication. The specifics of how that process operates changes as one changes the actors and settings, but the process remains constant.

The Communication Process Dissected

Senders and receivers: Since this work focuses primarily on human communication, the individual is the basic unit of analysis. The individual is both sender and receiver of communication simultaneously. There is no way one cannot be. We both receive and send off messages all the time—twenty-four hours a day.

Messages: *Message* is a communication term, used in the strict sense to mean any stimulus that can be perceived by the nerve endings in any of our sensory receptors. Each discrete "bit" of data that fires even one or two nerve endings in any of our receptors can be viewed as a message. More commonly, we think of a message as being a pattern of perhaps hundreds of thousands of discrete bits of data that make up an intelligible whole, but depending on the circumstances, the individual bits of data themselves can be viewed as being messages. The stimuli by themselves have no meaning. People attribute meaning to the stimuli, thereby transforming them into messages.

Nonhuman messages: Unquestionably, the greatest number of messages we receive, every moment of the day, are from nonhuman sources. The eyes pick up everything within their line of vision; the nerve endings on the skin react to temperature as well as touch; the ears pick up all the sounds around us; the nose picks up a variety of smells—all at the same time. We may be receiving messages only subconsciously, but we are receiving them nonetheless.

Human messages, verbal and nonverbal: The human animal is continuously sending out a multitude of messages simultaneously. The vast majority of the messages we send are nonverbal, and we are most often not even aware that we are sending them. Everyone is communicating so many different messages at the same time (even if they are not trying to mask them) that it is difficult, in the extreme, to know to which messages one should attend.

Subliminal messages: *Subliminal* means beneath the threshold, or "limen," of awareness. Subliminal messages are that vast number of messages we send and receive without being conscious of the fact that we are either sending or receiving. The work of the neuro-linguistic programmers has focused primarily on the nonverbal messages all of us send and receive all of the time.

Sensory receptors: Sensory receptors are those body mechanisms that allow us to take in information from the external environment. While Aristotle identified five senses—sight (eyes), sound (ears), smell (nose), taste (tongue), and touch (hands)—modern research indicates that there are many more.

Decision making: For every single bit of data picked up by our sensory receptors, a decision has to be made by us with regard to it. Is it to enter our consciousness, remain subconscious, or be totally ignored? Is it to be merely stored or acted upon immediately? If it is to be acted upon, how? There are a number of processes at work in each of those decisions, and it should be remembered that they are all operating simultaneously and at incredibly rapid rates of speed.

Censor screens: Obviously we cannot attend equally to all of the stimuli to which we are exposed. Some stimuli are so important or so salient to us that regardless of level of intensity, we are likely to pick them out first. Hence the first range of decisions the brain has to deal with, are what to focus on and what to block out. That process is taken care of by our censor screens.

Decoding: Coding has been called "a culturally defined, rule-governed system of shared arbitrary symbols used to transmit (and elicit) meaning." Meanings are not transmitted, symbols are. Decoding is the process by which the human checks his or her data-storage bank to determine the meaning, if any, he or she has learned to ascribe to a particular symbol.

Data-storage bank: The data-storage bank in everyone's brain is the world's most complex, sophisticated, and fastest information and retrieval system. It contains not only information about everything we have ever learned or felt but also information about how to go about learning what we do not yet know.

Superego screen: To prevent the public expression of our most primitive instinctive urges, every human constructs for himself or herself what I call a superego screen. It is a filter we impose between the instinctive animal reactions we have to certain stimuli and the actual reactions we allow ourselves to make. I call it a superego screen because it contains all of the information we have learned from our identity groups about what reactions to stimuli are expected and accepted by those groups.

Encoding: Encoding is the reverse of decoding. It is the process by which we decide what symbols to use to present the particular message we want to send. Normally we choose those symbols that we believe the recipient of our message will be able to decode.

Transmitter: Our entire bodies are transmitters of messages—our voice, our eyes, our face, our heads, our hands, our skin, our muscles. Each part of our body is capable of transmitting messages. To the degree that we can use all or most of our transmitters to communicate the same message simultaneously, we will certainly be more effective in getting our message across.

Conscious messages: Conscious messages are those we consciously choose to send. They can be verbal or nonverbal. The range and magnitude of ways in which we can send conscious messages is enormous. Probably the major limitations on how we send conscious messages are the constraints of the situation, the distances involved, the number of people to whom the message is being sent, their attitudes toward us, the context in which the message is being sent, and the limits of our imagination.

Involuntary messages: Involuntary messages are those messages we send that we cannot control. Both crying and laughing may be involuntary responses to stimuli, but we learn through the groups into which we have been socialized which is appropriate in which situation.

Subconscious messages: All of us send messages without being consciously aware that we are sending them. Although I have no "hard" empirical evidence to substantiate it, I am fairly certain that the vast majority of all the messages we transmit are subconscious messages.

Channels of communication: Every message in every communication must be sent over a channel. Without a channel, there is no way for a message to travel. One of the major problems in the communication process—but often one of the easiest to overcome—is the lack of sufficient channels of communication. Once the channel exists, there is at least the possibility that the parties will use it. Without the channel the certainty is that no communication will occur.

Noise: In the communication sense, noise is anything that interferes with the transmission of a message. Every communication system contains noise. Noise is another of those problems in every communication system that is *relatively* easy to overcome—provided we know it is there.

Role of feedback in communication: Perhaps the most important method for overcoming the deficiencies of the communication process is feedback—the return to the sender of data about the results of his or her communication effort. Communication with feedback often takes at least twice as long as communication without it, but the difference in degree of similarity between the message sent and the message received tends to rise sharply when feedback is introduced.

NOTES

[1] Paul Watzlawick, Janet Beavin, and Don Jackson, "Some Tentative Axioms of Communication," in C. David Mortensen, ed., *Basic Readings in Communication Theory* (New York: Harper & Row, 1973), p. 37.

[2] Porter and Samovar tell us that Sri Lanka is not the only place where people gesture no nonverbally in a different way. " . . . an Abyssinian is apt to express no by jerking the head to the right shoulder; a Dyand of Borneo may express it by contracting the eyebrows slightly; and Sicilians express no by raising the head and chin." Richard E. Porter and Larry A. Samovar, "Communicating Interculturally," p. 22 and also see Roman Jakobson, "Nonverbal Signs for 'Yes' and 'No,'" pp. 235–40; both in Samovar and Porter, eds., *Intercultural Communication: A Reader,* 2nd ed. (Belmont, CA: Wadsworth Publishing Co., 1976).

[3] George A. Barnett and D. Lawrence Kincaid, "Cultural Convergence: A Mathematical Theory," in William B. Gudykunst, ed., *Intercultural Communication Theory: Current Perspectives,* which is also the *International and Intercultural Communication Annual,* vol. VII (Beverly Hills, CA: Sage Publications, 1983), p. 173.

[4] Brent D. Ruben, "A System-Theoretic View," in ibid., p. 141.

[5] H. D. Lasswell, "The Structure and Function of Communications in Society," cited in Kim Giffin and Bobby R. Patton, eds., *Fundamentals of Interpersonal Communication* (New York: Harper & Row, 1971).

⁶ Gudykunst, *Intercultural Communication Theory*, p. 46.

⁷ Although some scholars would make a distinction between a theory and a model, it is not important for our purposes to do so here.

⁸ Gudykunst, *Intercultural Communication Theory*, p. 46.

⁹ Claude Shannon and Warren Weaver, *The Mathematical Theory of Communication* (Urbana: University of Illinois Press, 1949). See particularly Norbert Wiener, *Cybernetics* (Cambridge: Technology Press of MIT, and New York: John Wiley & Sons, 1948); and his *Human Use of Human Beings* (New York: Houghton Mifflin, 1964); also Colin Cherry, *On Human Communication: A Review, A Survey, and A Criticism* (Cambridge: MIT Press; New York: John Wiley & Sons, 1957; and New York: Science Editions, 1961). See particularly Karl Deutsch, *Nationalism and Social Communication, An Inquiry into the Foundations of Nationality* (Cambridge: Technology Press of MIT, 1953) and his *The Nerves of Government* (New York: Free Press, 1963).

¹⁰ As initially developed by Shannon, Cherry, and Wiener particularly, the model applies to machine/machine and human/machine communication as well.

¹¹ Mortensen, ed., *Basic Readings*, p. 1.

¹² Dean C. Barnlund, "A Transactional Model of Communication," in Johnnye Akin, Alvin Goldberg, Gail Myers, and Joseph Stewart, eds., *Language Behavior: A Book of Readings in Communication* (The Hague: Morton, 1970), p. 50.

¹³ See Bernard Berelson and Gary A. Steiner, *Human Behavior: An Inventory of Scientific Findings* (New York: Harcourt, Brace & World, 1964), p. 93.

¹⁴ Compare, for example, ibid., p. 95, with Wilson Bryan Key, *Subliminal Seduction* (New York: Thomas Y. Crowell, 1968).

¹⁵ E. H. Hess, as reported in Berelson and Steiner, *Human Behavior*, pp. 103, 104.

¹⁶ See particularly Richard Bandler and John Grinder, *Frogs into Princes: Neuro-Linguistic Programming* (Moab, UT: Real People Press, 1979); and Robert Dilts, John Grinder, Richard Bandler, Leslie C. Bandler, and Judith DeLozier, *Neuro-Linguistic Programming*, vol. I, *The Study of the Structure of Subjective Experience* (Cupertino, CA: Meta Publications, 1980). I am indebted to Dr. Edward Rindler for bringing these works to my attention.

¹⁷ The only exception the NLP people have found thus far are the people from the Basque region of Spain, which leads them to believe that those people share some genetic trait that no other group of people in the world known to them share.

¹⁸ Dilts et al., *Neuro-Linguistic Programming*, pp. 79-85.

¹⁹ Caution to the reader: You may not have the preference you think you do. I used to think I had a visual preference because I often need to see something in writing before I understand it. Yet after reading about neuro-linguistic programming, I now realize that when I look at something I don't "see it," but rather I sound out the words and therefore "hear it" in my head as I read.

²⁰ Key, *Subliminal Seduction*, pp. 15-16.

²¹ Ibid., p. 16 (italics in original).

²² Ibid., p. 15.

²³ Ibid., p. 14.

²⁴ Reported to me in a personal communication from Anthony Solow.

²⁵ At a lecture given at the University of Pittsburgh in the late 1960s.

²⁶ This may not be as startling an argument as it first appears. Recall Figure 1.2 in chapter 1, on perceptions, and the section called "Relationship of Stimulus to Surroundings." It is, indeed, likely that oranges and reds would appear very different in northern light—where there is no intense sunlight—than they would at the equator.

²⁷ Berelson and Steiner, *Human Behavior*, p. 100.

²⁸ Joseph H. deRivera, *The Psychological Dimension of Foreign Policy* (Columbus, OH: Charles E. Merrill, 1968), pp. 42-43.

²⁹ Berelson and Steiner, *Human Behavior*, p. 100.

³⁰ G. W. Allport and L. Postman, *The Psychology of Rumor* (New York: Holt, Rinehart

& Winston, 1947), as reported in Otto Klineberg, *The Human Dimension in International Relations* (New York: Holt, Rinehart & Winston, 1964), p. 42.

[31] Ibid., p. 42.

[32] This second experiment was reported to me in a personal communication.

[33] L. E. Sarbaugh and Nobleza Asuncion-Lande, "Theory Building in Intercultural Communication: Synthesizing the Action Caucus," in Gudykunst, *Intercultural Communication Theory*, pp. 48 and 60. See also Ralph E. Cooley's article in the same book, "Codes and Contexts: An Argument for Their Description," pp. 241–51.

[34] See Sheila J. Ramsey, "Nonverbal Behavior: An Intercultural Perspective," in Molefi Kete Asante, Eileen Newmark, and Cecil A. Blake, eds., *Handbook of Intercultural Communication* (Beverly Hills, CA: Sage Publishing Co., 1979), p. 135.

[35] See John C. Condon and Fathi S. Yousef, *An Introduction to Intercultural Communication* (Indianapolis: Bobbs-Merrill, 1975).

[36] See Shirley Weitz, ed., *Non-Verbal Communication: Readings with Commentary* (Oxford: Oxford University Press, 1974); Julius Fast, *Body Language* (New York: Pocketbooks, 1971); and particularly the Ramsey article in Asante et al., *Handbook of Intercultural Communication*.

[37] Albert Mehrabian, *Silent Messages: Implicit Communication of Emotions and Attitudes,* 2nd Edition (Belmont, CA: Wadsworth Publishing Co., 1981), p. 3.

[38] See Edward T. Hall, *The Silent Language* (Greenwich, CT: Fawcett Publications, 1959).

[39] See his chart in ibid., p. 163.

[40] See the study by S. E. Jones and J. R. Aiello in *Journal of Personality and Social Psychology,* cited in Stanley E. Jones, "Integrating ETIC and EMIC Approaches in the Study of Intercultural Communication," in Asante et al., *Handbook of Intercultural Communication;* also Kenneth R. Johnson, "Black Kinesics: Some Non-Verbal Communication Patterns in the Black Culture," in Samovar and Porter, *Intercultural Communication,* pp. 259–68.

[41] Personal communication to the author.

[42] Edward T. Hall, *Beyond Culture* (New York: Anchor Press/Doubleday, 1976), p. 61.

[43] Ibid., pp. 63–64.

[44] See, for example, Donald Cushman and Gordon C. Whiting, "An Approach to Communication Theory: Towards Consensus on Rules," in *Journal of Communication* 22 (September 1972), 217–38.

[45] The term is Deutsch's, but the oversimplification of Freud presented here is mine.

[46] See, for example, Fast, *Body Language,* and Weitz, *Nonverbal Communication;* Mehrabian, *Silent Messages,* Ramsey's "Nonverbal Behavior," and Dilts, *Neuro-Linguistic Programming.*

[47] See, for example, John T. Malloy, *Dress for Success* (New York: P. H. Weyden, 1975).

[48] Key, *Subliminal Seduction,* p. 19.

[49] The Barnlund model is taken from Dean C. Barnlund, "A Transactional Model of Communication," in Akin et al., *Language Behavior,* pp. 44–61.

[50] Ibid., p. 58.

[51] See Harold Levitt, *Managerial Psychology,* 2nd ed. (Chicago: University of Chicago Press, 1964), chap. 9.

CHAPTER FOUR
THE ROLE OF POWER
IN COMMUNICATION

THE POLITICS OF HUMAN BEHAVIOR

Harold Lasswell described politics as the study of "who gets what, when and how,"[1] and that is the sense in which I propose to use the term here. When I speak of the political process, I do not mean who is running for office or what bills the legislature is trying to pass, although those matters are certainly part of the political process. Rather, I will be using terms like *power* and *influence* in the broadest sense to mean how people, groups, and nations try to get what they want from other people, groups, and/or nations. How do they go about trying to fulfill their needs, goals, and values? What happens when the group's needs are not the same as the individual's or the nation's? The answers to these and similar questions are what the study of power is all about.

If I am correct in my contention that virtually all communications have a goal or a purpose—conscious or otherwise—then obviously to one degree or another all communications become, in part, an attempt to exercise influence; all behavior becomes, in part, "political" behavior. *It would be an overstatement to say that all human behavior is power oriented. It would not be an overstatement to say that there is an element of an attempt to exercise influence in all human behavior.* The part of behavior that is power-oriented is that part that attempts to exercise influence over others or to prevent others from exercising influence over us.

In Lasswell and Kaplan's terms there is no question but that every group, organization, and nation has most of the "welfare values" (well-being, wealth, skills, and enlightenment) and "deference values" (power, respect, rectitude, and affection) that the individual does. Indeed, they are very specific about applying their model to both individuals and groups. But again please note: while each individual, group, organization, and nation may have these values, each will have them in different degrees, and each will rank order them very differently depending on the nature of the group (its personality, if you will), the group culture, and the context of the situation. Accordingly, it is highly relevant to the study of intercultural communication to try to understand the power aspects of different relationships.

POWER: WHAT IS IT?

Power has been a central theme of Western political philosophy and political science since the writings of Aristotle. Lasswell and Kaplan make the point that "the concept of power is perhaps the most fundamental in the whole of political science: the political process is the shaping, distribution and exercise of power (in a wider sense . . . of influence in general)."[2] Although power has been discussed and analyzed from a number of perspectives, power is probably best understood as an interpersonal process.

In *Power and Personality* Harold Lasswell treats the relationship of the individual personality to the striving for power:

> That men want power is a statement we can accept as true in every society where power exists: and this is not to say whether everybody wants it with the same intensity or whether the drive for power is innate or acquired. For the purpose of analyzing the social process, power is unmistakably a value, in the sense that it is desired (or likely to be desired).[3]

Quoting Tawney's definition of power as "the capacity of an individual, or group of individuals, to modify the conduct of other individuals or groups in the manner which he desires," Lasswell and Kaplan note: "The making of decisions is an interpersonal process: the policies which other persons are to pursue are what is decided upon. Power as participation in the making of decisions is an interpersonal relation."[4]

One simply cannot deny that power exists as an operative factor at every level of interpersonal, intergroup, and international relations; that it has always existed; and that it always will exist in these relationships. Although social scientists have been frustrated in their attempts to analyze power because it is so difficult to measure, it nevertheless must be analyzed and discussed and understood if we are ever to be in a position to cope realistically with the complexities of those relationships.

As used in this book, power is a relative term. In a positive sense, it is the ability to influence others to behave in a manner desired by the one wielding the power. In a negative sense, it is the ability to prevent others from exerting influence on one's own behavior. Is power, then, the same as influence? Not quite. Power is the *ability* to exercise influence and the *ability* to prevent influence from being exercised over oneself. Whether the individual, group, or nation will choose to use the power it has in a given situation is another point entirely. That relates to what was said earlier about power as a value. Some individuals, groups, and nations—at different times and/or in different contexts (for whatever reasons)—may choose not to use the ability they possess. But if they have that ability to exercise influence—whether they use it or not—then I consider them powerful. If in fact they do not have the will to use the power they have—as distinct from ability—that is a different matter. In that case I would argue that to the degree they are lacking in will, everything else being held equal, to that degree their power is diminished. More will be said about *will* under "Components of Power" below.

People, groups, and nations tend to try to maximize their power in order to prevent others from being in a position to influence them and because they want to be in a position to influence others when they perceive the need and/or opportunity. To the degree that representatives of groups or nations are chosen (by whatever process) to be leaders, they are chosen because their constituents believe that those individuals will protect and/or advance the interests of the group. If the leaders come to be seen by the people they are supposed to represent as not exercising maximum influence to obtain desired group goals, those leaders are very likely to be replaced by others considered more capable of doing the job. The union leader who is perceived by the rank and file as accepting of too many of the demands of management runs just as great a risk of being replaced by a more "militant" leader as does the head of a government when he is perceived by his constituents as not representing *their* interests.

Nations seem to be the entities that make the broadest definition of what are "legitimate" ways to exercise influence. Every religion in the world and every state has some sort of "thou shalt not kill" prescription written into its basic law. An individual may not kill another individual from the same nation, merely because he believes it is in his own interest to do so. But if he kills as an agent of the nation to achieve what is believed to be in the national interest, there is rarely any punishment. Under certain circumstances (such as in time of war) if one of "us" kills enough of "them," instead of being punished, he will be considered a hero and may even get a medal. However, killing (coercion) is only one of the ways of exercising influence—and in fact it is the way that is used least often. Every day of every year, every individual, group, organization, and nation exercises at least some influence over other indivudals, groups, organizations, and nations, and only rarely do they rely on coercion as the means of achieving their ends.

Because there are many different ways in which influence may be exerted, there are many different manifestations of power. One speaks of the power of the pen or the power of the purse or the power of an army. But power is contextual. That is, the pen, or the purse, or the army is powerful only if it is used in an appropriate context. A brilliant, logical discourse may influence the behavior of people who hear it in the quiet of a lecture hall, but it could not possibly have any impact on them if they were in the midst of a battlefield. They simply would not be able to hear it. Conversely, in a world where increasing attention is paid to the battle for the "minds of men," chemical mace, napalm, and nuclear weapons may be totally inappropriate as instruments of power in a great many contexts.

Individuals, groups, and nations have power, in part and under some circumstances, because of their ability to coerce, but in *greater* measure and in many *more* circumstances they have power because they are able to *persuade* other individuals, groups, or nations to want the same things they want. And most often persuasion takes noncoercive forms. To present arguments in a way the other party can understand and accept as being in his or her or its own best interest is perhaps the most common and most effective form of persuasion. (That is why a chapter like this is essential in a book on intercultural communications. Successful communication with another individual, group, or nation means, if nothing else, that you were able to *persuade* the other to understand your message the way you intended it to be understood. If you have convinced others to do or think something you wanted them to do or think because you were successful in convincing them that it was in their interest to want the same thing you wanted, you have been successful indeed. Clearly, the more different, culturally, the other person, group, or nation is from you, the more difficult the process of exercising that influence will be.) If I am doing something only because I feel you are forcing me to, I will probably do it only half-heartedly in the first instance, and the moment your back is turned I probably won't do it at all. But if I am doing something because I am convinced that it is in my own best interest to do it, you can be certain that I will do it with persistence and perseverance. Thus what many scholars and practitioners fail to see is that power rests as much or more on the ability to persuade as it does on the ability to coerce. Influence can be, and often is, exercised without the persons being influenced even aware that it is happening. Certainly people will do what others want—within limits—in order to gain access to the things (material or nonmaterial) they desire. That is why in relations between weak and powerful individuals, groups, or states, coercion is for the most part not necessary to achieve the long-term policy goals of the more powerful. As early as 1934, Charles E. Merriam wrote:

> Power is not strongest when it uses violence, but weakest. It is strongest when it employs the instruments of substitution and counter attraction, of allurement, or participation rather than of exclusion, of education rather than of annihilation. Rape is not an evidence of irresistible power in politics or in sex.[5]

An attractive instrument of power is anything (material or nonmaterial) possessed by one individual, group, or nation that another desires, and seeks to obtain by doing what the possessor desires. Obviously, there are limits on what one will do in order to achieve certain goals, but those limits are relative and contextual. In order to achieve a higher education—if that is perceived by the individual as important and/or desirable—one may sacrifice a great deal (leisure, money, time), but rarely will one sacrifice his or her family.

If a person is hungry and another person produces more food that he can consume, the hungry person is much more likely to pay the price the person with food asks (which means doing what the person with food wants) than he is to hit him over the head to get it. The hungrier an individual, group, or nation is, the higher a "price" it will pay to get the needed food. A moderately hungry man is not likely to kill in order to obtain food, but a starving man is very likely to do so.

This is not to say that coercive instruments never work. Obviously, they do—particularly in the short run. But they often create hostility, which may be more damaging to the long-run interests of groups than any apparent short-term gain may have been worth.

One further point on the nature of power. It is often charged that power, or "power politics," is evil or immoral. Others sometimes argue that it is noble or virtuous. This simply is not a useful way of viewing the matter. Whether their ends are base or noble, there can be no doubt that people will use power to serve those ends. But power, as such—like effective communication—is neither good nor bad. People who have power may confuse themselves with gods, but power itself is simply an existing capacity, to be reckoned with as a fact of life.

The Components of Power

Looking at the subject of power from this perspective, one can argue that either domestically or internationally, in terms of interpersonal, intergroup, or international relations, the five basic components of power are wealth (material and human), organization (formal and informal), information (basic and specific), status (ascribed and acquired), and will (conscious and subconscious).[6]

Now all of these components are themselves values that individuals, groups, and nations may aspire to. Indeed, power itself is a value to which individuals, groups, and nations aspire. We might as well recognize that although all of us aspire to different values in different proportions and with different rankings, many of the values to which we aspire are power values. Thus we are introduced here to another of those circular causality loops. Power gives us the ability to achieve many of the values to which we aspire, but since many of those values are themselves power values, to the degree that we achieve those values we have acquired additional power.

What makes the wedding of intercultural communication theory to political science theory so fascinating to me is my conviction that we cannot understand one without understanding the other. The two are completely intertwined and dependent upon each other. We know that each individual and group ranks values differently. What we do not know—because no one has bothered to study it until now—is how each of us (and each of our groups) ranks those values in each context. It is an incomplete political science that ignores the attitudes and values of the individuals and groups it purports to study. It is equally as incomplete a field of intercultural communication that ignores the influence (power) component of the attitudes and values it purports to study.

In presenting this analysis, I take as a basic premise that the exercise of power is a process. That is precisely what Lasswell and Kaplan discussed in their book. Since it is a process, it should be possible to apply the model not only to interpersonal and intergroup relations but to interstate relations as well. Thus it is on all levels that components of power will be discussed.

Wealth: Material and human It is not coincidence that historically the countries considered the most powerful have at the same time also been the most wealthy. Nor is it accidental that the individuals and groups possessing the most material wealth within their societies usually wield the most influence and are considered the most powerful. Nor is it accidental that the poor or unskilled individual, the poor group, and the poor nation normally wield the least influence in their respective spheres.

It is a basic fact of human existence that individuals, groups, and nations having material wealth are usually in a position to influence others. The reason for this, of course, is that those who are not wealthy usually want some of the things wealth can make possible. Thus they will often do what the possessors of wealth want them to do in order to have a share in that wealth. If the "have-nots" did not value the manifestations of wealth, there would be no chance for the "haves" to exert influence. In that sense, it is the "have-nots" who give the "haves" power by allowing themselves to be influenced. Overwhelmingly individuals, groups, and nations seek to maximize their wealth. And—though it may not be their conscious goal—they are at the same time attempting to maximize their power, since wealth is one of power's components.

What is this wealth that is so universally sought? Wealth, in the broadest sense of the term, is both material and human. By material wealth I mean not only money and the possessions that money can buy, but I mean also the means to produce the goods and services that other people are willing to give up some of their own wealth in order to acquire. Thus, of course, control of the means of production can mean wealth, if the thing produced is wanted by others. (More about that in a moment.) Human wealth, on the other hand, refers to talent and abilities possessed by individuals and groups. In *Weak States in a World of Powers,* I included knowledge as a form of human wealth, but since I now consider information—including knowledge—as a separate component of power, I exclude it from discussion here. But talent of any sort is a human aspect of wealth.

Like power, wealth is both relative and contextual. In an agricultural society it is land; in a nomadic society it may be horses; in an industrialized society it may be factories, mines, and mills; and in a technological society it may be technological skill. The skill of a priest in moderating the forces of the unknown may be highly valued by certain people in certain societies at certain times. At those times those priests could be said to possess wealth. At different times or in different societies, the same priests might be considered to possess little or nothing of value. What one person, group, or state values, another may despise. The explanations and medications of the witch doctor may be highly valued by the tribe taught to believe that he can cure but may be scorned by Western urbanites, taught to value only the explanations and medications practiced by the medical doctor. Conversely, the technological skill required to run enormous, complex industrial organizations may be utterly scorned in a desert where survival is dependent upon the ability to use a camel.

The individual, group, or nation that controls whatever is both *scarce and sought after* may be said to possess wealth. This is simply a definition of wealth in terms of supply and demand, but those are useful terms in which to consider it because they demonstrate the relative and contextual nature of wealth. If no one seeks what you possess, you are not wealthy. Conversely, if there is a great demand for what you possess, you are in a position to influence the behavior of the seeker. There may be a number of reasons in any given situation why the possessor of wealth chooses not to exercise one's power, but so long as one possesses what others desire, he or she is in a position to exercise influence at any time.

A distinction must be made between *manifest wealth* and *latent wealth*. An individual, group, or country that possesses vast resources of some sort but cannot use them is not wealthy. When a way is found to utilize those resources, the individual, group, or state may indeed become quite "wealthy," but until those latent material or human resources are mobilized (that is, made manifest) they cannot really be considered wealth. A person with great innate intelligence but no formal education has latent wealth. But no one will seek it until it has been mobilized (in this case trained) into a skill that other people want. Zaire, Brazil, and Indonesia are considered by geographers to contain probably the greatest concentrations of sought-after natural resources of any countries in the world, but that does not make these countries the wealthiest in the world. Let them convert the latent wealth into manifest wealth, however, and their position in a ranking of the world's wealthiest countries will change enormously. Notice that the economist defines a state's wealth as "total goods and services *produced* in the country." It is the act of converting latent resources into manifest goods and services that makes wealth in economic terms.

During the centuries when no one sought the "thick, black, liquid substance" that existed under much of the Arabian deserts, those lands were not considered wealthy. Only after the substance was found useful and oil was actually extracted from the ground did those countries begin to become wealthy. As more and more other sources of energy become available, the bargaining position—relative wealth— of the possessors of that oil will be lessened. Notice that all groups define for themselves what it is that is sought after. That is precisely what we were referring to in our discussion of values in chapter 1. That being the case, we can perhaps better recognize why it is that intercultural power transactions are sometimes so very frustrating. I may be trying to exercise influence over you by offering you A, B, and C, when in fact what you really want are X, Y, and Z. Because I value A, B, and C highly (i.e., because they are sought after in my culture), I just tend to assume that you do too. I may have had some X, Y, and Z that I could have offered you, but it may never have occurred to me that that is what you might want. Those American Indians who reputedly "sold" Manhattan Island for twenty-four-dollars' worth of trinkets must have valued those trinkets (which were scarce) more highly than the land (which was abundant) they gave in return. (There are those who would say the Indians got the better deal, but given my urban value system, I would dispute it.)

Organization: Formal and informal   That organization is a crucial component of power is not a new discovery. George Washington and Nikolai Lenin both knew that very well, as has every revolutionary before and since. Indeed, they are not alone in this understanding. Anyone who has ever done any political work, whether in a club or a fraternity, for a city or on a national level, has come to recognize the importance of organization to power.

By organization, I do not necessarily mean formal structures with presidents, vice presidents, committees, and so on, although formal organizations of one sort or another certainly can be major possessors of power. A group, to be powerful, need not have a formal arrangement; sometimes informal organization can be equally effective. This is particularly true of small groups, whose members can communicate with each other fairly rapidly, often on a face-to-face basis. They can thus easily calibrate their views on a particular problem and plan a common strategy. This is true, for example of oligarchies, business groups, and communes, where the members have a similarity of perception to begin with and many opportunities for direct personal contact.

The basic role played by an organization is in the mobilization of human and material resources and the exchange of information for the achievement of particular goals. These goals may be clear and explicit or poorly defined and implicit. They may be understood differently by different segments of the group. But if most of the members can be mobilized for what each believes those goals to be, then the group can coordinate efforts in such a way as to maximize the influence it can have on its environment, national or international.

Just as with power itself, an organization's ability to exert influence is both relative and contextual. The European Economic Community wields considerable influence in European economic matters but is much less influential in political affairs. A political organization can exercise considerable influence getting someone elected to political office, but an organization of conservationists may be more influential in getting water pollution legislation passed. An organization of workers may exert some influence over its members' behavior as workers but may exert little or no influence over their behavior as Catholics, veterans, sports fans, conservatives, or any of the perhaps dozens of other categories to which a worker might belong. Organizations compete with each other for the loyalty and attention of many of the same individuals.

Before there can be effective organization, a common identity must be established. That identity very often precedes organization. The usual progression toward action in the political process is that a number of individuals perceive some aspect of the external world more or less similarly; communicate that similarity of perception among themselves, thus forming an identity group; and then organize for the accomplishment of certain goals thought to be important to the members. *The crucial aspect of organization, from this perspective, is the establishment of channels of communication through which perceptions, values, goals, strategies, and so on, can be calibrated, synchronized, reinforced, and translated into concerted, directed action.* In order for that to happen, however, the members of the group must understand the common language or "code." Words and symbols have to mean more or less the same things to the members of the groups for effective communication to occur. This is why it is relatively easy for a number of people who already perceive some aspect of the external world similarly to coalesce into an identity group and ultimately to develop some form of organization that enables them to take part in the political process more effectively.

Information: Basic and specific   "Knowledge is power" is an adage as old as time itself. It is no less true because it is old. If someone knows that an opportunity or a threat exists (before others do) he can take advantage of that opportunity or can protect himself from the threat. If he does not know about it, there is simply no way that he can react. Indeed, as we saw in the communication model presented earlier, the fact that an event occurred—whatever it is—remains outside the perceptual ken of individuals, groups, or states if it does not reach their sensory receptors. If a ball is traveling at great speed toward the back of my head and I do not see, hear, or "sense" it, I am liable to get very badly hurt by the time I receive the message—i.e., when it makes contact with my head. If someone else sees it happening and warns me *in time,* I can take appropriate action to avoid being hurt. But I need information, and I need it in time to take some action relative to that information.

It is important to make a distinction between basic and specific information. By basic information I mean our general level of knowledge. Obviously, the more basic information we have, the more effectively we can utilize whatever specific information we might gather. By specific information I mean just that—those messages that are specific to understanding of a particular problem or task. It is not an accident that better educated people—and groups and countries with better educated populations—seem to have more "influence" than less educated people, groups, and countries. I would argue here that at least one of the reasons this is so is that better educated people and groups have the basic information necessary to enable them to better use the specific information that they need in different situations. They know more codes and thus can decipher more messages, and if they don't know the codes themselves, they probably know where to find the people who can decipher them. They are in a much better position to seize opportunities when they arise—because they know about them—and to avoid serious threats to their well-being, again because they know about them and can therefore take appropriate action.

In a sense, the same distinction could be made with regard to learning about culture. To the degree that we understand what culture is and how it operates, we are better able to understand particular things about specific cultures. It is impossible for anyone to learn everything there is to be known about any specific culture (because so very much is buried so deep in our subconscious), but the more we understand about how culture operates generically (basic information), the easier it will be for us to know how to learn about any particular culture (specific information).

In my discussion of the components of power in *Weak States* I assumed that information was like wealth, in that it had to be mobilized in order to do anyone any good. The ball heading for my head is a fact. The message (information) that it was doing so remains latent until someone sees the fact and relays the information to me (which implies the existence of a channel). I also assumed that like wealth, it was both scarce (one rarely has enough) and sought after (everyone wants it). Upon reflection and the advice of students, I now see that information really ought to be considered as a separate component of power.

In the first place, whether a particular message is information or noise depends upon the individual's perceptions, attitudes, values, and in some cases, interest at a particular time. If I really want to know what is happening on the international scene at a particular moment, the horse-racing results being announced on the radio may be interfering with my receiving that information. On the other hand, if I have placed a two-dollar bet on a particular horse in a particular race, that particular message may be the one I am looking for, and thus it becomes information, while news of the overthrow of some government in a faraway country may be the noise. One person's information may be another's noise—depending upon his or her interest. And it depends on one's interest at that particular time. At some other time I may indeed be more interested in what is happening in that faraway place than I would be in the races. When that switch in interest occurs, so does my definition of what is information and what is noise.

Second, if I don't know about something, I will probably not know that I don't know and therefore won't realize that I am "missing something." Go back to the example of the ball heading toward my head. If I don't know that one is coming toward me, I will probably not seek the information. Yet it sure would have been useful information—if I had only known that it was coming! My definition of wealth specifically states that something has to be both scarce and sought after to be considered wealth. Since I would not have sought after the information that the ball was coming—no matter how valuable that information might have been to me before it hit—information as a category cannot be considered as being the same as wealth.

Further, information is not always scarce. Indeed one of the problems with information—in some circumstances—is that we have too much of it. That is technically called "information overload." It occurs when information is coming into our receptors faster than we are able to process it. This situation may occur for individuals or for small or large groups. Computers are not the only information-processing machines that can and do break down under the pressure of too much information simultaneously—individuals and organizations break down also. Leave aside for a moment the question of deciding which information is more relevant or more correct. The question of sheer volume of potentially relevant information is far greater in some situations than our ability to cope with it. And when our capacity to process incoming information breaks down, we lose the ability to attend to *all* incoming data—no matter how potentially important to us the data may be. We must have information about our external (as well as our internal) environment in order to function properly. But the situation caused by information overload can have the same effect as not having any information at all. It does us no good if we are unable to process it; we must have the ability to make decisions about which is relevant and which is not.

Now this question of which information is relevant in which situation can be very tricky. Sometimes seemingly innocuous bits of data can be extremely important—if we know how to interpret them. Like most, that is a very large *if*. Indeed, it has only been recently—with the assistance of very sophisticated computers—that some governments and large corporations have been able to begin to sift through the millions of bits of discrete data that pour in daily to determine the relevance of each bit. By developing that competence however, they are beginning to be able to attend to information that prior to this was being buried under an avalanche of other bits of data. Now with the help of computers (and with the help of human experts who have told the computers what patterns to look for) these organizations are becoming more expert on spotting important trends early. That is only possible because they have begun to solve the problem of information overload.

Let's go back to the distinction between manifest and latent information. Information that I received about an event is manifest information—that is, I did after all receive it, regardless of how I processed it after I received it. Latent information (as I am using the concept here) is information I could have used, i.e., information that would have been useful to me, if I had received it in a form that would have enabled me to decode it—*if* I had received it. Latent information, in other words, is information I didn't receive because I didn't attend to it, even though it was there, or because I was unable to decode its meaning (not recognizing it), or because the message was below the threshold of my ability to register it consciously, or because the channels for me to receive the information were either nonexistent or insufficient for the task. Let us look at each of these problems in turn.

1. "Because I didn't attend to it." There are two common reasons for not attending to information one already has (assuming that one is not suffering from the inability to process information owing to overload). The first is not knowing one needs it. I am not going to be looking for a ball coming toward my head unless I have received some prior indication that I should. If without any reason I looked for a ball, I would probably be rightly diagnosed as being "paranoid." And if I were paranoid in this way, it would probably consume so much of my available attention (always on the look out for a ball to hit me) that I would not have sufficient attention available to look out for the cars going down the road or the holes in the

ground where I walked or the thousands of other dangers that might lurk "out there" in the environment. This concept is true of individuals, organizations, and states. No individual or group can allow itself to become consumed with fears of real or imagined potential dangers and still function effectively. Thus precisely because we cannot attend to all information simultaneously with equal intensity we *must* attend to only a portion. There simply is no way to attend to all incoming messages with equal attention. While we are attending to that portion of information that *seems most relevant,* we may be missing other information that could potentially be important.

But what is most relevant? Here we have the second reason people don't attend to information that is there. Recall our discussion of perceptions in chapter 1, of our tendency to look for that information we expect to find. If we expect to see a woman driving badly, we will view suspiciously every woman driver we see and will tend to ignore the ninety-nine who are driving well but will find very relevant the one person who reinforces our preconceived expectation. Or what about the Russians (if you are an American)? Everyone knows that they can't be trusted. Hence we had better have "our intelligence men" watch them very carefully. And if they become suspicious of us and send their spies to see what we are doing, and our intelligence men discover that, of course we will take the fact that they are spying on us as proof that we were correct in our suspicions in the first place and that we were wise to have sent our intelligence men. And so it goes. Who "they" are depends, of course, on who "we" are at any given moment in history, but the process remains unchanged.

The point is that we have all been conditioned by our cultures to attend selectively to information we want, or expect, to find, and pay selective inattention to information we don't want, or expect, to find. Put simply, this means that we all have a tendency to "see" what we want, or expect, to see and "not to see" what we don't want, or expect, to see. Often the information is there. Someone looking at the same data (but with a different mind set) might see it, but we don't.

2. "Because I was unable to decode its meaning." As noted in chapter 3, on the communication process, if one doesn't know how to decode a message, the effect is roughly the same as not having received the message in the first place. But it is not really the same. One can learn new "codes." In order to do that, however, one must first recognize that the code in question is not known and then go out and learn it. Once again, someone else looking at the same message—who does know the code—would immediately decipher its meaning. But for me, looking at a message and not being able to decode it means that the information contained in the message is only latent information.

3. "Because the message was below the threshold of my ability to register it consciously." Once again the information is there, but it remains latent until I am somehow able to raise the intensity of the signal so that I can receive it at a conscious level. In interpersonal as well as intergroup and international relations this is a major problem of communication, in large part because many of the messages sent may be subconscious on the part of the sender. Thus there is no way that a

sender can "increase the volume," so to speak, so that it can be consciously received. Yet many of those "low-volume" messages may be potentially extremely important to our relationship. I, as a receiver, may be consciously troubled that "something is not quite right" in a specific set of messages, but because they are latent rather than manifest messages I probably will not be able to "put my finger" on what it is that is being transmitted.

4. "Because the channels through which I would have received the information were either nonexistent or insufficient." Events occur every day that are extremely important to every person in the world, but if the channel of communication between the event and me is either nonexistent or insufficient, I simply may never learn about that event or perhaps will learn about it only after it is too late. The event has occurred; that is the information. But if I don't find out about it in time, the information remains latent information for me. (I'll say more about this in the section on international mass communications in the last chapter.)

Once again, as I use the term, manifest information is information I do receive and that I can process. What I do with it after I have received it is another matter. There can be no question that the more manifest information I have (in a form I can use), the more I will be able to influence people and events, which is, after all, how I have defined power in the first place.

Given all that has been said here there is no way that information cannot be considered a major component of power.

Status: Ascribed and acquired   There are some individuals or groups in every society who are able to influence the behavior of others because they have what is called prestige or status. In some societies it is a caste or aristocracy that wields such influence. In others it is certain families or individuals. Whether the prestige attaches to the person or to the office held by the person, the person is able to influence behavior merely because of his or her high status. These people are said to have authority. Those with prestige have influence over others because both they themselves and the people whom they influence believe it is legitimate—that is, correct and proper—for them to wield that power.

The most interesting aspect of status is that it depends as much on the beholder as on the beheld. That is, an individual with a Ph.D. from Harvard may have a considerable amount of status among college students, professors, and intellectuals generally but almost none among, say, southern or western blue-collar workers in America, to whom such a person is a "northeastern egghead," a pejorative term. Conversely, Pete Rose or Joe Nameth may have high status among sports fans—and hence influence (fans do buy the cereals leading sports players tell them to buy on radio and TV commercials)—but presumably none among intellectuals, unless they happen also to be sports fans. Who we perceive ourselves to be (and that, of course, influences our attitudes and values) determines to whom we accord status—and to what degree.

Sociologists, quite rightly, make several distinctions among types of status. For example, they distinguish between *ascribed* and *acquired* status. Ascribed status is that which accrues to an individual or group by birth. Someone born into an aristocracy in a particular society has high status merely by virtue of his or her birth and thereby is accorded the ability to exert influence in that society. Similarly someone born into a despised caste, class, or race in that society has low status and thereby no ability to influence others merely by virtue of his or her birth. Acquired status is that which accompanies the attainment of some skill or position valued by a particular society (or segment of society). Someone who becomes a priest in a Catholic or Buddhist society acquires high status and thus the ability to influence religious Catholics or Buddhists in their respective societies. Notice, however, that Catholic priests have very little status or influence in Buddhist societies and vice versa. The Ph.D. holder and the famous athlete have acquired high status and the ability to exercise influence among their respective "constituents." Because high status—whether ascribed or acquired—depends so much on its being perceived as such, it may be the least transferable, across cultural barriers, of all the components of power we are discussing.

Another distinction sociologists make is between the status accruing to an office and that accruing to an individual. The office of president, king, or pope carries with it high status and thus influence among particular populations, regardless of who the incumbent happens to be. Conversely, some individuals have high status—as did Mohandas Gandhi, Robert Kennedy, and Martin Luther King (toward the end of their lives)—whether or not they hold a prestigious office. Of course, if the occupants of high-status offices happen also to be accorded high *personal* status by their group or nation, they are in a much better position to exercise influence than if they bring to that office little personal status of their own.

Status and power are mutually reinforcing. That is, while it is true that power accrues to those individuals and countries that have high status in the eyes of some other individuals or countries, it is also true that high status accrues over time to those individuals and countries that have power. "Power seeks to project itself into prestige, and prestige to transform itself back again into power."[7] John D. Rockefeller and his robber baron counterparts in the U.S. and elsewhere acquired great economic power in their own time, but no one would have said that they had high status in the eyes of their fellow citizens. As time passed, however, and hired public relations experts did their jobs, the families gradually came to be perceived as having high status.

Will: Conscious and subconscious   The existentialist philosophers have argued that with enough conscious "will" an individual can do or become anything he or she chooses. That may be an extreme position, but it is an assertion that comes closer to truth than not. The probability that Lenin could one day become head of what for centuries had been the Russian Empire was remote in the extreme. Yet he had the will to endure incredible hardships and the determination (which includes both will and persistence, or tenacity) to put together an organization of equally dedicated individuals with the same overriding will to succeed in their objective, to make success possible. Mao Tse-tung's success in China against equally overwhelming odds is another example.

Similarly there have been thousands of individuals in the U.S. who started with no education, no wealth, no organization, and no status who had sufficient will to achieve their goals of economic, or political success. Horatio Alger stories may be more of an American myth than reality, but for hundreds upon hundreds of determined individuals and groups it was reality. While it is true that this may be easier to do in a socially mobile society like the United States or the Soviet Union, countless cases of individuals or groups who did succeed against overwhelming odds in other countries prove that it is possible. It could just be that greater expenditures of will are required in those countries.

In every country, however, there are individuals in every field of endeavor who are able to succeed against seemingly insurmountable odds simply because they are able to concentrate all of their energies toward achieving their desired objective. To be sure, there has to be a certain amount of human wealth present to begin with, but given two individuals with equal inherited endowments and unequal amounts of will, there is little doubt that the one with the greater will is much more likely to succeed—whatever that may mean in specific contexts. Whether we consider musicians, athletes, scholars, poets, or soldiers, the ones with the greater will are much more likely to put in the time and energy necessary to excel.

Until now we have been discussing examples of conscious will (determination). There is also a category of subconscious will. Many people and groups strive to achieve particular goals totally unaware of the degree to which they are driven. It may be achievement of some sort (like good grades in school or success in accumulating money) for which they strive, but it could also be other things. The person who has a high psychological need for affiliation with other human beings but is not aware of this need (on a conscious level) and spends much of life building close, warm interpersonal relationships is responding to subconscious will as much as the individual who needs to achieve economic wealth or power. When entire groups of individuals respond to these needs in predictable ways, we argue that the cultural values of their group impelled them to act in certain ways.[8]

Consider here for a moment the implications this has for power relationships between individuals and groups. On an individual level, if a woman is responding to subconscious needs or drives for power (if she values power highly, in Lasswell and Kaplan's terms) she will do those things she believes will increase her power vis-à-vis other individuals. Similarly, if a man is responding to subconscious needs for affiliation (if he values affiliation highly) he will do things he believes will increase his close personal relationships with other individuals. Because each of these individuals is responding to different inner values—of which she or he might be totally unaware, on a conscious level—their overt behaviors are most likely to be completely different. From the perspective of analyzing the components of power, the individual with high value for power is much more likely to achieve it than one who does not rank that value as highly. The same is true for groups and whole societies. Those groups that rank the value to exercise influence (power) above other values will subconsciously teach their members to practice those behaviors that will help achieve their subconscious power goals. Those groups that rank other values above power will subconsciously teach their members to rank those behavior patterns more highly. Not only does this make communication between individuals and between groups with these different value systems more difficult but it puts the individual or group that does not value power highly at a distinct disadvantage vis-à-vis the individual or group that does.

It has been argued that will may be a necessary, but not sufficient, component of power. That is, whereas each of the components of power, except will, can easily lead to the acquisition of one or more of the other components, several of my Third World students have argued that will does not fall into the same category. I have been told that to think so is a typically American perception. Their argument is that in the U.S., where the opportunity to acquire any of the other components is so great, we tend to make the assumption that the same thing holds true everywhere. But, their argument continues, in fact there is so little opportunity in most of the Third World that all the will you can imagine will not produce influence. Now I must admit that this argument may have merit. In the first place I am the first to admit my own perceptual biases. It is very possible that I am viewing these processes from too American a perspective. Second, it conforms to my own thinking in another article I have written on the relationship between opportunities and propensities to produce.[9] In that article I argued that "development" can take place only when the "objective" opportunity factors (like size of market, level of savings, and levels of domestic resources) are present *in conjunction* with "subjective" propensity factors (like individual perceptions of those objective factors and level of need achievement). Lacking empirical evidence, I am not at this point willing to take a decisive stand either way. But I would not want to overlook the effectiveness of will as a component of power even if we have to qualify it by adding the phrase, "in those places where the opportunity exists." Certainly in a great many interpersonal and intergroup relations the opportunity does exist, worldwide. After all, even in the most remote village of some underdeveloped country, given two boys with equal endowments of everything but will my hypothesis is that the one with the greater complement of will would eventually come to exercise greater influence over others than the boy with less will. If that is so, then will is certainly a component of power.

Effects of Perceptions on Power Relationships

Power sometimes accrues to individuals, groups, and states from still another source, which like status depends not so much on tangible attributes as on the viewpoint of others. In the chapter on perception I argued that people can behave only on the basis of their perceptions of reality; that it is possible that an objective, knowable reality does exist, but for determining the behavior of individuals, groups, and nations, objective reality may be considerably less important than perceived reality. This is not to deny that the existence of the atom and hydrogen bombs in the stockpiles of states is an important aspect of their power. It is. However, various perceptions of those bombs may be as important as the bombs themselves. For example: The United States and the Soviet Union both have nuclear weapons. Each country assumes that the use of those weapons—whatever the circumstances—would probably trigger the use of them by the other. That perception may be sufficient to deter both of these powers from using nuclear weapons. What is more, each nation perceives that there are limits to the actions they may take without provoking the other to use those weapons. Thus the Soviet Union will not invade West Germany, not because it does not have the physical power to do so but because it perceives that to do so would mean nuclear war (whether it actually does is relatively unimportant). It is the Soviet *perception* in this respect that prevents a Soviet invasion, just as it was American perception of likely Soviet retaliation that prevented an American attack upon China during the Korean conflict or American intervention in Hungary in 1956 or in Czechoslovakia in 1968.

Prior to the 1940s, the European powers were perceived in most of Asia and Africa to be nearly invincible. Thus, it was possible for less than thirty-five thousand British bureaucrats and soldiers to rule a country of perhaps 500 million Indians. To be certain, the British were masters at keeping their subjects divided—unorganized—and that was a major factor in their ability to control the subcontinent. But another major factor was simply that they were perceived to be unbeatable. The Indians did what the British wanted not because the British actually had the power to force them to do so but because the Indians *perceived* the British as having that power. They behaved toward the British *as though the British actually did have the power,* thus conferring that power upon them. The same was true of the Indonesians and the Dutch, the Vietnamese and the French, and the Filipinos and the Americans. When the Europeans and Americans actually collapsed at the hands of the Japanese in 1941 and 1942, the Asian perception of their former masters totally changed. At the war's end, nationalists in each of the Asian countries were ready to test the extent of European power. The British Empire found itself unwilling to face a test of arms, and independence was immediately negotiated. The French and the Dutch, on the other hand, still maintained a prewar perception of their own power vis-à-vis "the natives" and fought to maintain political control over their colonies. It was only after the military defeat at Dien Bien Phu that the French revised their self-perception vis-à-vis the Vietnamese and sought a peace settlement. The Dutch never faced a similar military catastrophy, but owing to American diplomatic intervention on the side of the Indonesians in 1949, they too came to perceive themselves as lacking the power to hold on to Indonesia.

On a more individual level, we are all aware of the countless daily situations in which we do things that we might very well prefer not to do because we perceive other people as having the power to force us to. Now it could be that those other people actually do have the influence, but only rarely do we test them to find out if they really do. I am thinking here of the millions of people who get to their jobs at the appointed hour or the millions of students who go to class when all of them would rather be doing something else. I am only too painfully aware that the boss does have the power to fire us for being late, and the teacher does have the power to fail us for not going to class, but would they really? Have we tested that power to find out? I submit that most of us do not because we are afraid of the consequences. Therefore, in effect, we are giving them the very power over us that we think they have. Having myself been both an employee and a student as well as a boss and a teacher, I know that in the former roles, I rarely tested my "superior's" power. In my other positions as boss and teacher, however, I know full well that I probably wouldn't do a thing if an employee were late or a student occasionally absent. Certainly I might be tempted to take some disciplinary action if my employee or student were habitually late or absent, but I am constantly amazed at how few individuals are late or absent, and attribute that not to my having the power to force them to be on time and present but rather to their perception that I have that power. Thus because of their perception of my power they have in fact given me power I would not otherwise possess.

The examples of how perceptions of power affect the behavior of people, groups, and states are endless. The point to be made here is that if one perceives another to have power, he or she will behave toward the other as though the other did in fact have power—regardless of whether objective reality fully supports his or her perception. Since power has been defined as the ability to influence behavior, the very perception of another as having power may thus be adding to that other's power.

Although this chapter has been less directly intercultural than those that came before it, in the chapters that follow we shall see the importance of this power factor in any number of intercultural communication settings at all levels of analysis.

PROPOSITIONAL SUMMARY FOR CHAPTER 4

Politics of human behavior: As applied in this work, terms like power and influence are used in the broadest sense to mean how people, groups, and/or nations try to get what they want from other people, groups, and/or nations. Politics is defined as the study of who gets what, when and how.

Power: As used here, power is a relative term. In the positive sense it is the ability to exercise influence over others. In the negative sense it is the ability to prevent others from exercising influence over us. Power is both relative and contextual.

The components of power: In this work five components of power are discussed: wealth (material and human), organization (formal and informal), information (basic and specific), status (ascribed and acquired), and will (conscious and subconscious).

Wealth: Wealth is defined as anything (either material or human) that is both scarce and sought after.

Organization: Organization is the means whereby individuals, groups, or nations can be mobilized quickly to achieve particular goals. In order for organizations to exist, there must be channels of communication and a common identity of membership in the group.

Information: The adage "knowledge is power" is true. Basic information refers to one's general level of knowledge. Specific information refers to those messages that are specific to understanding a particular problem or task.

Status: Ascribed status is that prestige which accrues to an individual or group by virtue of birth. Acquired status is that prestige which accompanies the attainment of some skill or position valued by a particular society (or segment of society).

Will: Conscious will is defined as the determination to put in the time and energy necessary in order to excel at any task. Subconscious will is defined as the drive people and groups have to achieve particular goals without being consciously aware of the fact that they have that drive.

NOTES

[1] Harold D. Lasswell, *Politics: Who Gets What, When, How* (New York: McGraw-Hill Book Co., 1936).

[2] Harold D. Lasswell and Abraham Kaplan, *Power and Society: A Framework for Political Inquiry* (New Haven, Conn.: Yale University Press, 1950), p. 75.

[3] Harold D. Lasswell, *Power and Personality* (New York: W. W. Norton and Co., Viking Press, 1962), p. 16.

[4] Ibid., pp. 75–76.

[5] Charles E. Merriam, *Political Power* (New York: Collier Books, 1964), p. 179.

[6] In *Weak States* I included only three components of power: wealth, organization, and status. Since that time I have been convinced by some of my students to include *information* and *will* as separate components of power. In this case those students may have exercised more influence upon me than I did upon them.

[7] Merriam, *Political Power,* p. 134.

[8] For fascinating discussions of the ways in which this "subconscious will" affects individuals and groups, see David C. McClelland, *The Achieving Society* (Princeton, N.J.: Van Nostrand, 1961); and Everett E. Hagen, *On a Theory of Social Change: How Economic Growth Begins* (Homewood, Ill.: Dorsey Press, 1962).

[9] Marshall R. Singer with Joy Sargent, "A Propensity and Opportunity Model of Development Applied to Malaysia," forthcoming.

CHAPTER FIVE
INTRA- AND INTERPERSONAL COMMUNICATION

INTRODUCTION TO PART II

Having discussed in broad outline the four basic concepts with which this work is concerned, I would now like to attempt to apply those concepts to individuals, groups, and nations to show how using them could improve communication at each level of analysis. I recognize that I cannot do this in a very scientific way because my discussion has been very general. Still, what I hope to do in the next four chapters is to suggest the kind of questions that should be asked at each level of analysis in order to help the reader improve his or her communication effectiveness. Hopefully, others who read this work will find the concepts I have been dealing with sufficiently stimulating and useful to motivate them to try to refine them further than I have been able to do, thus enabling us to apply them far more effectively than can be done at this stage of analysis.

FINAL PREMISE

If effective communication is the goal, it is necessary to apply each of the concepts discussed in the first four chapters of this work to the appropriate level of communication.

What do these concepts look like when specifically applied to communication relationships among and between individuals, groups, and nations? One way of making these applications would be to construct a four-by-three matrix, with each of the four concepts discussed in the previous chapters listed vertically along the left and each of the three levels of analysis (personal, group, and national) listed horizontally along the top. The only problem with doing it that way is that we would be leaving out the important distinction between intra- and interpersonal, intra- and intergroup, and intra- and international communication. Thus I propose a four-by-six matrix in which we attempt to ask the critical questions, to which answers must be found, if we are to communicate effectively at any level of analysis.

Depending on the level of analysis in which one is interested, one has to ask some specific questions if one hopes to communicate effectively. Clearly the more carefully and specifically we construct our questions, the more we should be able to learn about both ourselves and the others with whom we are trying to communicate. While I can construct some very general questions here to illustrate the kinds of information I think it is important to have about both myself and any other party in a communication exchange, it must be remembered that those questions can only be general until we know the context of the interchange. Once we know that, we can then make the questions much more specific.

Since it is virtually impossible to separate questions of culture and perceptions from questions of identity, I will consider them more or less simultaneously as I discuss this matrix. I am also taking the liberty of discussing power before I discuss communication, despite the fact that the first four chapters were not presented in that order.

I urge the reader to use chart 5.1 in part as a guide to the three chapters, on personal, group, and national communication, and also as a check list to be applied in specific communication contexts. Certainly you will not know the answers to all of the questions being raised, but I think when you actually try it, you will be surprised to find that you know the answers to a great many of them. Simply bringing these questions—and the answers to them—into conscious awareness should make all of us better communicators. At the very least, it should help us to understand the cultural barriers that must be overcome for more effective communication to occur. At best, it should help us to recognize the cultural similarities we already share and hence should help us in the building of bridges of trust to the other person or group.

Now let us try to apply the concepts of the earlier chapters to the personal, group, and national levels of communication.

CHART 5.1 **Basic Concepts Applied**

	PERSONAL		GROUP		NATIONAL	
	INTRA	INTER	INTRA	INTER	INTRA	INTER
WHAT ARE:	My	His/her	Our	Their	Our	Their
	Perceptions? Behaviors?					
WHAT ARE:	My	His/her				
	PERSONAL CULTURAL Perceptions? Attitudes? Values? Beliefs? Disbeliefs? Behaviors?		GROUP CULTURAL Perceptions? Attitudes? Values? Beliefs? Disbeliefs? Behaviors?		NATIONAL CULTURAL Perceptions? Attitudes? Values? Beliefs? Disbeliefs? Behaviors?	
WHO MAKES DECISIONS FOR:			Our group?	Their group?	Our nation?	Their nation?
			What are the personal and other group cultures of the people who make those decisions?		What are the personal and other group cultures of the people who make those decisions?	
WHAT ARE THE CONFLICTS IN: / Are there conflicts in values or interests within:	My values?	His/her values?	Our group?	Their group?	Our nation?	Their nation?
Between:			Between our groups?		Between our nations?	

Culture and Perceptions

126

Identities

	PERSONAL		GROUP		NATIONAL	
	INTRA	INTER	INTRA	INTER	INTRA	INTER
TO WHICH GROUPS:	Do I belong?	Does she/he belong?				
WHO ARE THE INDIVIDUALS WHO COMPRISE:			Our group?	Their group?		
WHICH ARE THE GROUPS THAT COMPRISE:					Our nation?	Their nation?
TO WHICH OTHER GROUPS DO:			Our members belong?	Their members belong?		
WHICH IDENTITIES ARE MOST IMPORTANT:	To me?	To him/her?				
WHAT ARE THE GOALS (PURPOSES) OF:			Our group?	Their group?		
WHICH IDENTITIES ARE MOST IMPORTANT TO:			Our members?	Their members?	Our nationals?	Their nationals?
	(In which contexts?)		(In which contexts?)		(In which contexts?)	

127

CHART 5.1 (continued)

Power	PERSONAL		GROUP		NATIONAL	
	INTRA	INTER	INTRA	INTER	INTRA	INTER
	HOW CAN I REALISTICALLY ASSESS:		**HOW CAN WE REALISTICALLY ASSESS:**		**HOW CAN WE REALISTICALLY ASSESS:**	
	My power?	His/her power?	Our group power?	Their group power?	Our national power?	Their national power?
	(In which contexts?)		(In which contexts?)		(In which contexts?)	
	Do I	Does he/she	Does our group	Does their group	Does our nation	Does their nation
	HAVE ENOUGH OF THE RIGHT COMPONENTS TO ACHIEVE:		**HAVE ENOUGH OF THE RIGHT COMPONENTS TO ACHIEVE:**		**HAVE ENOUGH OF THE RIGHT COMPONENTS TO ACHIEVE:**	
	My goals?	His/her goals?	Our group goals?	Their group goals?	Our national goals?	Their national goals?
	(In which contexts?)		(In which contexts?)		(In which contexts?)	

	PERSONAL		GROUP		NATIONAL	
	INTRA	INTER	INTRA	INTER	INTRA	INTER
WHICH CODES:	Do I know?	Does she/he know?	Does my group know?	Does their group know?	Does my nation know?	Does their nation know?
ARE THEY SUFFICIENT?						
WHAT IS MY/OUR IMAGE:	Of myself?	Of him/her?	Of our group?	Of their group?	Of our nation?	Of their nation?
IS IT REALISTIC?						
DOES TRUST EXIST:	In myself?	In him/her?	Within our group?	Within their group?	Within our nation?	Within their nation?
	Between us? (Can it be improved?)		Between our groups? (Can it be improved?)		Between our nations? (Can it be improved?)	

Communication

CHART 5.1 (continued)

PERSONAL		GROUP		NATIONAL	
INTRA	INTER	INTRA	INTER	INTRA	INTER
ARE THERE SUFFICIENT COMMUNICATION CHANNELS AVAILABLE:		ARE THERE SUFFICIENT COMMUNICATION CHANNELS AVAILABLE:		ARE THERE SUFFICIENT COMMUNICATION CHANNELS AVAILABLE:	
With myself?	With him/her?	Within our group?	With their group?	Within our nation?	With their nation?
AM I COMMUNICATING AS EFFECTIVELY AS I COULD:		ARE WE COMMUNICATING AS EFFECTIVELY AS WE COULD:		ARE WE COMMUNICATING AS EFFECTIVELY AS WE COULD:	
With myself?	With him/her?	Within our group?	With their group?	Within our nation?	With their nation?

Communication (continued)

130

	PERSONAL		GROUP		NATIONAL	
	INTRA	INTER	INTRA	INTER	INTRA	INTER
WHAT CAN BE DONE TO IMPROVE COMMUNICATION:	With myself?	With him/her?	Within our group?	With their group?	Within our nation?	With their nation?
HOW IMPORTANT IS THE MESSAGE:	To me?	To him/her?	To our group?	To their group?	To our nation?	To their nation?
WHAT LEVEL OF INTIMACY:	Do I want?	Does she/he want?				

131

INTRAPERSONAL COMMUNICATION

Intrapersonal Perceptions and Identities: Getting to Know Ourselves

It is purely axiomatic to argue that the more we know about ourselves, the more effective and accurate our communication is likely to be (all else being equal). The interesting thing to note is how much less we know about ourselves than we think we do. How well do we know what we are really trying to achieve every time we try to communicate or what our own personal and group cultures actually are?

In a useful conceptualization of how individuals communicate, Joseph Luft and Harrington Ingram developed what they called the Johari window to help analyze human interactions.[1] Left and Ingram argue that in every communication there is an "open area," which includes information known both to ourselves and most other people. On the personal level this might include such public information as our height, gender, and approximate age.

The "blind area" contains information that others know about us but of which we are not ourselves aware. This might include such things as nervous habits or prejudices we might have that are obvious to others but not to ourselves. For example: For years I have had the habit of constantly adjusting my tie while I was lecturing. I never knew I had that habit, but all of my students did. One day some of them put on a skit parodying all of their professors. The fellow who played me kept pulling on his tie, in exactly the way I do. The other students roared. I asked them if I really did that and they were amazed that I didn't know that I did. Since I found out about that particular habit, it is no longer totally blind, and I can try to control it. I'm not always successful, and I sometimes still do it (I'm told) but at least, now that I am aware of it I can try to do something about it.

In the "hidden areas" are those things we know about ourselves that we usually try to keep hidden from others, usually information about ourselves of which we are not very proud. Individuals, groups, and nations all have a great deal of information they try to keep hidden. The "unknown area," of course, contains information about ourselves that neither we nor others know is stored there.

In the Luft and Ingram model (see Figure 5.1)[2] the space taken up by these four areas changes depending upon our relationship with the persons or groups with whom we are communicating. We tend to have a much larger hidden area and a much smaller open area when communicating with a person or group we know only vaguely or really don't trust. The less one trusts certain people, the less one is likely to want to reveal about oneself. That is precisely because of our fear that they might "use" the information they have about us against us. On the other hand, we are much more likely to be "open" (to have a large open area) when communicating with someone whom we know well and do trust.

To the degree that an individual wants to operate more effectively, it seems to me that the blind and unknown areas have to be greatly reduced. To the degree that there is information stored in those areas about which we are unaware, we will

	Information Known to Self	Information Not Known to Self
Information Known to Others	OPEN	BLIND
Information Not Known to Others	HIDDEN	UNKNOWN

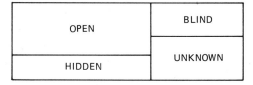

When Communicating
with Someone
We Distrust

OPEN	BLIND
HIDDEN	UNKNOWN

When Communicating
with Someone We
Know and Trust

OPEN	BLIND
	UNKNOWN
HIDDEN	

FIGURE 5.1   Johari Window. From *Of Human Interaction* by Joseph Luft, by permission of Mayfield Publishing Company. Copyright © 1969 by the National Press.

be less effective communicators. To the degree that we are able to become conscious of what is stored there, we are that much more likely to become more effective communicators.

Now what are those personal idiosyncratic and cultural perceptions and identities each of us has stored? In part, they are the way we have learned to view the world "out there." In part they are the reasons some of us see the number ten when we look at a symbol while others of us see a "plus sign" or "life after death." In part they are responsible for whether we think some things are good and others are less than good. In part they are responsible for our image of who we are—which itself is in part a result of the groups we identify with. And finally, in part they are the rankings we have made of the needs and values we have learned from those groups we have come to identify with. In sum they are the totality of everything we know and think and feel. All of this was discussed in chapters 1, 2, and 3 and need not be repeated here.

Getting to know, consciously, *how we perceive others* may be as important to effective interpersonal communication as getting to know our own perceptions.

I am *not* referring here to getting to know *their* attitudes and values. That is important, of course, and we will discuss it shortly. Rather, I am referring here to getting to know how *we* perceive others—including the motivations we attribute to others. For example, if I have biases against people who are short or tall, black or white, Catholic or Jewish, Communists or capitalists, Russian or German (or whatever), I ought to be consciously aware of that *before* I try to communicate with them. If those biases are there—and we would be less than human not to have some—then I think we ought to make them conscious, at least to ourselves. We may not be able to erase some of those biases entirely, but just making them conscious can help us to examine them more rationally and ask ourselves on what they are based, and whether they have enough merit to be retained, or whether we might not want to revise them.

Not all of these expectations are biases in the true sense of the word. Rather, they are incorrect attributions we make about how *they* are likely to think or behave in certain situations. Indeed, there is an entire field of studies within social psychology called attribution theory.[3] What this branch of learning examines is the motives we attribute to others—correctly or incorrectly—in order to explain their behavior.

There is nothing that another person does or does not do to which we do not attribute *some* motive. If someone from our culture extends his hand, we simply assume that his motive is to shake hands, and we react instantly by extending ours, without having to think consciously at all about "why he did that." Indeed it is precisely because we have learned so well to interpret the expected behavior of our own groups that we can function so easily with other people from those same groups. On some level of consciousness we think we know very well why *we* do what we do. The problem is that we have no yardstick but our own with which to measure why someone from another group does what they do. Thus we tend to judge them by the wrong measures, and of course, we are more likely to be wrong than right. We attribute attitudes and motives to others not necessarily because they are correct but rather because we think they are correct. We simply cannot help but think that they are correct if we are unaware that different people have different attitudes and values. Thus *it is our perceptions of them* that will determine our attitudes and behavior toward them rather than what they are actually like, or what their motives actually are.

To what degree are the goals and values to which I ascribe group related? In order to answer that, I really have to ask the prior question, With which groups do I identify? Having identified the groups of which I form a part, it is important that I try honestly to understand what the cultural values of those groups are. I will discuss that in a moment. The reader must understand that I am attempting to discuss them separately merely for analytic purposes. Actually they are inextricably intertwined and cannot be separated. Once I have determined the groups I belong to, I then must make the effort to determine the cultural perceptions of each of those groups. Once I have done that, however, I still have to attempt to determine how I deviate from the norms of each of the groups I identify with. What parts of

Intrapersonal Communication

When I first came across the term *intrapersonal communication* I didn't like it at all. My first reaction was: Most of us don't talk to ourselves, so why use a term like that? Having thought about it and worked with the concept for some years, I have come full circle and now believe that there may be no more important part of the communication process over which we do have some control.

There seems to be an incredibly large gap between the enormous amount of information about ourselves stored in our subconscious and the amount we are able to bring to conscious awareness. What is more, we seem to be surprisingly poor at listening to and interpreting the multitude of messages our bodies continuously send. To be sure, I can recognize the signals when my body tells me that it is too cold or too warm or whatever. At the point that I recognize the signal I can respond to it or not. If I decide to respond, it is I who make the conscious decision to either turn down the air conditioner, move to a warmer place, or put on a sweater.

What is more, there is always a plethora of conflicting internal messages that bombard us continually, to which we simply cannot attend simultaneously and to which we sometimes decide not to attend at all. "I'm cold," "I'm hungry," "I'm tired," "I'm thirsty," says the body. "Forget it for now," says you; "the teacher has assigned this chapter for tomorrow, and like it or not I am going to sit here and read it before I attend to anything else." Now, of course, any one of these messages could become so loud and create so much noise in your internal communication process as to give you no alternative but to attend to it. For instance, our eyes have a way of closing when we are tired that very effectively puts an end to our reading.

While most of us would not normally think of any of this discussion as intercultural, in fact, from one perspective it is. That is, there is, going on within us, all of the time, a competition for attention among our various identities. The fact that you sit and read these words instead of going out to play means that at the moment, at least, your identity as a student is taking precedence over your identity as a hedonist, and you are doing what a student is supposed to do. Sometimes, however, it is important to attend to those other identity needs first so that we can turn our attention—without internal noise—to the tasks that we must accomplish.

Most of our needs, goals, and values are, of course, subconscious and remain so most of the time. Indeed we simply cannot bring everything into conscious awareness simultaneously—nor should we. We couldn't function if we did. The neuro-linguistic programming people point out what should be an extremely obvious point, yet one that I think we sometimes overlook, when they say:

> The amount of information available from our ongoing experience greatly exceeds our ability to sense our experience *consciously*. In fact much of the process of learning and growing is our ability to sense regularity or pattern in our experience and to develop programs within ourselves to cope effectively with the world at the *unconscious* level of behavior. . . .

The vast bulk of our everyday lives is occupied with the execution of tremendously complex patterns of unconscious behavior. The ability we have to enjoy our experience and engage in the activities which each of us find interesting and pleasing would in large part be lost if we did not have the ability to program ourselves to carry out certain complex patterns of behavior for execution at the unconscious level of behavior.[4]

They then go on to cite research done by George A. Miller to argue that at any given moment the human mind has the capacity to deal consciously with "7 plus or minus 2 chunks of information."[5]

That is, as we turn our conscious attention from one thing to another, either from our external environment or from internal signals, something must drop out of consciousness, at least temporarily. No problem there. The important question, however, is whether we can call into conscious awareness those attitudes and values that have so subtly been put there while we were growing up. Therapeutic and hypnotic evidence indicates that we can. But therapy and hypnosis are extreme methods of getting at the information. It seems to me that some rather intense and honest introspection may be able to achieve at least some of the same results. Having once brought these attitudes, values, beliefs, or whatever into conscious awareness (out of the "unknown" in the Johari window example), we can deal with them one way or another. Once we realize what they are we may decide to change them or keep them exactly as they are, but at least our decision will be conscious.

INTERPERSONAL COMMUNICATION

Interpersonal Perceptions and Identities: Getting to Know Him or Her

Since every individual is culturally unique, every communication involving humans is, and must be, to some degree intercultural. In no way is that a problem. Indeed I am convinced that simply recognizing the fact can help us communicate much more effectively. For once we recognize the intercultural nature of all interpersonal communication, we can then apply all we know about intercultural communication to making those relations more effective.

For example, in chapter 1 we saw that even though Mary, Margaret, and Mildred shared many common group memberships, they did not share membership in all, and only, the same groups, nor did they identically rank the values of the groups in which they did share membership. We not only can but *must* remind ourselves to do the same with regard to the attitudes, beliefs, and disbeliefs of the people with whom we must communicate.

We simply cannot remind ourselves too frequently that everyone is culturally unique and that the perceptions and identities I have in my head are probably not the perceptions and identities that are in the head of the other people with whom

I must deal. Just reminding ourselves of this fact will force us to try, by whatever means possible, to determine just what it is that is in the other person's head. Interestingly enough, to the degree that we are "nonjudgmental" and can communicate to others that we will accept them no matter what their personal culture, the more likely they are to reveal more of their attitudes and values to us. I am absolutely convinced that one of the reasons Mr. Rogers's television program has been so successful for so many years is that he really convinces kids that he truly does like them just the way they are. They respond with their viewing loyalty.

The more different the value structure of the other person is from our own, the more difficult communication will be, of course. It is always difficult to understand why the other person does not see things the way we do. But I submit that regardless of how different the values may be, it is better to get them out into the open and look at them consciously than to allow them to go unexamined, thereby creating noise in the communication system.

One other factor that must be looked at consciously in any interpersonal relationship is the way other people view us. I once knew an older European professor who, deep down where it counted, was a caring, considerate individual. Unfortunately, his style of speaking was such that he came across as being terribly patronizing to everyone. (What portion of that style was cultural and what portion was personal is, of course, difficult, if not impossible, to determine.) Worse still, he somehow had the knack of making each person he spoke to feel as though it was he or she personally—or at least his or her group, in particular—to whom he felt superior. Female students, male students, black American students, white American students, African students, Asian students, European students, secretaries, even fellow faculty members and university administrators all complained that he was singling out their group to patronize. Unfortunately, no one ever told the poor man how he was being perceived by others, and therefore he was never able to do anything about it. I think that if someone he trusted had been able to tell him—in nonthreatening terms—he might have been able to do something about adjusting his behavior.

Do others see us as friendly, patronizing, or even hostile? Is that a correct evaluation, or is it incorrect? If it is incorrect, what can we do—if anything—to change their perception? On what are those perceptions of us based? These and a host of similar questions ought to be answered by us if our interpersonal communication is to be more successful.

As with everything else I have discussed in this work, the more we understand our own and the other person's cultures, the more effectively we will be able to communicate. The less well we understand, the less we deal with on a conscious level, the more difficulties and miscommunications there are bound to be in any relationship. If it is important enough for us to communicate, then there is really no choice but to spend the time and effort to try to understand the other person's perceptions, attitudes, values, and beliefs so that we can have some common codes through which to communicate.

Interpersonal Power

In a sense, we have already discussed the important questions that have to be asked here. Since power can be exercised only in the context of a relationship, all of the same questions that we asked about our own components of power have to be asked about the other person. What are his or her strengths and weaknesses? Do we have enough of the right components of power to exercise the influence we would like to? That can be answered only in the context of the relationship. I may have a large amount of a particular component, but if the other person I am trying to influence has more—and that is the critical component in this particular relationship—then I am not likely to succeed. Hence questions of whether one has enough of the right components to exercise influence over another person can be answered only in the context of a particular relationship.

What we have not yet discussed in this section is perceptions of power and the nature of the relationship. First of all, what is the power relationship? Is it superior/subordinate or peer? Do both parties in the relationship perceive it similarly? If one perceives it as the former and the other as the latter there could be trouble. Second, let's face the reality directly that the person with the preponderance of power is *usually* (but certainly not always) going to achieve her goals in the relationship. Even if I do not perceive her to have the preponderance of power appropriate for that situation, although she really does, she will be much more likely to exercise influence over me than the other way around. We might as well try to be as accurate as possible about our evaluation of the other party's power potential in relation to our own before we begin to expend a great deal of time and energy trying to exercise influence on an issue or in an area where we cannot "win."

Finally, it is important to know whether the relationship is one of objective or subjective dependence, counterdependence, or interdependence. I have discussed this concept more fully in another work,[6] but let me summarize the gist of it here. I make a distinction between objective and subjective dependence. Objectively, all of us are dependent on a great many people in order to have our needs met. That doesn't create any psychological problems for us so long as we feel that it is a perfectly natural situation from which we profit and also so long as there are other areas in our life where we feel others are depending upon us. (Mutual dependence or interdependence.) None of us in an interdependent world is ever totally independent of everyone else. We can become completely independent of one person or the other, but when we do that we are no longer in a relationship with that person. And if the person was previously supplying something we objectively need (like affection), we are likely to look for someone else to fulfill that need, and thus in a sense we merely shift our dependence from one individual to another.

The human animal is objectively dependent upon its parents for mere physical survival, perhaps longer than any other species of animal. Along with that physical dependence there is also a psychological dependence. Indeed in the earliest months, psychologists tell us, the child cannot even distinguish between itself and its parents. As it grows it becomes physiologically self-sufficient faster than it does psychologically. Unless the child is helped to become psychologically autonomous (and therefore interdependent with its parents), it is never able to develop a healthy sense of self-worth and thus remains *subjectively* dependent, psychologically, on first its parents and then on other surrogates. It is these subjective feelings of dependence that cause problems in later life, for eventually the child-turned-adult begins to resent the feelings of self-worthlessness and also the people he or she feels are responsible for those feelings. What that often produces is what I have called counterdependence: a lashing out at authority figures (either specific ones or any authority figures with whom the person happens to come into contact) simply because any authority figure makes these people feel inadequate.

So often in interpersonal power relationships we come across individuals who lash out at us for no apparent reason. When we examine the situation, we sometimes find that it was nothing we did or didn't do that caused the lashing out, but rather it occurred because we were perceived to be in a dominant power position, and hence we incurred the counterdependent person's wrath. These people are very difficult to deal with, but to the degree that they can be made to feel that we will help them become less dependent upon us, we may make communication with them that much easier. After all, none of us, as adults, want to feel totally dependent upon anyone.

Years ago during the Vietnam War, a student of mine went to Vietnam to work as a volunteer with a social-service organization. She was assigned to work with some Vietnamese nuns. Since she didn't know the Vietnamese language or very much about the culture, she became very dependent upon the one nun who spoke English and was teaching her both the language and the culture. The nun was apparently a lovely woman, who was trying very hard to make my student feel as comfortable as she could in a strange and difficult war-torn environment. After some weeks of being completely dependent upon this nun for everything, my student began to feel a strong resentment building toward the nun. Because she (the student) was familiar with these concepts of subjective dependence and counterdependence she recognized what was happening and was able to change the feelings. She wasn't able to change the power relationship—she still needed the nun and was still objectively dependent upon her, but the subjective feelings of dependence and the attendant anger disappeared.

If we perceive ourselves to be objectively dependent, we are not likely to be able to exercise much influence ourselves, but we should expect a considerable amount of influence to be exercised over us. On the other hand, if we know that someone is objectively dependent upon us and we want to avoid or at least mitigate counterdependence, it seems to me that we should do what we can to lessen the other person's feelings of *subjective* dependence.

Interpersonal Communication

In a very real sense, all human communication is a form of interpersonal communication.

In the first edition of *Theories of Human Communication,* Stephen Little-john said:

> Interpersonal interaction is involved in small groups, organizations and mass communication. It is incorrect to view the four contexts as separate entities. It is better to view them as a hierarchy of nested contexts in which the higher level includes the lower but adds some additional constraints and qualities.[7]

He then presents a figure to illustrate his approach. (See Figure 5.2.) While I have not divided the contexts of human communication exactly the way he has, his point is well taken. The basic unit at every level of analysis is the individual.

It seems to me that regardless of context or level of analysis, if there is another human with whom I want or need to communicate, I can do so most effectively by determining those group identities we share and then start to build from there. And while I am certain that most of us do this intuitively, what I am suggesting is that we make the effort more systematic and more conscious.

The place to start, it seems to me, is by first identifying the person with whom we are trying to communicate. What do I know about him? Using the Johari window model, there will be some things about him that are "open" and that therefore I will know immediately (or at least I will have some first impressions that will have to be checked later). Just looking at the other person will establish quite a few of his identities. From the way he dresses and talks I will probably be able to make some judgments regarding his level of education, his class background, and the like. I will probably be able to detect from his accent or dialect not only the country he is from but also the part of the country. (Assuming, of course, that I am familiar with the language he speaks and his country as well.) If he is from my own country, I might even be able to identify the city he is from. I might also, merely on the basis of his physical characteristics, be able to tell the ethnic group to which he belongs. Now, one has to know the country from which the other person comes fairly well to be able to establish so much within the first few minutes of conversation. Indeed, this illustrates at the outset why it is easier to communicate with someone whose cultures we know than with someone whose cultures we do not. If we know what to look for, we can decipher the codes immediately. Not knowing the codes makes it that much more difficult.

Aside from those immediately apparent "open" and "blind" bits of information about the most obvious identity groups the other person belongs to, which

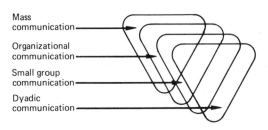

Mass communication

Organizational communication

Small group communication

Dyadic communication

FIGURE 5.2 From Stephen J. Littlejohn, *Theories of Human Communication,* 1st ed. Columbus, Oh.: Charles E. Merrill, 1978, p. 204. Reprinted by permission.

we pick up instantly, a few minutes of conversation could reveal his name (which will further help me identify his ethnic group), his occupation, whether he is married or has children, where he went to school, what he studied, and a host of other specific identities. A series of questions no more personal or probing than is normally acceptable at a cocktail party in America reveals enough about the other person for me to determine whether I am interested (a) in pursuing the conversation any further and, if I am, (b) in exploring further those identities or experiences we share in common. The "Oh, you lived in Boston, too" or "Gee, I love to sail, also" establishes those first identities we share in common, which can sustain the conversation through its first minutes. There is nothing magical about any of this. All of us do it all the time, every time we meet a new person. We do it so quickly and so subconsciously that we don't even think about what we are doing. I submit, however, that if we were to make the process more conscious, we would be more thorough and might better ask the questions, the answers to which are important for us to know if we want to communicate more effectively with this person.

Assuming that we do want to continue the conversation by establishing which group identities we share with the other person, we are "building bridges," so to speak. That is, we establish common identities, in effect, to say to the other person, "Hey, you are one of us," or perhaps more important, "I am one of you." What we are really doing by establishing these common identities, where we find them, is building trust. The more "we" groups we can establish that exist between us—or at least the more important they are to both of us—the more trust will be established. Aside from our earlier discussion about the importance of trust to a communication (see chapter 2), recall from our discussion of the Johari window model that the more trust is established, the larger the other person's open area becomes. Thus to the degree that we establish these "we" linkages, we can get to probe deeper and deeper and get to know more about the other person's attitudes and values. We may not know at all which identities are most important to our newfound acquaintance—meaning that we may not know how he ranks the attitudes and values we suspect him to have on the basis of what we know about other people of the same identities—merely by a few minutes' worth of conversation, but if we think about it for a moment, it is startling how much we can know about another person in a very short time. The first conversation with another person will in no way tell us all we need to know to communicate effectively, but it may establish whether there will be a second conversation. If enough common identities and interests are established, the likelihood is that there will be.

If often happens that many of the people we have to work with or must associate with are people with whom we do *not* share a great many similarities of either identity or perception. Still we must work with them. As we saw in chapter 3, it is much less difficult to communicate with someone with whom we do share many common codes. But if communicate we must, it probably pays for us to probe in order to find whatever common identities may exist. The more we can find, the more "bridges" we will have built toward the other person.

If we are going to be in a work relationship with someone whose value structure is different from ours, it is quite important to the successful completion of our tasks—whatever they may be—to understand the other person's values as well as we can. We don't have to accept those values as our own, obviously, but we had better understand them and try to accept them nonjudgmentally. Similarly, to the degree that our own attitudes and values conflict with the other person's, there are times when it can be useful to bring those differences out into the open and other times when we may want to keep our own concealed. That is a matter of strategy, but we had better know what those differences are.

There are a whole range of other questions that need to be answered in order to make interpersonal communication more effective. Not the least of these is the level of intimacy desired. Some people (particularly in the United States) feel strongly that far too much thought and not enough feeling goes into most interpersonal communication—particularly in urban industrial societies. Many of these people come out of the fields of "personal growth and development," Gestalt psychology, and sensitivity training. These people feel that Western men, in particular, have so depersonalized and dehumanized interpersonal communications that we have created high degrees of loneliness, isolation, depression, and general neurosis in our society. Those people quite rightly recognize that all of us have affiliation values, and they want us to be aware of those values in ourselves and in others.[8]

Now, while I think that it would be great if everyone had the psychological and cultural security to have intimate interpersonal communication relationships when they wanted them, I must admit that I cannot go along with the approach that *all* interpersonal communication ought to be more intimate. A truly intimate relationship requires trust, support, openness, affection, and a lot of hard work. I believe that there simply is not enough time or psychic energy available to convert every interpersonal communication into an intimate, personal relationship. Most of the routine communication required of us in the course of a normal day is, and probably ought to remain, impersonal.

While I am willing to agree that everyone has feelings and that it is much nicer to say "good morning" and "please" and "thank you" to everyone who waits on us, I do not think that it is necessary or wise to try to convert every interpersonal communication into an intimate relationship. I do believe that the context of the relationship ought to determine the level of communication effectiveness one ought to strive for. If one needs ten gallons of gas or two tickets to the theater, it seems to me that it is not the place or time to try to achieve personal closeness. But that is not to say that one ought to treat people like the gas station attendant and the box office ticket seller as though they were not persons at all. Between those two extremes there is a middle ground. One can be civil, polite, and even superficially friendly merely because the world would be a much nicer place in which to live and work if everyone were at least pleasant in casual interpersonal encounters of this sort. What is more, it often happens that when we go back to the same gas station week after week, we get to know the attendant, at least superficially. He or she becomes a familiar acquaintance with whom it can be quite pleasing to

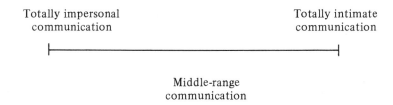

FIGURE 5.3   Types of interpersonal communication.

exchange pleasantries. There are, after all, shadings of relationships. What I am suggesting here is an "intimacy continuum." (See Figure 5.3.)

At one end of the continuum are totally impersonal communication relationships, and at the other end are totally intimate communication relationships. In between these two extremes there are an infinite range of possible behaviors. Indeed, there is no question but that the greatest portion of all communications in which we engage in a normal day, at work, at school, with our neighbors, and so on, fall into the middle category. The important part of communicating effectively is not to make all communication more intimate—as many current writers urge—but rather to choose the behavior appropriate to the situation.

The purpose of any communication is to achieve a goal. If the goal of communicating with a ticket seller in a box office is to buy tickets, then the communication "Two tickets, please" is indeed appropriate. It is simple, direct, clear, and polite—exactly what it should be.

In our modern industrial society people seem to be quite adept at dealing with totally impersonal communication. The most difficulty seems to appear as we move toward the other end of the continuum. Many people feel unable to establish close, warm, sharing, intimate relationships with people they would like to be close to. Close, emotionally honest, and supportive interpersonal relationships seem to frighten people—especially American men in relation to other men—and they thus tend to avoid those kinds of relationships, even though at some level of consciousness they may want them.

Let us turn now to another important rule in communication: *the more steps a communication must go through to reach its final intended destination, the more likelihood there is of distortion. The more culturally different the individuals concerned are, the more likelihood there is of distortion.* With all of the difficulty *any* two individuals have in communicating effectively, pause a moment and reflect on what happens to a message each time another person who is culturally dissimilar is added to the process. For the sake of argument let me say that we are sending one message through five different people: Alice, Bob, Carol, Dave, and Emily.

Let us also say that the message will be passed in a face-to-face communication, with feedback in each case, from Alice to Bob, then from Bob to Carol, then from Carol to Dave, then from Dave to Emily. Let us suppose that each individual shares many of the identity groups with the person from whom he or she is receiving the message. Let us also suppose that there is trust in each of the two-person communications and that each person is going to work very hard to relay the message as exactly as he or she possibly can. Remember that there can be no more effective communication than a face-to-face two-person communication in which the individuals share a large number of identity groups and in which there can be instant feedback (both ways) over a multiplicity of channels. There simply is no situation in which better communication can occur. Given all of that, even if we assume that there would be only a 10 percent distortion in each transmission of the message—which is probably a very optimistic assumption—there would still be a 40 percent distortion factor by the time the message reached Emily. Unfortunately for the communication process, in some circumstances the picture may be even gloomier than that: the decrease in the amount of message transmitted at each step of the way may increase at an exponential rate. That is, if we assume that 10 percent of the message could be lost in the transmission from Alice to Bob, we have to assume that 20 percent *of the original message* could be lost in the transmission from Bob to Carol; 40 percent could be lost between Carol and Dave; and by the time Emily receives the message from Dave, 80 percent of the original message could have been lost. Remember also that we are talking here about communication among people who are more or less culturally homogeneous. The more culture differences we add, the more distortion there is likely to be.

In actual fact the evidence seems to indicate that most details seem to drop out between any A and B communication, and that a "leveling off" seems to occur after that.[9] But that is on content that is culturally neutral. On material beyond one's perceptual experience or on material that is culturally threatening, my own research indicates that the distortion rate gets much higher. Once certain key pieces of the message disappear, great portions of the message became unintelligible. Worse, however, as the details begin to disappear, each person in the chain will normally infer new details to fill the voids, and of course these in turn get distorted.

Thus it is one of the most basic rules of communication that if one wants to minimize distortion (it cannot be eliminated), one must try to send the message through as few steps as possible, preferably on a face-to-face basis, between people who know and trust each other. This is simply a law of parsimony. Having said all of that, however, we will have cause in a moment to demonstrate instances in which it pays to violate that rule in order to insure that the message gets through.

There is in the literature on mass communication and influence a theory known as the two- (or multi-) step flow of communication. Messages from the mass media are not attended to equally. Quite the opposite. We attend most to those messages that interest us most and ignore or pay only minimal attention to the majority of other messages. Those who attend to particular subjects have been called "attentive publics" by Gabriel Almond.[10] There are many different attentive publics in the world attending to different subjects. Millions of people each day listen to religious programs, read the Bible, and subscribe to religious or "inspirational" literature. Christian fundamentalists attend to Christian fundamentalist messages while devout Catholics attend to Catholic messages. Rarely do either ever tune in or subscribe to the other's source of information.

People who have an identity as sports lovers almost always turn to the sports section of their newspapers before they look at anything else (indeed, some may not look at anything else). If they are really avid sports fans, that is what they will watch on television, listen to on the radio, and read about when they choose to read a book. They are also more likely than anyone else to subscribe to sports magazines. These people invariably become extremely knowledgeable about people, events, and trends in sports. They are likely to consume all of the mass-media output on sports and probably prefer socializing with other people who share their passion for sports and their knowledge of it. If you yourself are not a sports enthusiast but want some specific information about a sporting event, it makes most sense to talk to one of these enthusiasts. If he can't supply the answer on the spot (they usually can), he will know where to look to find the information.

Similarly there are other—usually different—people who are equally as enthusiastic about hi-fidelity sound equipment, gardening, philosophy, home remodeling, cooking, theater, art, politics, or what have you. The list is almost endless. Those people—that means all of us—attend to those stimuli from the outside world that, for whatever reasons, interest them. Because we do attend to those special areas we become more or less "experts" in those areas of interest. That is why other people ask us questions about our specialization. Since not all people are interested in the same things, each person will attend to what interests him or her. If we need information about a subject, about which we know very little, we will go to those people to get answers. Though they may distort the information about their area of specialization somewhat, in the process of relaying it to us, all of us prefer to go to others whom we trust for information about what we know interests them, rather than trying to become experts ourselves. No matter how distorted their filtering of information may be, we tend to value their opinions. That is why they are often called opinion leaders. Thus we see a two- (or multi-) step flow in the communication process from the media to the attentive publics, and from the attentive publics to other individuals who may want some information but are not themselves attentive to that subject. That is why personal communication through people we know and trust is so important. Voting studies, for example, have determined that relatively few people in America (or anywhere) read much about what the candidates have to say about issues in a campaign. Rather, they tend to be influenced by people they know and trust—who they know read more than they do—on how they should vote in any given election.

In terms of identities, what this means, of course, is that whichever identities one ranks highly, those are the messages to which one will attend. If someone ranks highly her identity as a member of a particular political party, of course, that is what she will attend to—particularly at election time. And if we don't rank that identity as highly but feel the need to know more about the subject, we will ask the people we know and trust to tell us rather than trying to digest huge quantities of printed or visual material ourselves.

This is precisely why these multiple groups to which we "belong," even if only peripherally, are so important in molding our behavior. We tend to trust, so we seek advice. And that is why networks of people whom we know and trust are so important.

Networks of people whom we know and trust are among the most important channels through which messages flow. Probably the most important channels of communication for human behavior are the networks of people who know and trust other people. People are persuaded to buy a certain product or vote for a certain candidate or to do or think all sorts of things very largely because of the personal influence that is exerted—sometimes very subtly, sometimes not so—by people we know and trust.[11]

We have already seen that the most important network in the life of most people is the family. Beyond the immediate family, in a great many cultures, the next most important group is the extended family or kinship groups. In Western cultures that is less true. There it is often people we call friends or acquaintances whom we know and trust. In either case, however, these people are capable of influencing us (and we them) precisely because we know and trust them. In either case it is trust that makes the system work.

Before we look at some illustrative cases, let us consider the extent of these personal-acquaintance networks. All of us are constantly reminded of how "small a world" it is every time we meet someone who knows someone else we know. Indeed we keep saying that the world is constantly "getting smaller." More than two decades ago, Ithiel deSola Pool, then of the Massachusetts Institute of Technology, decided to investigate that proposition seriously to accurately determine just "who speaks to whom?"[12] Underlying that reasearch was a basic hypothesis that if one were to go through enough steps, everyone in the world would be interconnected in an informal communication network with "everyone else." Indeed one is forced to that conclusion because the opposite conclusion is untenable. That is, if one were to conceive of the world as a series of discontinuous groups, each communicating among themselves but not across the boundaries of their group, one might have a picture that looked approximately like Figure 5.4.

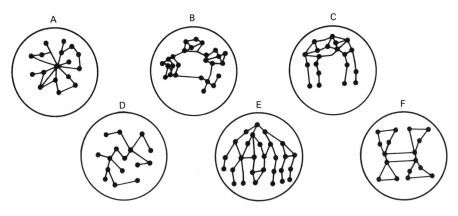

FIGURE 5.4

Logically that creates no problem and may even have been the case millenia ago when people did live in communities totally isolated from each other. But as soon as one person from A (say Athens) traveled to B (say Babylon) and got to know only one person from Babylon, he was instantly tied to Babylon's communication network and thus—going through enough steps—was within easy communication distance to everyone in Babylon. That is not to say that our traveler from Athens got to know everyone in Babylon but rather that the person in Babylon he did get to know spoke to other people in Babylon and knew many of them well (in my terms, was part of many identity groups in Babylon). Those people in turn were each part of their own network of acquaintances and identity groups with whom they communicated easily, and so on, so that, in fact, everyone in Babylon was linked by communication networks with everyone else in Babylon.

Now at least since Magellan, if not since Alexander the Great, and before, merchants, warriors, students, proselytizers, and travelers—and in our own day, anthropologists, missionaries, and Peace Corps volunteers—have gone out to virtually every other community in the world, thus tying each of those communities—at least indirectly—with the others. What is more, because of the multiplicity of identity groups one can think of and the inevitable overlapping of people from all over the world in many of the same identity groupings, this becomes increasingly possible. Conceptually it is possible to imagine small isolated communities being totally isolated from the rest of the world, but for the most part we are forced to the conclusion that, in fact, linkages probably do exist among virtually all the groups in the world. In that case, Figure 5.4 has to modified to look at least like Figure 5.5.

Having logically established the communication interconnections that exist in the world, the next task that Pool and his associates directed their attention to was to establish empirically the number of steps required to reach everyone within a given country and then the number required to reach everyone in the world. They established that anyone in the U.S.—sending messages exclusively through personal

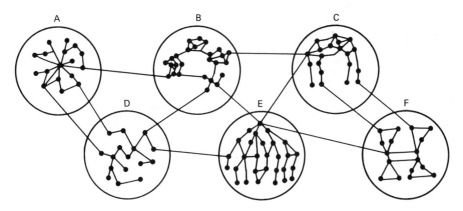

FIGURE 5.5

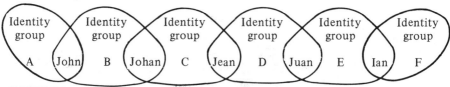

FIGURE 5.6

acquaintances—could reach anyone else in the U.S. in six steps, at a maximum, and that anyone in the world could reach anyone else in the world in fourteen steps.[13]

Before we discuss the implications of the MIT studies more explicitly, let us consider again the impact of face-to-face communication among individuals who are "one of us"—i.e., who share some identity group in common with us. Consider Figure 5.6. John, who is a member of identity groups A and B, may want to pass a message to Johan. Because they share common membership in group B (and thus presumably speak B's language, and value B's belief systems) they may be able to communicate at a relatively high level of understanding. Further, because both are members of group B there is likely to be a higher degree of trust between them than there would be if they were not both members of the same identity group. Having received the message from John, Johan can transmit the same message to Jean because Johan and Jean are both members of group C. John would have had difficulty communicating with Jean because he wouldn't necessarily speak C's language or share C's values, attitudes, or perceptions. What is more, as a C, why should Jean trust an A like John?

Assuming relatively equal socialization into each of the groups, Johan, being bicultural (a member of both groups B and C), would have no more trouble communicating with Jean than he had with John. But whereas he communicated with John in B language, he would communicate with Jean in C language. (I don't necessarily mean only verbal languages here.) Similarly, the same message could be passed on to Juan by Jean, speaking D language, while Juan passed the same message to Ian in E language, and so on.

Earlier, I argued that the more steps a communication must go through before it reaches its destination, the more distortion there is likely to be. Thus I postulated the rule to go through the minimum number of steps possible in any communication in order to minimize distortion. That rule is certainly correct. But now we are faced with another rule that says that communications between individuals (from groups) who trust each other are likely to be much more accurate—and accepted—than between individuals (from groups) who do not. Faced with two rules that are equally correct but contradictory, how do we know which one to follow? We don't know, for all situations. Each situation may be different, and we just have to use common sense to know which rule is more applicable. For example, if the groups concerned really distrust each other significantly or are totally different in their values, then it is probably a "better bet" to take our chances with the distortion and communicate through individuals who at least trust each other. After all, if John and Jean don't know each other's language, or don't trust each other, very little communication will occur anyway. It is better to use an intermediary who may distort somewhat but who at least will be trusted enough by Jean to get a hearing and who will get the message in a language (cultural or otherwise) he understands and presumably can relate to. Indeed, all of the literature in communication indicates that this is the most effective way to get messages accepted from one cultural group to another. Within a group of people who know and trust each other, on the other hand, eliminating extra steps is probably the best course of action.

Instead of merely reporting the results of the MIT research (mentioned above) to my classes, I usually present it in the form of a series of questions, the answers to which graphically illustrate some very important communication phenomena. I ask my class how many steps they would have to go through to get a message to the president of the United States using only a network of face-to-face communication among people who knew and trusted each other.[14] Some of the American students in the group invariably answer "hundreds," "thousands," or on occasion even, "There is no way I could get any message, from me, through to the president." Others, usually more reluctant to respond, ultimately answer "three," "four," or "five." I ask those who have responded with the smaller figures to identify the path the message would take—i.e., the individuals who would transmit the message. I then get answers like "Our Congressman is a good friend of my father" or "I worked last summer in Senator X's office." The first responses in attempting to trace the steps in the face-to-face communication network almost always focus on political figures. But that is only natural because I am asking them to get to a political figure. After we have discussed the process a while, two things usually happen. One, some students begin to think of other "influential" people whom either their friends or family know well; or two, some of the students who previously had remained silent or had at first thought that they were very far removed from anyone in positions of political influence suddenly remember someone they know, who knows someone, who knows someone else.

When we start putting on the blackboard some of the very ordinary people many of the students see regularly and know quite well (like their parents, professors, local ward captains, or neighborhood merchants), they are amazed at how few steps are actually required to reach the president. An example of a typical network is shown in Figure 5.7.

While the students may not know the congressman personally, there is little doubt that the congressman and the ward captain would know each other. (Whether the congressman "trusted" the ward captain is another matter and would depend completely on their personal relationship. If the congressman did not trust the ward captain the message would obviously stop there. But if he did trust her there is

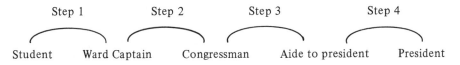

FIGURE 5.7

every reason to assume that it would be transmitted to the next step in the network.) Exactly which aide to the president the congressman would approach with the message is often unknown to the student. Often it would depend on the content of the message. For example, if it was about the energy problem, the congressman would be much more likely to go to an aide who specialized in energy matters and whose opinion the congressman knew the president valued. If the congressman really wanted to get the message through to the president, it would make little sense for him to approach an aide to the president on, say, foreign affairs, with a message on energy. On the other hand, if the content of the message was foreign affairs, that might indeed be the aide the congressman approached.

When I ask how many steps are required to reach the president of a major U.S. industrial firm, or the president of a university, or a member of the Joint Chiefs of Staff, the process is almost identical. The difference of course is that their choice of the first step is different. The first step is usually decided by the sector of society with which the person we want ultimately to reach is identified. That is not a bad starting place, but it may not be necessary.

In one class, having discussed many different ways of reaching important decision makers in many different countries, one student said, "OK, so you can get a message through to important people. What about getting a message through to, let us say, a farmer in Oklahoma?" Now there I had to admit that I was stumped. I really had no idea of where I ought to begin. But at that point a young student with whom I had begun to develop a very warm and trusting relationship raised his hand and said, "I trust you, and I graduated from the University of Oklahoma School of Agriculture." It is here that I point out to the class that it is precisely this "not knowing whom their friends know" that prevents them from using the communication channels they actually do have available to them.

The good communicator knows that it is better to take the chance of some additional distortion creeping into the message—by adding an extra step somewhere in the process, if necessary—than to take the chance that the message will stop at a hostile (or less than trusting) receiver. If the sender of the message is really interested in seeing that message reach its ultimate destination, it doesn't matter that another step is added.

Empirical tests have repeatedly shown that people who attribute a statement to someone they trust are likely to believe it, while if they attribute the same statement to someone they distrust they tend not to. No surprise there. That is the kind of result one would expect to find, but the effects of this result are far more important to effective interpersonal communication than one might expect. What is implied, at least in part, is that in some, if not most communications, the message itself may be less significant than the attitude of the receiver toward the source of the message. If we trust the sender, we tend to trust the message. If we distrust the sender, we tend to distrust the message—regardless of content.

Now what is the significance of all of this to interpersonal communication? The significance is that *the more* intra*cultural we can make any interpersonal communication, the more effective it is likely to be.* Sometimes that may mean trying to build bridges of trust to another person by identifying—and strengthening—the bonds of group identities we may share. That means constant probing and openness and willingness to understand—and accept for the other person—values and attitudes with which we may be in complete disagreement. It means a willingness to accept the validity of another person's beliefs and the willingness to recognize that ours are not as absolute as we once thought they were. Doing that is in itself a sign of openness, and most often (though not always, of course) openness on our part will be met with openness on the part of the other person. With openness can come increased understanding—thus serving to strengthen and accelerate the spiral of trust and enhanced interpersonal communication. It also takes a great deal of very hard work.

PROPOSITIONAL SUMMARY FOR CHAPTER 5

Intrapersonal perceptions and identities: The more I know about my own perceptions and identities, the better communicator I should become. But do I have a clear, conscious image of my own perceptions and behaviors? Do I know my own personal cultures? Do I know which identities are most important to me in different contexts? Am I aware of the conflicts and potential conflicts in my values? I should try to find answers to these, and questions like these, if I am to become a better intercultural communicator.

Johari window: A visual conceptualization about the information that is known to us and that which is known to others. That section of the window that is known to both others and ourselves is called *open.* That section known to us but not to others is called *hidden.* That section known to others but not to ourselves is called *blind.* Finally, that section known neither to ourselves nor to others is called *unknown.*

Intrapersonal power: How can I realistically assess my own power in specific contexts? Do I have enough of the right components of power to achieve my personal goals in differing contexts?

Intrapersonal communication: Which codes do I know? What is my image of myself? Is it realistic? Do I trust myself? Am I communicating as effectively as I could with myself? How important is the message to me? What level of intimacy do I want?

Interpersonal perceptions and identities: What are his or her perceptions? The more I know about those perceptions and identities, the better communicator with him or her I should become. Do I know his or her personal cultures? Do I know which identities are most important to them in different contexts? Am I aware of the conflicts and potential conflicts in his or her values? I should try to find answers to these and similar questions if I am to become a better intercultural communicator.

Interpersonal power: How can I realistically assess his or her power in specific contexts? Does he or she have enough of the right components of power to achieve his or her goals in differing contexts?

Interpersonal communication: Which codes does he or she know? What is his or her image of himself or herself? Is it realistic? Does trust exist between us? Are there sufficient channels of communication available between us? Am I communicating as effectively with them as I could? What could be done to improve communications? What level of intimacy does he or she want?

Steps in the communication process: The more steps a communication must go through to reach its final intended destination, the more likelihood there is of distortion. The more culturally different the individuals concerned are, the more likelihood there is of distortion.

The two- (or multi-) step flow of communication: Messages from the mass media are not attended to equally. We attend more to those messages that interest us most and ignore or pay only minimal attention to the majority of other messages. When we want or need information about subjects we normally do not pay attention to, we turn to people we know and trust who do pay attention to those subjects for information and/or advice from them.

Networks of people we know and trust are channels of communication: Probably the most important channels of communication for human behavior are the networks of people who know and trust other people.

NOTES

[1] Joseph Luft, *Of Human Interaction* (Palo Alto, Calif.: National Press, 1969).

[2] The diagrams have been altered somewhat by this author to conform to the description I have used in the text, but their spirit remains unchanged.

[3] See Harold H. Kelley and John W. Thibaut, *The Social Psychology of Groups* (New York: John Wiley & Sons, 1959); and Richard Nisbett and Lee Ross, *Human Inference: Strategies and Short Comings of Social Judgement* (Englewood Cliffs, N.J.: Prentice-Hall, 1980).

[4] Dilts, Grinder, Bandler, Bandler, and DeLozier, *Neuro-Linguistic Programming,* pp. 52–53.

[5] Ibid., p. 54.

[6] Singer, *Weak States,* Chapter 2.

[7] Stephen W. Littlejohn, *Theories of Human Communication,* 1st ed. (Columbus, Ohio: Charles E. Merrill, 1978), p. 204.

[8] See for example, John Stewart and Gary D'Angelo, *Together: Communicating Interpersonally* (Reading, Mass.: Addison-Wesley Publishing Co., 1976).

[9] Gordon W. Allport and Leo Postman, *Op. Cit.*

[10] Gabriel A. Almond, *The American People and Foreign Policy* (New York: Praeger Publishers, 1960).

[11] For a recent study of research trends in network analysis, see June Ock Yum, "Network Analysis," in William B. Gudykunst and Young Yum Kim, eds., *Methods for Intercultural Communication Research* (which is also called *International and Intercultural Communication Annual,* vol. VIII) (Beverly Hills, Calif.: Sage Publications, 1984).

[12] I was first exposed to this research while still a graduate student at MIT. Since then Pool has published his findings in collaboration with Manfred Kochen. See Ithiel De Sola Pool and Manfred Kochen, "Contacts and Influence," *Social Networks* 1 (1978-79), 5-51.

[13] Ithiel De Sola Pool, "Communication Systems," in Pool, Wilber Schramm, Fredrick W. Frey, Nathan Maccoby, and Edwin B. Parker, eds., *Handbook of Communication* (Chicago: Rand McNally, 1973), pp. 3-26.

[14] The MIT researchers were actually more interested in studying the networks themselves than in assessing the influence that could flow over them. Accordingly, they did not ask about knowing and trusting. In those studies "knowing" someone was all that was required. Knowing was defined as your knowing their name and their knowing yours. Pool and Kochen, "Contacts and Influence."

CHAPTER SIX
SOME CONCEPTS
ABOUT GROUPS

Absolutely the first thing that has to be said in any study of communication within or between groups is that groups, as such, don't communicate: people do, either collectively or in the name of their groups. Thus in a very real sense, all intra- and intergroup communications are at some level also interpersonal communications.

Perhaps because some formal groups, such as various organizations, corporations, bureaucracies, and all nations, have a legal identity separate from the people who comprise them, we sometimes forget that it is, after all, people who do the communicating for them. Thus if we want to communicate more effectively, either within our own groups or with other groups, we had better get to know as much as we can about the people with whom we will be communicating. Regardless of how much we may know about their group or national cultures (and the more we know about those, the better we should be able to communicate) it is imperative to know as much as we possibly can about the personal perceptions of the people we must actually communicate with. What are their personal cultures? With which groups do they identify most closely? To what degree do their attitudes and values deviate from the attitudes and values of the groups they form a part of?

Go back to Figures 1.8 and 1.9 presented in chapter 1. At the center is the individual. This individual is a part of all of the cultures that surround him or her. In the discussion in chapters 1 and 2, the assumption was that most of those cultures represented were large identity groups, but actually some of them undoubtedly are some of the small groups and formal organizations of which the individual forms a part. At least one of those circles will represent the nation. When the officials of two nations or two corporations sit down to negotiate, the fact that they are both members of the identity group called fathers or husbands of urbanites or any of perhaps a hundred different identity groups they share is useful information to have. But, presumably, in the context of that specific encounter their different role identities as officials of the particular group called nation (or of a particular organization) will become their primary identity during that encounter, and therefore their behavior is likely to represent the culture of the organization or group they are officially representing more than any other. Other individuals representing the same two organizations or nations but bringing to the situation different identities and values, would surely behave somewhat differently, but the organizational culture would still dominate their behavior in that situation. (It has sometimes been argued that if we had women heads of state instead of men, there would be less tendency to go to war to settle disputes [a] because women are less pugnacious than men and [b] because their identities as mothers would make them much less likely to risk the lives of their sons in battle. Alas, however, the limited experience the world has had with women prime ministers has indicated that Golda Meier of Israel, Margaret Thatcher of Great Britain, and Indira Gandhi of India—to mention only three of those we have had to date—all have chosen military solutions to international disputes as readily as their male predecessors did. Clearly none of them were going to let their identities as women and mothers interfere with doing what they perceived any prime minister in their position would do, and that was to fight.)

Next, let's try to get a better "handle" on what we mean when we talk about groups. Groups come in an incredible variety of types and sizes. They can include everything from husband and wife to a country of hundreds of millions of people. Their purposes can be as diverse as making love or making war. Therefore, before going into a discussion of *intra-* and *inter*group communication, it is important for us to differentiate at the start those characteristics that groups have in common. What is more, many of the different characteristics of groups will have a profound impact on the type of communication they conduct and the way communication occurs both within and between groups.

The problem with trying to categorize groups is that there are just so many ways of conceptually viewing them. For some purposes size may be the single most important factor to take into account when discussing groups. (We will get to that in a moment.) For other purposes, however, it may not be.

TYPES OF IDENTITY GROUPS

Identity groups could be viewed from any number of different perspectives. Some people, including Talcott Parsons, have chosen to identify them on the basis of their world outlook. Others have chosen to categorize them on the basis of size or purpose. As I see it, there may be some merit in viewing them on a continuum con-

Involuntary   Voluntary

FIGURE 6.1   Type of Identity Groups

cerning the degree of control the individual has over the characteristics that define them. (See Figure 6.1.)

All of the identities I will consider here are based on some experience the individual will have had as a result of being part of the groups discussed. Looking at it this way, however, allows us to see the degree of control the individual had over membership in any particular group.

On the extreme left of the continuum would be those identities the individual inherits and that are immutable—and thus over which he or she has no control. I'm thinking here of those physical characteristics one normally associates with race or ethnicity. We inherit them, and there isn't too much we can do to change them. To be sure, there are operations that can be performed on the eyes, nose, and other parts of the anatomy to try to change those characteristics but (a) our children will still inherit essentially the same characteristics we inherited, and (b) having tried the operation, we would probably be more closely tied to the identity group of people who have tried to change immutable physical characteristics. Now, these physical characteristics really are not very important in and of themselves. What makes them important is the way other people react to them. For whatever reasons, I submit that racial, tribal, and ethnic identities—over which we have virtually no control—are among the most important identities people hold. Again, it is not the physical characteristics themselves that are important but rather the attitudes, values, and perceptions that are associated with being born a member of one group and—just as important—not being born a member of some other group. Of course the society into which one is born is important in this respect too. For while in some societies certain racial, ethnic, or tribal characteristics are completely immutable, in others they are not. For example, in Malaysia one can become Malay (an ethnic and cultural group) regardless of physical characteristics—if one is adopted early by a Malay family and is raised as a Muslim, speaks Malay language, and practices Malay customs and traditions. Similarly, in Guatemala an Indian can become Maestizo if she or he is educated, speaks and reads Spanish fluently, and dresses like a European—i.e., wears shoes. There are other places where that situation is true also, but those are the exceptions. Overwhelmingly, the world over, one is identified—and identifies oneself—as a member of a racial, ethnic, or tribal group on the basis of his or her physical characteristics.

Another set of physical characteristics that have a profound influence on the individual identity, of course, are gender characteristics. To be born male is totally different from being born female. Despite variations in behavior from place to place, the fact is that worldwide, to be born female is pretty much to be born a second-class citizen. Here too, as with other physical characteristics, the meaning may reside less in the physical characteristic itself than in how societies treat that characteristic, but the fact is that if one is born a female, one is treated fundamentally differently than is someone born a male. While here, too, there are operations possible, people who have those operations become less a member of the opposite sex and more a member of that small and select group of individuals who have had gender-change operations.

Also in the category of involuntary, inherited characteristics I would include both extremes of the very, very bright and the extremely mentally retarded. While neither of these characteristics is necessarily inherited directly from their parents, they are inherent characteristics that cannot be changed and therefore belong here. In this category, too, should be included those who have some form of birth defect or deformity, which if serious enough, will probably become one of the major behavior determinants and primary identiy-group rankings in their lives.

Moving slightly to the right on our continuum are those identities we inherit by being born into our particular family. Certainly they are involuntary. While theoretically they are not immutable, in fact somewhere in excess of 95 percent of the people born into a particular economic class, religion, language group, or nationality will remain in those groups all of their lives. Yes, a child taken from his Animist parents in Zaire at birth and raised by a Christian family in Kansas will be much more Christian than Animist. But for the overwhelming majority of the population of the world, the child born into a family will be raised by that family and taught the language, religion, ethnic, and/or tribal identity of that family. What's more, though most of these characteristics could theoretically be changed by the child after he or she grows up, once the child has learned the cultural values of those groups, they can probably never be completely shed.

Based on what we know about the importance of these group identities to human behavior, I think we can argue that for the overwhelming majority of people in the world, these involuntary inherited group identities (along with the immutable group identities that are, after all, themselves inherited) probably affect—if not, indeed, determine—90 percent of the behavioral choices that all people make in their lives. At this point I am afraid that this is just an educated guess because I am unaware of any empirical research to either substantiate or dispute that assertion. I hope that in the years ahead considerably more work will be done on this subject so we will not need to make merely educated guesses. However, if this assertion is true, then these involuntary inherited group identities may be the very ones which are most important to human behavior.

Moving farther to the right on the continuum in the direction of voluntary group identities, one comes to that whole range of experiences that are a blend of voluntary and involuntary experience groups. For example, it may well be family values that make one family decide to send their children to a parochial school and a different family send their children to a public school, but the children involved really didn't have much choice in the decision. Whether they had a choice in the decision or not, however, the fact is that graduates of the two school systems will have been through two dissimilar life experiences. The same could be said of the one child who is sent out to the fields to work at an early age compared to the child who is sent to school. Neither child has much choice in those decisions; yet those decisions and the experiences associated with them will markedly determine the child's identities, attitudes, values, perceptions, and behaviors for the rest of his or her life.

Although somewhat more to the right on our continuum (because the children are older and therefore have a bit more control), it is certainly family values that determine that children in one family ought to receive a university education, and totally different values, in a different family, that say a child should go out and get a job as soon as she or he is able. The fact is that university graduates do learn to view the world differently from high school dropouts. But while each of these groups has learned different world views, let us not overlook the fact that those who have gone through a university education do tend to share a good deal of similarity of perception with others who have had the same experience. Not only do university graduates have an experience-based identity with all other university graduates, but graduates of a particular university share with other graduates of that same university an identity they do not share with graduates of some other university. Because of a lack of empirical data it is not possible for us to say with any certainty at this point whether a biology major and a history major who both graduated from Yale would share greater similarity of perception than would a biology graduate from Yale and another biology graduate from the University of Chicago. But that is not really at issue here. What is clear is that the two Yale graduates will share a degree of similarity of perception and identity as Yale graduates, while the biology graduates in our example would share different perceptions and different identities as biologists. Both of these identities, by my definition, will have been formed in part because of pressures placed on the child by his or her family and peers, and in part the choice to attend Yale or study biology would have been one of his or her own making.

On the extreme right-hand side of the continuum are those groups that one becomes part of completely by choice. Now, I fully recognize that no human is totally a free agent. We are all the products of our life experience and the groups that have had the most impact on us. To the degree that we have any choices to make at all, I'm talking here about the groups we join because of whatever element of free will we may have. For example, take "religious believers" or "nonbelievers" or political idealogues of various varieties and intensity. Three siblings could, after all, be born into the same Baptist family, but for whatever experiential and psychological reasons one could become exceedingly devout, one could be totally nonpracticing (and indeed even downright hostile to the believers), and the third could simply not care one way or the other. In a sense each has "chosen" his or her group identity.

The degree of volition an individual had in becoming a member of a group *may be* very important in determining a person's attitudes and values, but it may not be. One must be extremely careful before making generalizations. Think for a moment, for example, of the "true believer"—usually a person who has been converted to a "cause." The cause could be religion, ideology, nationalism, or even an approach to life (the psychological approach, for example). For these people the ranking of that single identity becomes all consuming. Whereas most other people adjust their ranking of values to the context in which they find themselves, these people see virtually everything in terms of that one single identity. "What does the Bible say about situations like this?" "What are the class implications of this situation?" "What does this do for my people?" or "What would Freud have said about that?" are not uncommon reactions of true believers to virtually all situations. While in the middle ages many people were raised with religion as their single overarching identification (through which virtually everything could be explained and for which virtually every human behavior was prescribed), since that time most people rank highly a great many different identities, each of which presumably is ranked differently in different contexts. The true believer, on the other hand, views virtually all contexts and interactions through the filters of that *one* identity she or he has adopted and made paramount and virtually exclusive. In many cases those identities are consciously and voluntarily embraced. The reasons any particular individual adopts any one identity so single-mindedly may be subconscious, but the "embracing of the faith" is often conscious and voluntary.[1]

In a sense, one could argue that the individual who went to Yale, as opposed to Chicago (or even the one who became a biologist instead of a historian) chose to do so and therefore should be considered more as an example of a voluntary than an involuntary experience, and that may indeed be correct—provided it really was the individual's choice. In many cases, however, we know that the school one attends and sometimes even the field one studies is less a matter of personal choice than response to family or other pressures. Now, I admit that in this particular example we may be dealing with a borderline case (because one could argue that the individuals concerned could have "chosen" to resist external pressures instead of having "chosen" to agree to them), but I don't want to get bogged down in semantic definitional problems. I believe that it may be conceptually useful to retain the notion of a continuum of identity groupings ranging from the completely involuntary to the completely voluntary, with some mixture of the two in between. Once the person has had the experience, there is no question but that his or her perceptions and identities—i.e., his or her personal culture—will be much more similar to someone else with the same experience, regardless of the degree of choice involved in the decision.

The point of this entire discussion is that people acquire group identities via life experiences. Some of those identities are acquired involuntarily, and others are acquired more as a matter of personal choice. Once the experience is there, however, whether voluntary or not, the individual's identities, attitudes, values, beliefs, and perceptions generally will have been markedly fixed for the rest of his or her life—which means that communicating with another individual with a different set of equally fixed identities requires bridging a great many cultural chasms.

Another whole type of identities that ought to be examined in this context is role identities. This category of group identities runs the whole range from involuntary to voluntary but are different from the others we have been discussing in that a lot more has been written about them.

As I discuss them here, role groups are those that are determined by our interpretation of the various "parts" we find ourselves acting during the course of our lives. Thus a man can be a son in relation to his mother, a husband in relation to his wife, and a father in relation to his daughter. In each of these roles he has learned that the identity demands and receives different sets of behaviors. While each societal culture may teach different accepted and expected behavior patterns for each of the roles, regardless of the societal culture in which we have been raised, we have absolutely no difficulty in moving from role to role and from behavior pattern to behavior pattern, sometimes in matters of only moments. Similarly in a work situation, all of us play the roles of superior or subordinate, depending on whether we are talking to, or doing something for, those we work for or those who work for us. Are we different people in each of those roles? No, of course not, but we do behave differently in each.

While each of these role identities certainly has some degree of similarity of perception attached to it, one must be careful not to generalize too much about them because of the other societal identities we may also possess. There is no doubt that all people—regardless of where and how they were brought up—recognize some similarity of perception for each of those roles. But how much is just not certain because it depends on so many other factors. For example, I once posed this hypothetical problem to a multinational group of midcareer male civil servants I was teaching: Suppose you are on a ship that is sinking. Your mother and your wife are also aboard the same ship. There is only one life jacket and you can't keep it for yourself. To whom will you give it? Two of the participants responded immediately and almost involuntarily, saying "no question," while a third said aloud, "God forbid." Now since one of the two who said "no question" was from Britain and the other was from Egypt, I sensed that they may not have meant the same thing by their verbally identical responses, so I asked them to elaborate. The gentleman from Egypt said, "Of course I would give it to my mother. I have only one mother and I can always get another wife." Whereupon the Englishman said, "Oh my God," and then went on to say, "Look, I chose my wife. I had nothing to say about whom I was born to." Thereupon there ensued the most incredibly heated discussion about why each value system was superior to the other, which of course convinced neither. The gentleman who said "God forbid" was from Lima, Peru (an urban center in a Third World country). For him both role identities (as son and husband) were equally ranked, and he would have had very great difficulty trying to decide between the two.

OTHER WAYS OF VIEWING GROUPS

In a fascinating study of all living systems—using a systems approach—John Grier Miller considered seven different levels of analysis. He started with the single cell, then went to the organ, the organism, the group, the organization, the society, and finally to what he called the supranational system.[2] He argued that every system has functions that have to be performed and that these functions are usually carried out by specific subsystems. He argued that at every level of analysis each subsystem is specifically designated to perform different functions. He counted nineteen functions that each system had to perform. While we need not concern ourselves with each of the nineteen subsystems that he discussed, what is most interesting from our perspective is that every level of analysis has some functions to perform and uses some or all of the subsystems in order to perform them.

I have cited Miller's work not because I intend to use a systems approach to looking at groups—although that is not a bad approach—but rather to illustrate several points. I want to build upon Miller's approach in order to present my own typology of groups. Miller's approach is useful in looking at groups once they have become groups in the traditional sociological sense.

W. J. H. Sprott enunciated that sense when he said in his classic work:

> A group, in the social psychological sense, is a plurality of persons who interact with one another in a given context more than they interact with anyone else.[3]

But perceptual groups, as I have used the term in this work, are not groups in the traditional sense. As I noted earlier, since individuals who belong to that collectivity do not communicate among themselves, they might be thought of as a "pregroup." As soon as they do communicate about the fact that they perceive some aspect of human existence similarly, they become what I have called an identity group. Now while every group has an identity—and is thus an identity group—not every identity group is a group in the traditional sense. That is, identity groups—as such—do not make decisions, maintain boundaries, or perform most of the other functions that Miller claims all "groups" are supposed to perform. An informal group may develop on the basis of some shared identity, and the people involved may begin to perform some of those functions, but as I have used the term thus far, identity groups per se are abstractions at a higher level of analysis.

As soon as a number of persons get together to perform any function, they have become at least an informal group. Every functional group has goals and an informal group is no exception. Often those goals are unstated and implicit. They can be as informal as a group of friends who get together periodically to study or chat over coffee. Sometimes an informal group is so informal the members are not even aware that a group has indeed been formed. Whatever the goal, however, and however implicit or subconscious it may be, in order to achieve that goal, certain functions have to be fulfilled. At a minimum, arrangements have to be made about where and when to meet. This implies that there has to be some direct internal communication within the group. Those channels may be sporadic and informal, but they are channels nonetheless. As soon as those channels become so formalized as to require different individuals or subgroups to perform specific tasks to carry out group functions, I would argue that they have become formal groups, or organizations.

What I am proposing here is a categorization of groups based on the kind of communication patterns that exist. The major distinction between groups, viewed this way, would be their primary mode of communication. If they rely solely on informal communication channels to perform group functions, I would call them informal groups, or simply "groups." If they have available to them routinized and formal channels of communication to perform those functions, I would call them formal groups, or simply "organizations." Having said that, however, it must be realized that both formal and informal groups do use informal communication channels where they exist. But since informal groups have no regularized channels of communication available to them, they must rely solely on informal channels. As soon as formal channels develop—no matter that they sometimes use informal channels as well—they have become (by this definition) formal organizations.

I would consider the staffs of various institutions, such as schools, hospitals, libraries, fire departments, or bureaucracies, also to be formal groups. Whether the fire department is volunteer or paid need not concern us here. Neither should whether the institution is public or private. All of the institutions I have mentioned here have formal, regularized (and many of them even have prescribed), channels of communication; therefore, I would call them formal groups, or organizations.

By viewing groups this way it allows us to compare all sorts of different groups and to ask the same kind of questions of them all. We can ask the same questions about groups of friends, workers, veterans' organizations, unions, private corporations, public bureaucracies, national states, and even international organizations. Every group, from an informal association on up, has by virtue of this definition certain functions that must be performed. Two of the things that distinguish groups, then, are (1) which of those functions they perform and (2) *how* they perform them. By this definition, every group has goals—or values (which after all, are what goals are). The values and ranking of values that each group accepts are one of the major characteristics that distinguish one group from another. The preferred ways in which groups perform the functions that are needed to achieve their goals also distinguish one group from another. That is why every group—in the traditional sense of that word—may be said to have its own culture. That is what makes every intergroup communication also an intercultural communication.

SIZE OF GROUP

Size of group has a major impact on the way individuals communicate within a group and on how groups communicate with other groups. What happens to interpersonal communications when the number of participants in the interaction increases from two to, say, three, four, six, or more? For one thing, we simply cannot pay as much attention to each individual in a group as we can in a one-to-one relationship. Instead of focusing all of our attention trying to communicate with just one other individual in a group setting, that attention must be divided as we give and receive messages from the entire group. Therefore, almost automatically this means that communication within a group cannot possibly be as accurate as can a two-person communication. There is also another reason why it cannot be as accurate. In a two-person communication—even of the more impersonal variety—the two individuals, while in the process of communicating, are also calibrating each other's perception of the other to make it more accurate. This requires virtually constant feedback on the part of both participants as each communicates. In a several-person communication interchange, there are just that many more varying perceptions, attitudes, and values that have to be calibrated. Since every person is culturally unique, the addition of each extra individual adds different cultural dimensions to the group and thus makes the task of calibrating meanings that much more intercultural and hence that much more difficult.

Decrease in "air time" is also a factor. In a two-person communication each of the participants theoretically can have 50 percent of the air time to do the sending of messages. (Actually we know that this is just not true, for all of us receive messages all of the time we are sending them, but never mind. When we are attending to the messages of just one other individual, that allows us to focus in on that person much more than we could in a group.) In a three-person interaction we theoretically have only 33 1/3 percent of the possible air time, while in a four-person interaction we have only 25 percent, and so on in descending proportion to the number of people present. In reality, however, the problem is even worse than it appears in mathematical terms. If I say something in a conversation with one other person, that person can feel free to ask for feedback until she or he understands any given message I may have sent. In a conversation among three people, they are simply not going to feel as free to ask as many questions as they each may need to in order to correctly understand the message. It would require just so much time for feedback that the conversation would "get nowhere." Each of us knows that instinctively and accordingly "settles" for less precise understanding of someone else's message in every group discussion. Thus it is virtually inevitable that the more people one tries to (or must) communicate with simultaneously, the less effective communication will become.

Another thing that has to happen as we increase the number of people in a communication relationship is that the distance and position among them has to change. Three people simply cannot stand or sit as close to each other as two can—unless one is content to face the other's back. But you cannot look someone in the eyes when you are facing the back of his or her head. Thus as numbers in the communication relationship increase, of necessity so do distance and intimacy of position. Therefore, the second casualty of increased numbers is intimacy. The more people we add to any group, the less intimate and the more impersonal every communication has got to become. No small group relationship can possibly be as intimate as can a two-person relationship. The more people involved in any communication, the less intimate—and hence the less open and honest—it is likely to become. Thus almost by definition every group interaction has got to be less intimate, less open, less trusting (and thereby less honest), and more intercultural than any interpersonal communication can be. With all of these factors working simultaneously, it is no wonder that no *intra*group communication can ever be as accurate as any *interpersonal* interaction can potentially be.

Further, in a one-to-one relationship there is no problem of alliance formation. As soon as another person is added to the relationship, suddenly alliances become not only possible but inevitable. Everything else being equal, Alice will agree some of the time with Bob and some of the time with Carol. The more Alice agrees with Bob, the more Bob is likely to feel the need—consciously or subconsciously—to reciprocate and agree with Alice. The more that occurs, the more Carol has got to feel rejected or left out and that there is an alliance against her. These may be "floating" alliances that change from issue to issue, or they may be more permanent alliances covering a number of issues, but there can be no question that they inevitably form. Thus in any *intra*group communication relationship, all of the participants, conscious of the possibility of the formation of alliances within the group, are likely to try to behave in ways that will win allies or at least not alienate potential allies. Again it seems to me, this only adds to a lack of honesty, openness, and trust within any group.

In some multiperson groups (of more than three) if Alice and Bob seem to be agreeing on too many issues with which Carol disagrees, there is always the possibility of Carol's forming an alliance with Dave and Emily and perhaps Frank (if it happens to be a six-person group). The number of persons with whom one forms alliances is sometimes less important than the reverse of not having anyone to ally with. It is precisely in those situations in which one of the individuals feels completely isolated that that individual is likely to display the most defensive—and probably the most dysfunctional—behavior. Once an alliance has been formed and an individual feels either left out or "ganged up" on, she or he is likely to display very dysfunctional behavior indeed. If the individual feels too isolated from the rest of the group she or he may simply withdraw from the group entirely. More often, however, the individual stays in the group, at least for a while, and tries to disrupt virtually anything the group tries to do. As long as the individual has at least one ally, she or he is much less likely to withdraw from the group entirely. As long as she or he receives validation from at least one other member of the group she or he is not likely to feel totally isolated and thus is much less likely to withdraw.

Suppose you have a group from which the individual or minority faction cannot withdraw, such as a work group or a minority racial group. If individuals or factions feel that there is not even the option to withdraw, and if they have reached the point where they feel that they have no hope of ever becoming the majority themselves or of ever convincing the majority to take their perspective into account in the making of decisions, then behavior regarded by the rest of the group as dysfunctional may not be viewed as dysfunctional at all by the minority. If we don't like where our group is headed, and we can't convince the other members to change course, then it is not at all dysfunctional behavior (from our perspective) to be totally disruptive and prevent the group from going anywhere.

Let's go back to the discussion of the development of factions within groups, which I argued is inevitable. When do these factions become so different in their perceptions that we are not so much discussing *intra*group communications as we are discussing *inter*group communications? I would argue that when the members of a faction begin to value their own perceptions, attitudes, and values *more* than they value those of the larger group, of which they presumably form a subset, at that point (and perhaps only on that issue) they probably have become a group unto themselves. When a group splits and becomes two different groups—even if only on one specific issue—then they are two distinct groups, not one, and communication between them becomes *inter-* rather than *intra-* group and therefore that much more difficult. I believe that it is useful, however, to argue that when an issue becomes controversial enough, or the opposition to it becomes intense enough, or it lingers unresolved long enough, one or both sides may begin to view themselves as "those of us who support X" as opposed to "those of us who oppose X." At that point an identity group—surrounding that one issue to be sure, but an identity group nonetheless—may be said to have formed, and until that issue is resolved to the satisfaction of the entire group—if it ever is—all communication concerning that issue between "us" and "them" will have all the characteristics and problems of *inter*group communication.

If that one issue becomes central enough to the entire group, of course, the group could become permanently split. And often that is exactly the case. In many more instances, however, in most groups there are "floating coalitions" that form on different issues. Thus, Alice, Bob, and Carol may oppose Dave, Emily, and Frank on issue one, but on issue two, Alice, Bob, and Dave may oppose Emily, Frank, and Carol, while on issue three, Bob and Frank may oppose everyone else. It is inevitable that this sort of thing happens in groups all the time. On the other hand, if Alice, Bob, and Carol repeatedly find themselves opposed by Dave, Emily, and Frank on most issues, it will not take long for "us" to recognize who we are and that "they" will usually oppose what we propose. At that point whether the group has "officially" split or not, for all practical, operational purposes it has. The question then becomes, What—if anything—can be done to assist all of the members of the larger group to begin to function as a unit again?

In many organizational settings nothing is ever done. Units function inefficiently, and no one is certain why. Actually they function inefficiently because they are not units at all but rather are conglomerates of subunits, often more opposed to and frightened of each other than they are of the external units that they are supposed to be dealing with as a unified whole. It does sometimes happen that some external threat (whether budget cuts in an organization or some other threat that affects *all* of the members of the unit) is perceived to be sufficiently threatening to *all* (or most) of the members of the unit that they can begin to work together as a single group in the face of the threat. The trouble with that approach, of course, is that as soon as the threat recedes, so does the unity of the group.

The question is in no way different from the one that was asked in chapter 2 on identities: At what point does one rank one's identity as an X more highly than she ranks her identity as a Y? She may still be part of both the faction and the group, but in those contexts where she ranks her identity as a member of the faction above her identity as a member of the group, that faction itself has become a group. At that point we may be talking more about *intra*group communication than about *inter*group communication. This is totally a matter of perspective. Which level of a system are we interested in? In discussing a group as a whole we are still discussing *intra*group communication. But every large group is composed of many smaller groups. When our level of analysis becomes communication between two of the smaller subgroups, then of course we are discussing *inter*group communications. As soon as we go back to discussing communication within the larger group as a whole, we have switched back to an *intra*group discussion.

The point is that this is strictly a level-of-analysis problem. What is important for any intelligent discussion is to try either (a) to keep our level of analysis constant or (b) to at least be conscious of the level we are discussing and to try to see how that level relates to other levels within the total system.

ENVIRONMENTAL AND HISTORICAL
IMPACT ON GROUPS

Environmental and historical factors often have a major impact on the perceptions and behaviors of groups. Either the group deals with them—consciously or subconsciously—or it dies. This is as true for private corporations, fraternities, and universities as it is for whole societies. I submit that the more conscious any group can make these environmental and historical constraints, the better able the group will be to cope with its environment. For some—perhaps many—groups, however, these factors are rarely looked at consciously. Let me give just one example of an environmental factor—life expectancy—and see how two different groups (in this case whole societies) dealt with it but not in a conscious way, to the best of anyone's knowledge.

Life expectancy in Ireland during the nineteenth century hovered somewhere around fifty years of age. In those days the country was a land of relative deprivation. There was not a lot of food to go around. Indeed, it has been said that in the nineteenth century Ireland's major export was Irishmen—simply because there was not enough food for everyone to eat. Now the Irish are predominantly a very religious Catholic people. One of the implications of that identity is the value that artificial birth control is not acceptable. Given that cultural value, how did the Irish cope with the problem of overpopulation? No one really knows how, or even precisely when, the group confronted this environmental problem, but somewhere along the line they did. And the way they did so was rather clever, I think. Somehow it evolved that it was inappropriate for Irish women to marry before the age of thirty or so. Take the plain biologic reality that women can have children roughly between the ages of thirteen and fifty. That would be thirty-seven child-bearing years. Given that artificial birth control is not acceptable to the Irish, if Irish women married young, just think of the overpopulation problem that Ireland would have had. To the best of our knowledge, no group of elders or other authority figures sat around and said "Look here, we have a problem, you know, and if we don't make it culturally unacceptable for women to marry before the age of thirty we will be in serious trouble." No, it just doesn't work that way. Rather, cultures evolve and change to meet environmental needs or they perish. Now contrast that with India.

India in the nineteenth century was even more economically deprived than was Ireland. It was so bad that average longevity at the turn of this century in that country was approximately twenty-eight years.[4] Faced with that environmental reality, if India had adopted the same "acceptable" marriage age for women as the Irish did, the society would have perished long ago. Instead, faced with that reality, somehow it evolved that the preferable age of marriage for an Indian woman was around twelve or thirteen. That way, not one precious potential childbearing year was lost. If the woman couldn't expect to live beyond twenty-eight, at least she had fifteen or so good years in order to propagate the species. And indeed, since more than half of all the children she had were certain to die before the age of five, not one of those precious years could be wasted if Indian society was to survive.

Please don't misread these examples. I am not saying that these societies—or anyone in them—made conscious decisions on how to deal with their environmental reality. Rather, I am saying that the cultures adapted to their environments, and that if they had not, they might have perished. While I realize these are extreme cases, I present them precisely because they illustrate my point. What I am arguing is that every group is confronted with environmental realities of one sort or another. Every group must deal with those realities in one way or another, or it will perish. Some groups may not adapt as well as others. There is no rule that says every group must survive. Throughout history many have not.

How about the impact of historical factors on group perception? There are a whole host of historical questions one ought to ask to see what impact history has had in determining the attitudes and values of the group. For example: How did the group start? When did it start? Do we know? Who were originally involved? What did the founders see as the basic aims or purposes of the group? What were the attitudes and values of the original members? What kinds of things have happened to the group since its inception that could have altered its attitudes and values? It is simply not possible to understand black American perceptions and ignore the slave experience. It is equally impossible to understand Jewish attitudes and values and not consider the impact of the diaspora in ancient times or of the Holocaust in more recent times. One doesn't have to have lived through the experience to be affected by it. It is sufficient to know that if one had lived during that particular period and had belonged to that particular group, he or she would have been directly affected. The questions one will ask will, of course, depend on the group. But no one can deny that historic memory is a major determinant of group attitudes and values.

Since every group has a history, that means that every group also has a history of relations with other groups. We cannot erase that history, but neither can we ignore it. If two groups have a history of mistrust, that is reality, and anyone who wants to do something about the current relationship between the groups must start from where the two groups actually are in relation to each other. If one wants to improve relations between two groups, it is important to go back into the history of how the two groups have related to each other in the past and see where mistrust and misperceptions started to see if they can't be undone. So often, well-meaning attempts at improving communication between groups have failed because the people trying to improve those communications (often new people to the group) have not paid enough attention to the history that has gone before.

"WE" VERSUS "THEY"

I argued in chapter 2 that any identity group comes into much sharper focus when juxtaposed against a threatening "they." That point is important enough to inter-cultural communication to warrant further discussion here.

Virtually every group perceives itself (and members of the group) as being essentially "good." (Some exceptions to this rule will be discussed in a moment.) "We" may recognize individual differences among ourselves and admit that not all of us are perfect, but by and large we consider ourselves trustworthy, loyal, helpful, friendly, courteous, kind, obedient, cheerful, thrifty, brave, clean, and reverent. In addition, we are intelligent, industrious, and generally nice people. Regardless of what we may be engaged in at any particular time, we genuinely believe ourselves to be acting from the best of motives. Of course we want what is best for everyone. It just usually happens that our definition of "what is best" is based on a subconscious definition of self-interest, rather narrowly defined. The industrialist sees the country's best interests as being served by allowing in-dustry to accrue huge profits, which will "naturally" (the industrialist genuinely believes) be reinvested, thus creating jobs for workers and well-being for everyone. The worker, on the other hand, sees the country's best interests as being served by insuring high wages for the worker, which will, just as "naturally" (the worker just as genuinely believes), mean that the workers will have more to spend on things the industrialist produces, thus creating well-being for everyone. Of course, both perceptions are equally as valid (remember our discussion of differing reality worlds?), but each accuses the other of being out to improve "their" position at "our" expense.

Whoever we are, we tend to trust one of us, more than we trust one of them. If we know nothing about two individuals, save that one of them is a member of one of the primary groups with which we identify and the other is not, we are likely to be trusting of the one who belongs to our group and to be suspicious of the other.

Every group tends to see itself as noble, just, honest, and virtuous—and "them" as the opposite. The ancient Athenians—like everyone else before and since —divided the world into two classes of people: we and they, Athenians and non-

Athenians. Do you know what word the Athenians used to describe someone who was not from Athens? *Barbarians.* Even the word *they* is itself mildly pejorative. The degree of hostility expressed toward other groups increases as the group becomes more specific. Thus while *they, stranger,* and *alien* all have mildly pejorative connotations, words like *spic, mic, honkie, kike, nigger, wop,* and *queer* are both specific and strongly hostile. Recall that the Jews consider themselves "God's chosen people." That leaves everyone else to be considered "less than chosen by God." The Chinese call themselves the Central Kingdom—meaning that they are at the center of the earth. Clearly everyone else is peripheral, in their view. The Germans were told—and presumably believed—that they were the Master Race. What did that make everyone else?

I have been told that the Filipinos—a Catholic people—have a charming myth about Genesis. According to the myth, when God decided to create Adam, He formed a bit of clay into the figure of a man and put him into the oven. Unfortunately He left him in too long and he came out burned to a crisp. He put that man down in Africa. Then He formed some more clay into another figure of a man and again put him into the oven. This one He took out too soon. He put this half-baked model down in Europe. He fashioned a third figure of a man and took him out when he was a beautiful golden brown. This one He put down in the Philippines.

Now while we may all chuckle at this little bit of Philippine folklore, how is it different in kind from the Judeo-Christian notion that God made us in His image? Note too, if you will, the male chauvinism in the very term *His image.* No different in kind from the pre-Copernican view of the universe with the earth at the center.

While it is certainly true that virtually every group has this overinflated view of themselves and a somewhat dimmer view of everyone else, there are exceptions to that rule. People who have long been subjected to domination by other groups often come to accept the standards of beauty and other values held by the dominant group. Thus British values, dress, and manners have been accepted in large parts of the world formerly ruled by them as the standard of excellence by which all others are measured. The same is true for French and Spanish cultures in areas they once dominated. In the U.S., despite the recent emergence of black pride and slogans like "black is beautiful," hair straighteners and skin lighteners still sell well among blacks. Blonde is still the hair coloring that sells most in the U.S., and many people suffer severe discomfort and considerable expense to have their noses clipped to Anglo-Saxon proportions (I've never heard of a case of someone having an operation to have a nose made larger). Far more important for human behavior than these dominant attitudes toward beauty, however, are other belief systems and ways of viewing the universe—and themselves—that subjected peoples may unknowingly have taken from the dominant group. The most debilitating of these beliefs may be the suspicion that "they"—usually the Europeans in Asia or Africa—are, in fact, superior to us. This leads to a kind of ethnic "inferiority complex" on a very basic level of beliefs, which can dominate much of one's behavior in extremely counterproductive ways.

That having been said, however, the evidence seems quite overwhelming that we tend to view our own groups as being pretty good, while we tend to view "them" less favorably. Now this is extremely important for successful communication, since as we have seen again and again throughout this work, we tend to trust messages received from one of "us" and tend to mistrust messages from one of "them." The more different or threatening we see them as being, the less we are likely to trust them.

Going back to what was said earlier about subconscious behavior, precisely because we are consciously unaware of the importance to us of some of our identities, some of our behavior in certain contexts may be motivated by identities that are "inappropriate" to the role we are supposed to be playing. Allow me an anecdote to illustrate my point. A number of years ago I was teaching at a university in New York City of which the student body at the time was 85 percent white, middle-class, Jewish-American. The chairman of the political science department, in which I taught, was a third-generation American of German-Jewish ancestry. He was not a religious man at all and indeed hardly thought of himself as Jewish. In another time one might have said of him that he was trying to "pass" as a non-Jew.

One year we were recruiting for a junior position on the faculty, and the choice narrowed down to two individuals. One had his Ph.D. from Harvard, the other from Yale. Both were extremely bright, personable, clean-cut, attractive young men. Both had published, and both were reputed to be good teachers. Having gone through all of the regular procedures then in operation, the committee (headed by the chairman) decided in favor of one of them. Since they both seemed so very evenly matched, when later asked on what they had based their decision, the chairman replied, "I can't quite put my finger on it, but there is something about X that we all felt we liked." Of course, it turned out that Mr. X was of Jewsih ancestry. When that was pointed out to the chairman, he was furious that anyone would think that he had shown favoritism "to one of us." Yet in fact— subconsciously—that is precisely what he had done. Indeed, it had to be more than coincidence that of the professors in the political science department at that school approximately 90 percent were of Jewish background. Just as it could not have been an accident that the history department at the same school, which by "accident" had had white Anglo-Saxon Protestant chairmen for twenty years, was predominantly white Anglo-Saxon Protestant.

This anecdote and hundreds of thousands like it all across America (and, indeed, the world) explain why it is that for so many years well-qualified racial minority groups and women just didn't "make it" professionally. Now that the matter has been raised to the level of consciousness something can be—and is being —done about it. But that is only so with regard to feelings toward minorities we recognize. Unfortunately, there are dozens of other groups toward whom we harbor unconscious negative biases. If we are honest with ourselves, we will have to admit that we are more negatively disposed toward "them"—whichever group they happen to be—than we are toward one of us. Not only do we tend not to hire "them," we tend to not even associate with them, if we can help it.

Misperceptions in Conflict Situations

That "we" are good and "they" are less than good in a great many situations is an attitude anyone studying interpersonal, intergroup, or international relations must take into account. The student of intergroup or international conflict must also consider the likelihood that the more intense the conflict, the better *we* become and the worse *they* become. During times of relative calm it is fairly easy and often quite satisfying to consider ourselves objective enough to find fault with our own identity groups and to find at least some merit in other groups. All that changes, however, when *we* perceive our group to be seriously threatened by *them.*

In international affairs, particularly where national identity is strong, notice that *they* have "spies" while *we* have "intelligence men." Notice, too, that *we* have never declared an aggressive war; *they* fight aggressive wars while *we* fight wars of self-defense. It was Britain and France, after all, who declared war on Germany in 1939, merely because *we* Germans went to the rescue of other Germans being massacred and mutilated by the Poles. What was Germany to do? *We* had to defend good Germans in the good German city of Danzig (at the time occupied by Polish troops) from destruction. And once the U.K. and France declared war, there simply was no choice for Germany but to defend itself.

Ralph K. White, in a brilliant monograph entitled "Misperception and the Vietnam War," has explored this subject in depth.[5] In systematic fashion he has provided an analysis of six forms of misperception that commonly appear in intense conflict situations. While these forms of misperception are undoubtedly most intense during crisis periods, they probably exist to varying lesser degrees whenever any group perceives even minor threats to itself.

White's six forms of misperception are (1) the diabolical enemy-image, (2) the virile self-image, (3) the moral self-image, (4) selective inattention, (5) absence of empathy, and (6) military overconfidence.

White describes each of these more or less as follows: The diabolical enemy-image is the view that they are "out to get us." They are devious, deceptive, and downright treacherous. They will say one thing and do something else. They simply cannot be trusted. Anyone who thinks otherwise is naive at best, a fool or a traitor at worst.

The virile self-image: They may have more men or guns than we do, but any one of us is braver and a better fighter than any ten of them put together. Just look at any late-night World War II movie on television, and you will see how easily a handful of our men destroy a battalion of theirs.

The moral self-image: We are peaceful, innocent, and virtuous. Right and justice are on our side. Indeed, God is on our side. We have to win eventually because we are the ones who are moral. If we lose, the world will be turned over to the forces of evil. We have a moral obligation not just to ourselves but to the whole world to oppose them.

Military overconfidence relates to the virile self-image. Not only are our men better fighters, but if it comes to war—no matter how badly prepared we may be at the moment—we will win. Indeed, this is one of the attitudes that most often lead to war. After all, it does take two sides to fight a war, and usually one side wins. If the side that lost had made a realistic appraisal of their military capabilities before the war, they probably would have not entered it in the first place.

I have chosen to discuss selective inattention and absence of empathy last and at greater length than the other four factors White identified because they are so significant for every aspect of intercultural communication and human behavior. Part of chapter 3 deals with selective attention. Selective inattention is, in a sense, the other side of that coin. Instead of analyzing which bits of data individuals with different perceptual sets choose to *select* and why, White asks which bits of data—from the host available—individuals with different perceptual sets choose to *ignore* and why.

> Call it resistance, repression, ignoring, forgetting, non-learning, inhibition or curiosity, evading, card-stacking, perceptual defense, blind spots, or just plain not paying attention. By whatever name, it is omnipresent. Absence of empathy—i.e., not paying enough attention to the thoughts of others—is probably its most serious, most war-producing manifestation, but it has many other. Whatever is inconsistent with the black-and-white picture (that is, with the diabolical enemy-image and the moral self-image) and whatever is inconsistent with the virile self-image tends to drop out of consciousness. Space perspective, especially whatever has to do with distant onlookers, tends to be restricted. Time perspective is restricted. Important distinctions (e.g., between different meanings of "aggression," between Munich and the . . . situation in Vietnam, between a holding operation and surrender) tend to be blurred or ignored. Individuals who raise issues that one does not want to think about are often not answered in terms of the issues; they are denounced as traitors, cowards, or naive dupes of the diabolical enemy.[6]

It is precisely this inability to "view events from the other nation's perspective" that White refers to as absence of empathy.

> To avoid misunderstanding it should perhaps be repeated that the word "empathy" as used here does not mean sympathy. It does not mean a sneaking sympathy for the Communist cause, but a tough-minded effort to understand the viewpoints of both enemies and onlookers as a basis for realism in coping with enemies (without war if possible) and achieving cooperating with onlookers. . . . One aspect, however, calls for further discussion: what Newcomb has called "autistic hostility"—the tendency to express hostility by cutting off communication (and with it, the possibility of achieving empathy), with the result that the hostility is perpetuated or even reinforced, and a vicious circle results. Autistic hostility is present to an extreme degree in the paranoid psychotic who believes himself persecuted and therefore cuts himself off from empathic communication with all or almost all of his fellow human beings. It can occur in any quarrel between individuals. It also tends to develop on both sides of any acute group conflict.[7]

Selective inattention and absence of empathy are just two of the more serious difficulties that occur when members of one group view members or actions of a different, hostile group. All the general problems of perception and communication inherent in any interpersonal, intergroup, or international relationship are invariably exacerbated in nearly direct proportion to the intensity of the threat perceived by the units in a conflict situation.

It could be that the only real hope for those who would like to resolve group conflict is to have each of the groups in a conflict situation identify with some third, larger, identity of which both form a part. Thus for example, while American industrialists and American workers may be at each other's throats, so to speak, in the absence of some other threatening group, let the U.S. be attacked and suddenly they coalesce behind their American identity and work together to fight a common foe. Notice, however, that it takes some other threatening "they" for the industrialists and workers to unite in that American identity. What is more, very often that threat to our third, shared, identity is only temporary, and once that threat is removed we may return to our old animosities. I am afraid that the implication for those who cherish the hope that one day all humans will rank their human identity above all others is that it would take an invasion from outer space before that could occur. Too many of us simply tend to focus more on the differences that divide us than we do on the human qualities that we share in common.

PROPOSITIONAL SUMMARY FOR CHAPTER 6

Groups don't communicate; people do: Groups, as such, don't communicate; people do, either collectively or in the name of their groups. Thus in a very real sense, all intra- and intergroup communications are, at some level, also interpersonal communications.

Types of identity groups: One way of analyzing identity groups is to view them on a continuum concerning the degree of control the individual has over the characteristics that define them. Viewed this way, those identities can range from the ones that are inherited and immutable (such as gender, race, and other physical characteristics), to those one chooses (such as political preference or profession).

Informal groups: Informal groups are distinguished by the fact that whatever their functions or goals, they rely *solely* on informal communication channels to perform those group functions. Sometimes an informal group is so informal, the members are not even aware that a group has been formed.

Formal groups: Regardless of goals or functions, formal groups are distinguished from informal groups by the fact that they have available to them routinized and formal channels of communication to perform their group functions. Formal groups may, and often do, use informal communication channels as well as the formal ones, but only the formal groups have the routinized, formal channels of communication, as well.

Size of group: Size of group has a major impact on the way individuals communicate within a group and on how groups communicate with other groups.

Environmental and historical impact on groups: Environmental and historical factors often have a major impact on the perceptions and behaviors of groups. Either the group deals with them—consciously or subconsciously—or it dies. The more conscious any groups can make those constraints, the better able the group will be to cope with its environment.

"We" versus "they" in conflict situation: Everything else being equal, "we" tend to view ourselves as essentially good and "them" as something less than good. What is more, we tend to trust "us"—however that "us" is defined—more than we trust "them." The more intense the conflict between groups, the better our own view of ourselves tends to become, and the worse our view of them tends to become. Also, the more hostile we perceive them to be, the less likely we are to trust them.

Misperceptions in conflict situations: Ralph K. White has identified six forms of misperception that are common in intense conflict situations: the diabolical enemy-image, the virile self-image, the moral self-imate, selective inattention, absence of empathy, and military overconfidence.

NOTES

[1] Personal communication; I am indebted to Professor Marvin Koenigsberg of Brooklyn College, CUNY, for this insight into "true believer" behavior.

[2] John Grier Miller, *Living Systems* (New York: McGraw-Hill Book Co., 1978).

[3] W. J. H. Sprott, *Human Groups* (Harmondsworth, England: Penguin Books, 1958), p. 9.

[4] I recognize, of course, that the figure was so low because of the high infant mortality rate, but that in no way affects my argument. Nearly the same infant mortality rate—not quite as bad—was present in nineteenth-century Ireland.

[5] Ralph K. White, "Misperception and the Vietnam War," *Journal of Social Issues* 22, no. 3 (July 1966), entire issue.

[6] Ibid., pp. 134–35.

[7] Ibid., pp. 132–33.

CHAPTER SEVEN
INTRA- AND INTERGROUP COMMUNICATION

Back in the late 1960's when I first tried bringing together the people teaching intercultural communication in the various departments and schools of the University of Pittsburgh, I was struck by the cultural differences among these people who, in some other ways, shared so very much in common. The male professors from the professional schools all came to the meetings in jacket and tie. The male professors from the speech communication department never wore ties or jackets. The professors from the professional schools were usually addressed by their titles by the student members of the group; the disciplinary department students almost always addressed their professors by their first names. The people who were more cognitively oriented always wanted to talk about accomplishing the task at hand. The human relations people and the organizational development people, on the other hand, wanted to talk about the processes by which we would arrive at our decisions. Indeed, even the codes that each of the groups used did what codes always do—they facilitated communication among "us," but made communication with "them" that much more difficult.

Since I had been teaching for some time that every group has a culture of its own, I shouldn't have been surprised by these cultural differences, yet I was. Indeed, very often some of those differences prevented the group from successfully achieving its goals.

At about the same time, not one, but two professional organizations in the field of intercultural communication were started (Society for Intercultural Education Training and Research—SIETAR and International Society for Educational, Cultural and Scientific Interchanges—ISECSI). When I was asked by someone to give a logical explanation of why there should be two separate organizations in such a small and such a new field of intellectual endeavor, I told the person that it made as much logical sense as did the existence of two Koreas, two Germanys, and, at the time, two Vietnams.

INTRAGROUP

Intragroup Perceptions and Identities:
Getting to Know Our Own Group

J. Van Mannen and Edwin Shein describe organizational culture as follows:

> Any organizational culture consists broadly of long-standing rules of thumb, a somewhat special language, an ideology that helps edit a member's everyday experience, shared standards of relevance as to the critical aspects of the work that is to be accomplished, matter-of-fact prejudices, models of social etiquette and demeanor, certain customs and rituals suggestive of how members are to relate to colleagues, subordinates, superiors and outsiders, and a sort of residual category of some rather plain "horse sense" regarding what is appropriate and "smart" behavior within the organization and what is not.[1]

In order to determine the perceptions of any group, one of the first things we have to do is to determine who the members of the group are. In social science jargon this is sometimes called identifying the universe. Once the social scientist knows the universe, she can then extract a stratified sample from that universe in order to test for whatever it is she is interested in finding out. That is the first step the intercultural researcher would take in order to determine the attitudes and values of the group. While the practitioner may not have the time or money to do as thorough a job as the researcher, it behooves him to do something similar, if not nearly as rigorous.

One of the reasons it is so important to know who comprise our group is that then we may be able to get to know something about the other cultures that members of this group bring with them from their other group memberships. Recall from our discussion of premise 8 in chapter 2 that group culture is that peculiar symbiotic relationship between the collectivity and the individuals who comprise it. Their collective culture becomes the group culture at the same time as the group culture becomes, in part, their personal culture. Hence to know the culture of any group one has to know the perceptions, attitudes, values, identities, and belief and disbelief systems of the members of the group.

Once it has been determined—by whatever means—who the members of our group actually are, then we can explore with them directly to determine answers to questions such as, What are the personal needs and/or values of the members?

How do those goals jibe with the capabilities of the group to meet them and/or with the goals of the group as a whole? What are the attitudes of members of the group on critical issues affecting the effective functioning of the group? To what degree are the attitudes of the individual members in congruence with the expressed attitudes of the group?

Dinges and Maynard say:

> The analogy of organizations to cultures is particularly useful in comparing and contrasting the interactions among members of organizations when they differ significantly in their socialization backgrounds. Formal organizations often mirror the implicit social organization in a given culture. The potential for conflict is great when culturally different organization members attempt to fulfill their organizational roles based on prior socialization experiences that differ greatly from those expected in the current organizational setting (e.g., leadership-subordinate relations).[2]

Elsewhere Edgar H. Schein says: "Organizations exist in a parent culture, and much of what we find in them is derived from the assumptions of the parent culture." But he warns that we must recognize that different organizations will stress or "amplify" different aspects of the same "parent culture," and thus organizations even within the same parent culture can be quite different.[3]

Having discovered what the needs and values of the individual members are, we can ask to what degree the group as a whole is meeting—or can be expected to meet—those goals. We can ask if it is realistic for the members of the group to expect the group, as such, to be able to satisfy their personal needs/values. If not, is there anything that the group could do to assist its members in helping them to satisfy those goals elsewhere?

After all, if there is conflict between the personal values of the individual members and the collective values of the group, that ought to be brought out into the open and dealt with. Our group might not be able to fulfill those goals or to resolve those conflicts, but by bringing those conflicts into conscious awareness and examining them honestly it is entirely possible that, at least, some of those conflicts can be resolved. It is very important for any group—as a group—to make conscious whatever value conflicts may exist within the group so that the group can try to solve them and then get on to whatever business it is that the group is supposed to be addressing itself to. The more contented the individual members of our group are—all other things being equal—the more effectively our group, collectively, should be able to function.

Just as the individual has its open, blind, hidden, and unknown areas, so too, does a group. Joseph Luft, one of the developers of the Johari window, recognized that in his book *Group Processes*.[4] He argues that for every group there are some things that are known both to members of the group and to others (open area). There are also things known to the group but not to others (hidden areas). There is also a blind area that is known to others but not to members of the group, while there is an area that is unknown to members of the group and to others. To the degree that a group wants or needs to operate more effectively, it seems to me that the blind and unknown areas have to be greatly reduced. That is, if there are internal problems of any sort within the group of which the group is unaware, it does the group no good to remain unaware of their existence. Rather, it seems to me that exposing them is the first step to overcoming them.

Every organized group has some sort of decision-making process—and, indeed, must. In order to understand our own group attitudes and values better, we have to determine how the decision-making process in our group works and who the people are who make the important decisions for our group. Once we know that, we can analyze *their* attitudes and values, and we can ask if those are the same attitudes and values held by the rank and file of the group or whether there are conflicts. Although theoretically one might assume that they have to be more or less the same, from everything else that has been said here about the importance of group perceptions in molding the perception of the membership of the group, the fact is that sometimes they are not. After all, the group leadership (sometimes called elites) may be part of many different other groups of which the rank and file are not a part. Depending upon the organization, of course, and how decision making occurs within it, there are some groups in which the distinction between leader and led is very great. In those kinds of organizations—by definition—the rank and file is not a part of the leadership group and therefore cannot share the same attitudes and values of the leader. The implications of this are enormous for some groups.

Go back to what we said earlier about definitions of self-interest. It is not at all uncommon for the leadership of some groups to define what is good for their own personal self-interest as being in the self-interest of the entire group. And they very often genuinely believe it. They very often genuinely believe that it is the interest of the group as a whole that they are trying to defend and foster. Upon investigation it is very often discovered that the leaders' definition of group interest very closely coincides with what by other definitions might be called personal self-interest of the leaders. But the leaders—almost without exception—will deny that they were pursuing selfish and personal values in the way they defined group goals. Rather, they honestly believe that what is good for them is also good for the group.

Think for a moment of the managers of industry who feel that it is important for the firm to reduce unit costs by increasing productivity so that they can more effectively compete in the marketplace. In order to do this they may believe that they must either automate some aspect of production (thereby putting some of their employees out of work), increase the number of units each worker produces, or lower workers' salaries. From management's perspective it is important to please the Board of Directors and the stockholders and thus get credit for doing a good job of managing. The workers on the other hand, may value job security above all else and might be perfectly willing to produce more units of whatever it is they produce, *provided* it means job security for them. But management simply wouldn't know that unless they asked the workers what it is they value more.

The point of this discussion, however, is to try to determine whether or not there are value and attitude differences between the leadership of any group and the rank and file, who usually believe that there should not be. The only way we can determine that, of course, is first to identify who it is that makes the decision for the group and then try to determine *their* attitudes and values.

If we are to determine whether conflicts exist between members' individual values and the values of the group as such, then it is very important to ask all of the same kinds of questions—of the group as such—as were asked of individuals in the group. After all, every group has both goals (values) and needs. These vary, of course, depending on the kind of group that one considers. The goals of a group of friends who meet weekly to play bridge are vastly different from the goals of a business corporation or a branch of the armed forces, but every group does have implicit or explicit goals. Certainly they have functions that have to be performed in order to insure the maintenance of the group. The performance of those functions are themselves goals. More often than not the goals of an informal group will be implicit (and perhaps even subconscious) and therefore unstated, while the primary goals of more formal groups are usually explicit.

What is often overlooked, however, is that every group has multiple, and often conflicting, conscious and subconscious goals. Every group also has needs. Thus, implicit or explicit, one of the unstated goals of every group is to meet the needs of the group—as a unit—as well as to meet the needs of the individual members of the group. Because of this it is virtually certain that every group will have a multiplicity of goals simultaneously. Indeed, it is not at all uncommon for some of the implicit group and individual goals to be completely contradictory. The strong probability is that group goals will not be the same—or at least will not be ranked in the same order—as the individual goals of the members of the group. The group goals may more accurately coincide with the individual goals of the leadership of the group, but that may be because (a) the leadership may have molded the group goals to meet their own personal goals and/or (b) because they may have come to so completely identify with the group that they have adopted the group goals as their own personal goals. Despite that, however, we must not confuse the goals and needs of the individual members with the goals and needs of the group as such. I would argue that most often they are not the same.

Now there is something of a paradox here since we have already argued that groups as such don't act, the people who comprise the group do. I believe that paradox can be solved, however, by viewing the people who act for groups as playing the organizational role. That is, when an individual is put into the role of having to speak for what is needed by the group she may submerge her own personal goals and/or needs and address the goals and needs of the organization or group. Corporations and other formal organizations do have a culture quite distinct from the members who comprise it. An organizational culture does develop, and for those who identify closely with the organization or group it is not at all difficult to submerge their own goals and needs and to give a higher ranking to the goals and needs of the organization. That is precisely what was meant by the term *organization man*.[5] The organization comes first. Indeed it is not at all uncommon for some people to feel so strongly about some groups as to be willing to die for them. In those cases the groups' goals and needs have become the individual's. In those cases, also, role identity may be said to have taken precedence for behavior above all other identities.

Just as every human has somewhat different values and ranks them differently, so too does every group. Every group, informal and formal, has basic needs. If those needs are not met, the group simply will not survive. For a family or a tribe, they can be as basic as finding enough "wealth" to provide food, clothing, and shelter for its members. For a formal organization, some basic resources are necessary merely to keep it "alive." It may not need food and clothing, but it probably needs at least some money or other resources to achieve its primary goals—whatever they may be. It usually needs a shelter of some kind for its members to meet in. What is more, every group—formal or informal—also has survival (or safety) needs. Indeed, the safety needs of informal groups and formal organizations seem to be as great as those needs are in individual humans. At its most basic level no group can tolerate "internal warfare" among its members.

While no group is ever likely to have just a single goal, some groups are more single-purpose than others. If a group is more single-purpose, the likelihood is that it will be smaller and will probably be more dedicated to that single purpose than a multipurpose group could be. That is because neither an individual nor a group can be equally dedicated to a multiplicity of purposes simultaneously. Precisely because a multipurpose group does address a multiplicity of purposes, it is likely to attract a larger number of members than a single-purpose group, but that probably means poorer internal communication. Some people may join the group because of purpose A, while others will be attracted because of purpose B, C, D, or E. Each individual attracted for a specific purpose is likely to work hardest to achieve the purpose for which she or he was attracted to the group and may merely "just go along" with the other purposes or may even reject some of them. Even holding size constant, there is little doubt that a multipurpose group simply cannot be as effective as a more single-purpose group can.

Intragroup Power

For some reason people generally find it easier to think about groups and nations exercising influence as opposed to individuals doing the same. The question, "Does our group have sufficient power to achieve its goals?" is not an unusual one for us to ask. We constantly ask ourselves whether group resources are sufficient for achievement of its purposes. That kind of question we find quite "natural." But while the question may not be alien or surprising, I am afraid that often we may ask it in its grossest form without considering which component is most appropriate for achieving which value. That is, I suspect that many groups believe that because they have sufficient resources of one sort, they do not stop to question whether that resource is the appropriate one to use to achieve a specific value. "We have enough people on our side who support what we want to achieve so we can't lose." Well, that *may* be true, but are they properly organized? Do they have sufficient skills to achieve that particular goal? Do they have the material equipment they need? Unfortunately, these and questions like them are just not asked frequently enough.

"We know we are right; therefore, we can't lose" and "God is on our side" are two other statements (in exaggerated form, perhaps) that one frequently hears variants of. Now, moral and religious values are fine, and I don't mean to deprecate them, but in real life I am afraid that the "good guys" don't always win. We may consider ourselves good, right, or virtuous, but I am afraid that "they" consider themselves to be all of those things as well. Often groups fail to achieve their purpose simply because they haven't properly taken into account all of the components of power that would be necessary to achieve their goal in *a specific context.* Because we are "right" in no way assures us of success. Other groups are not going to do what we want them to do merely because "we" think that we are right. We have to convince them that we are. That means exercising influence over them. That means having sufficient amounts of the correct components (vis-à-vis them) to do so. That is precisely what power is all about.

While I do not propose to go through each of the components of power as they apply to groups here, there are two in particular that I want to say a word about. Recall that organization is one of the components of power. The better organization, the greater ability our group should have to achieve its goals. Now recall that the only way to achieve effective organization is to have sufficient internal channels of communication so that all parts of the group can communicate with all other parts of the group that they need to. While doing an assessment of the components of power of our group, I suggest that we not overlook asking ourselves not only whether the channels of communication exist but also *how well* each segment of our group can, and does, communicate with the important other segments of our group. If there is no trust within the group, then, to that degree our communication channels will not work, and to that degree we are deficient in organization.

Another question—which really relates to organization—that I believe ought to be looked at is the power relationships within the group. Are there power struggles within the group among different sectors of the leadership? If so, to the degree that they exist the group is weakened. Are there power struggles going on between the leadership of the group and the rank and file in general, or between the present leadership and certain segments of the rank and file that would like to become part of leadership? Once again, while some struggles of this sort may be inevitable in virtually every large group, to the degree that they exist they weaken the group. If the group hopes to achieve certain goals vis-à-vis other groups, before it does so it might do well to resolve whatever power struggles can be resolved. Sometimes merely by bringing into conscious awareness the fact that they exist can facilitate the internal compromises necessary to resolve them.

We have already established that every group has needs and values—goals. Once we have made conscious and explicit what those goals are, then we are in a position to ask ourselves what amounts of which power components would be necessary in order to achieve those goals. That cannot be done in a vacuum but only in relation to the environment and/or to other individuals and groups. Therefore we must assess our power potential in relation to theirs. How much of whatever it may take in a specific context will we need to achieve our goals, compared (a) to the magnitude of the task and (b) to what other groups may have? We may have a good idea or a good product, but we had better know whether some other group doesn't have a better one. At least they may think that theirs is better. And if they have more resources than we do to make other people aware of their product or idea, no matter how good ours is, theirs is the one others are likely to "buy."

Forgive the repetition, but power is relative and contextual. We had better know the context in which we are trying to operate and to whom it is relative as we go about trying to assess whether we have enough. That implies that we must make an honest and accurate assessment not only of our own power capabilities but of theirs as well.

Intragroup Communication

Questions concerning intragroup communication are not different in kind from those asked about *intrapersonal* communication. Is our group acquiring adequate information from the external world? Are our group censor screens blocking out information that our group should be attending to? Are they preventing information overload? Do members of our group know all of the codes they ought to know in any specific communication context? Does our group have sufficient data-storage capacity? Can we recall important information when it is needed? These and many similar mechanical questions must be attended to by any group if it is to function effectively.

Questions that may be even more important concern things like whether there are sufficient *internal* channels of communication so that members of the group can be mobilized rapidly to achieve group goals when the need arises. Recall that informal groups don't have formal channels of communication available to them to meet their needs but formal organizations do. If those channels are insufficient or are not being used, the group could be in trouble.

I would be willing to wager that everyone reading this can think of at least one example in which an informal group, of which you were a member, did not meet as scheduled because one of the other members, who was supposed to "spread the word" on where or when you were to meet, "messed-up," for one reason or another. If that person repeatedly forgot to communicate, or did so inaccurately, the group would soon learn not to rely on him or her to perform that function.

Is there adequate communication—both ways—between the group leadership and the rank and file? Is there sufficient feedback within the group so that accuracy of messages can be tested? Is there sufficient trust within the group so that important messages can flow freely from the top down and from the bottom up?

Once again if that trust is not there, communication within the group suffers accordingly. Either the group deals with the issue directly, to solve the problem, or it withers and dies. My own experience with informal groups leads me to believe that many informal groups do dissolve, precisely because the members are not willing to deal directly with the issue of lack of trust. We are often so afraid that someone's feelings will be hurt if we discuss the issue, that we say nothing, and the group simply disintegrates.

The formal channels of communication in any organization are almost always from the top down—from upper management to middle management to lower management to workers—just as formal communication the other way is supposed to be through "proper" channels from the bottom up. Fortunately for the functioning of any organization, informal communication channels always form, and more often than not, it is these informal channels among people who know and trust each other that keep the organization operating. I say fortunately because in every large organization decentralization and subdivision on geographic and/or functional lines must take place.

Every large firm, for example, would have at a minimum, a production division, a market division, and a financial division. I know of few large corporations that have *effectively* built into their formal structures a way for people in the various divisions to communicate with each other—except at the top. Most decent planning committees of most large corporations have, at the top, at least occasional meetings of representatives of each of the major divisions of the company to discuss overall corporate planning. In actual fact, however, these formal communication channels often function very poorly. One reason, of course, is that the head of the production division, for example, isn't really going to know too well what is going on in his division. The reason he won't have an accurate picture of what is going on—even if he came "up from their ranks"—is that the nature of his managerial function takes him out of his division and away from the work he used to do when he actually worked in the division. Human nature, being what it is (and it is amazing how similar this aspect is, regardless of culture), his subordinates are not likely to report to him what is really going on in his division, but rather, are likely to report what they think he will want to hear—just as he is likely to report to *his* superiors what *he* thinks they are going to want to hear. That seems to be built into the very nature of superior/subordinate communication everywhere one looks.

Now, given the hierarchical nature of every large organization, no subordinate is going to report to her superior "how bad things are" in the unit for which she is responsible. What is more, because there are rarely formal links *at the bottom* of each of these divisions, without some informal communication channels, each would function in almost total isolation of the other. Indeed, each of these divisions attracts people with different kinds of skills, temperaments, and personalities to begin with, and then reinforces the differences between them. Here is the paradox that every organization must face: In order to function effectively *as a division,* it is important that those people working in the division share a high degree of identity and therefore communicate effectively. The more effectively they identify with the subunit (in this case the division), the less effectively they are going to communicate with the other components in the same larger unit. Thus what may be good for the division (probably in the short term) may not be good for the parent organization (probably in the longer run). The organization would be most effective if the various subunits could effectively coordinate their activities, but that would require as effective communication *between* the subunits as exists within each subunit—a situation that probably can never exist. (I hope the reader sees now that the question of what is *intra*group and what is *inter*group depends completely on the level of analysis one is considering.)

One of the ways large organizations do survive is by decentralizing. That is, they make some subunits almost completely self-sufficient, allowing them to act virtually as separate self-contained units, with only minimal ties to the parent organization. That cuts down enormously the communication problems that would be involved in trying to run the total organization from the center. But it also means that many of the decentralized units may go off in directions that the parent organization would rather not see happen, but is incapable of preventing.

An interesting technique that some corporations have begun experimenting with, rather successfully, to overcome these intergroup communication problems is the introduction of what are sometimes called "Quality Circles" or "Quality of Work Life Committees." In either case, committees are set up comprising representatives of management and workers to discuss and help resolve problems within the organization. The problems may range from how to improve the cleanliness of the restrooms all the way up to how the plant should be run. The main purpose of these committees is to establish more trust and communication between workers and management, and there is considerable evidence that they work.[6]

Another way that some of the communication problems of large organizations are overcome is through *informal* channels of communication. That is, presumably Mr. Curious in division A may know and trust Mr. Interested in division B, because they live near each other or go to the same church or some other fortuitous circumstance. Because they know, trust, and speak to each other on a regular—even if informal—basis, when they do talk about work-related things they presumably can acquire some awareness of what is happening in the other division.

In a study done by Agarwala-Rogers of a commercial firm in India she found that, in fact, several cliques of individuals who did know and trust each other did exist, but with but one exception, those informal cliques followed almost exactly the formal division organization of the company (see Figure 7.1). When one thinks about it, that is almost what one should expect. We do tend to communicate—even informally—more with those who work in the same division as we do.

Two other techniques that some formal organizations have experimented with to try to overcome some of these communication problems within organizations are "Management by Objectives" and "Matrix Management." Management by objective is a technique whereby an organization tries to determine precisely what some of its specific objectives are, and then brings together the individuals and/or units involved in achieving those objectives (often management and workers) so that they can more effectively communicate, and thus, presumably, better achieve those objectives. Although there has been some criticism of this approach to management (as there is whenever any new approach is tried, in any field), there

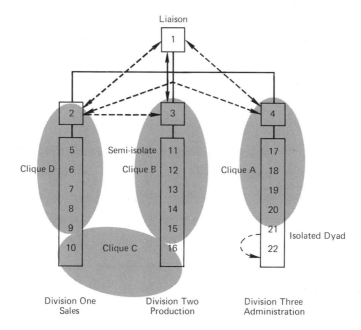

FIGURE 7.1 Communication networks in organizations. Reprinted with permission of The Free Press, a Division of Macmillan, Inc. from *Communication in Organizations* by Everett M. Rogers and Rekha Agarwala-Rogers. Copyright © 1976 by The Free Press.

is also considerable evidence that these committees do help solve some of the internal communication problems within formal organizations.[7]

Matrix management is a concept that has been applied to some large, formal organizations that have to deal with two different approaches to problems: for example, functional and geographic. In this case what an organization would do would be to list its functional organization along the horizontal of a matrix and its geographic organization along the vertical. At each of those places where the horizontal and vertical intersect, management teams would be set up to assure that channels of communication exist to deal with any problems that may arise or to brainstorm together on how best to meet the objectives of the organization given the dual needs of a functional, as well as a geographic, focus.[8]

While some large multinational corporations and some governmental agencies have tried to implement this approach, it has sometimes been reported that it does not work as well in practice as it does in principle because of "turf battles," as well as differences in attitudes and values between the representatives of the two overlapping foci. That is, geographic people often see the problem primarily from the perspective of the geographic region for which they are responsible, while functional people tend to see the problem primarily from the perspective of their function. Nevertheless it is an interesting attempt on the part of some large organizations to overcome the problems of intraorganization (or intragroup) communication.

This much is certain: the larger any group becomes, the more we increase the likelihood of introducing diverse perceptions, identities, and values into it. The more diverse perceptions we introduce, the more likely is factionalization to occur. The more factionalization exists in a group, the less effective or accurate communication can be. It is a fairly rigid law: the larger the group, the less effective—and accurate—communication within the group can be, hence the less "well organized" it can be. Having said that, however, it must also be said that increased numbers of people in a group can also increase the number of different experiences the group has to draw upon in order to come up with creative responses to common problems. Thus while increased membership can create communication problems, it can also generate more creative problem-solving capabilities.[9] But again, all other factors held constant, size alone is the major enemy of effective communication in organizations.

INTERGROUP

Intergroup Perceptions and Identities: Getting to Know Their Group

Everything that was said above about getting to know our own individual and group perceptions applies here. Indeed, having gone through the exercise of having asked ourselves about our own and our group's perceptions, attitudes, and values should enable us to ask the same question for each of the other persons and groups involved in each *inter*group communication that is important to us.

Just as we started there by identifying who the persons were with whom it was important for us to communicate, so too should we start here by asking which are the groups it is important for our group to communicate with. Once we have identified those groups, then we can apply the same methods and ask the same questions about their group that we asked of our own. Who are the people involved —particularly the people who make the decisions for their group? What are their personal attitudes and values? What are their group's attitudes and values? Can we understand those perceptions better by understanding some of the factors that have helped determine those attitudes and values? Just as we did in the other sections, we can start by acquiring that information which is "open" and freely accessible to us. From there, by studying them carefully, we can probably discern additional information by studying what we know about them that they may not even know about themselves—their "blind" areas. Depending upon the level of trust and/or hostility that exists between the two groups, it may or may not be possible for one of us (preferably one of us whom they are more likely to trust) to speak to them and ask some questions. Of course, if there is intense hostility between our two groups, that simply may not be possible. Many of our very important *inter*group communications are not hostile, however, and there is no reason why more groups don't engage in getting more information about them except that it never occurred to them to do so. The amount of information that is often available about other groups is sometimes astounding. It's just that very often in *inter*group communication neither side makes the effort to find out what they can.

The importance of learning about their group culture—including their verbal and nonverbal languages—probably cannot be overstressed. One of the most common problems encountered by people from one group trying to deal with someone from a different group is that "they just don't think the way we do." That is quite correct. It shouldn't be surprising. What would be surprising is if they did. Thought patterns are buried so deep in what Rokeach has called the central regions of our belief system that it simply never occurred to us that anyone would think differently—nor is it at all easy to try to understand different thought patterns. Yet we must if we are to communicate effectively.

In an interesting article on the thought processes of different linguistic groups, Robert B. Kaplan has observed that while English writing—and thinking—is linear (a statement on which there is virtually unanimous agreement among logicians, linguists, anthropologists, and other scholars), those who speak and write Semitic languages (Arabic and Hebrew) seem to use various kinds of parallels in their thinking, and the writing and thinking of Chinese and Koreans (whom he lumps together as Orientals in his study) is marked by indirection. That is, a "turning and turning in a widening gyre." Kaplan has graphically represented the major groups he studies. (See Figure 7.2.) Now, while one must be careful not to fall into the trap of believing that *all* Chinese and Koreans think by a process of indirection, that *all* English-speaking people think in a linear manner all of the time, and so on, the fact is that most probably do, most of the time.

Similarly, the more different from us they are, the more likely we are to find that their belief system is, in fact, one of our disbelief systems. How then are we to cope with the differences? I submit that there is only one way, and that is by trying to understand rather than to judge. That's very difficult precisely because, as I noted earlier, it's virtually impossible to separate attitudes and values. Yet we must if we are to communicate effectively with someone from a group quite different from our own. We don't have to like another group's values or way of thinking to communicate effectively with them, but we certainly do have to understand them.

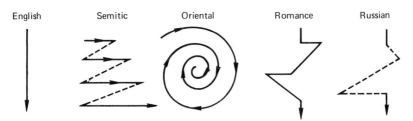

FIGURE 7.2 Thought processes of different linguistic groups. From Robert B. Kaplan, "Cultural Thought Patterns in Intercultural Education," in *Language Learning,* Vol. XVI, nos. 1 and 2, 1966, p. 15.

Please do not misread what I am trying to say. I am *not* arguing that all group conflict is a matter of differences in values or ways of thinking. Indeed, some group conflict may be generated precisely because both groups value and want the same things. It could be a piece of real estate, a market for their product, whatever. It is entirely possible—and it often does happen—that two groups compete for exactly the same goal. In those cases I would argue that there is a conflict of interest, probably with each group seeing the other's gain as their loss. If, indeed, two groups do see the issue that way, then understanding the other's values will do little to ease the conflict. Rather, the conflict will probably be settled in pure power terms. Which group is better able to influence the situation to their advantage? I submit, however, that many group conflicts that are perceived by both sides to be conflict-of-interest arguments are, in fact, at least partly conflicts in perception. Alpha group people think Beta group people want what they want—let's call it X—and do what they think they have to, to prevent Beta from getting X. Upon investigation it sometimes turns out that, in fact, Beta was only a little interested in X, but rather wanted Y much more. Because Alpha was opposing Beta, Beta thought that Alpha wanted Y very much. Therefore Beta people spend their time, energy, and resources trying to block Alpha from getting X and Y. Had the conflict been understood correctly from the beginning, Alpha could have had X and Beta could have had Y by mutual agreement, and both sides could have saved their energy and resources for fulfilling some of the other values each undoubtedly hold.

Intergroup Power

Although I touched briefly on intergroup power in my discussion on assessing our own group's power, allow me to say a word more about it here. Every *inter*group conflict has a specific context. Therefore, before we start to pursue a group goal—whatever it is—we ought to ask ourselves some questions not only about our own power potential in that context but about the potential of the other groups we will probably have to compete with in order to achieve that goal. Assuming that the values are the same, and that the competition is actually over the same goal, then there are still some questions to which we ought to have answers *prior* to entering into competition with other groups to achieve the same goal. The number one question, it seems to me, is how much of which components of power will be required to achieve that goal, *despite the competition from other groups.* Obviously, it would require the expenditure of a great deal less power if other groups did not compete with us to achieve that goal.

Do we have sufficient power to win our "prize"—whatever it is—alone? If not, must we join together with some other group or groups in order to achieve it? If we must, what will be the cost to us? *They* are not likely to help *us* achieve our goal for nothing. Perhaps the cost will be splitting the prize with them. If so, what kind of a split will they accept: 50-50? or 60-40? or 80-20? Who will have to settle for the 20? If the prize is not the reason they are willing to help us, what is? What will they want in return? Are we willing to pay that price? In short, is the effort going to be worth the victory—assuming that we have assessed both our own and our adversary's power capabilities correctly? Many *inter*group struggles are entered into without having gone through this kind of "power analysis" sufficiently, if at all. That is why some groups lose. Obviously, if they knew ahead of time that they were going to lose, they wouldn't have bothered. But groups do lose all the time, and I believe that they do so because decision makers in the group did not accurately assess the power that would be required to achieve the goal vis-à-vis other groups. Had they done an accurate power assessment *before* entering into conflict and recognized that they would lose, they could have offered their adversary a "deal," whereby they would not fight at all—which would have made attainment of the prize much "cheaper" for the adversary—in return for, say, 20 percent of the prize.

Not every goal that is sought after is of the type that has to be divided. Many different groups often join together in America to try to get certain kinds of legislation passed, for example. They may want that legislation for different reasons, but they all value the same legislation, and therefore they are all willing to work for its passage. Very often no one group working alone could achieve their goal simply because they do not have sufficient resources by themselves—whichever ones are required. But by combining with other groups and "pooling resources," so to speak, goals that each of the groups want can be achieved. Accordingly, many groups enter into "coalitions" or "alliances" with many other groups much of the time. By coordinating efforts, each group has to expend fewer resources than would be required if they tried to achieve that goal by themselves. Now while "everything does have its price" (we may have to accept a wording of the legislation we do not prefer in return for their support), it often still does pay to join with other groups—if we can—to achieve our goals. (Please note: this requires evaluation of the attitudes and values of a host of other groups to determine which are close to our own and might join with us, and which are not.) It requires that much less expenditure of resources on our part. But we had better be fairly clear before we start what the price of cooperation with other groups will be. It could be that when we find out what they want from us in return for our support, we would rather achieve our goal without them. I do not mean to turn this section into an essay on the costs and benefits of coalition formation. I do want to stress, however, that in assessing our own power potential to achieve our own group's values, we had better carefully consider not only how much of a particular component we alone—or with other friendly groups—can muster, but also how much *they* alone or in coalition with *their* friendly groups they can muster, and therefore how much we are likely to have to be able to expend in order to achieve that goal.

Since information is a component of power, the more information we have about them, the better power position we will be in to influence them. Getting to know *their* value structure may be critical to the successful attainment of *our* values, vis-à-vis them. If we understand their value system we can deal with it, even if we don't like it. Probably the greatest cause of *inter*group communication breakdown is not not *liking* their value system. Rather, it is not understanding it. Aside from all we have said in communication terms about the importance of accurate information for successful communication, just think of the implications of this in power terms.

Intergroup Communication

Let's start by recognizing that most intergroup communications are neither unsuccessful nor hostile. Groups do operate quite successfully—for the most part—and that is a direct result of their ability to communicate effectively with other groups in their environment. But let's not forget that it is not groups as such that are communicating, but rather people who are communicating as representatives of their groups.

When Mr. Allshiney of the Ajax Corporation communicates with Ms. Bright of the Babo Corporation or with Mr. Clean of the Comet Corporation they may come from different corporate cultures, to be sure, but there are probably a hundred other cultural groups that they do share in common. Most likely they are all from more or less the same linguistic, national, educational, social, economic, or even religious groups—meaning that they probably share a great many common perceptions and codes among themselves. They probably have also all been socialized into the cultures of both their industry and their work-functions. After all, it is not usual for the janitor of one group to speak to the vice-president or the accountant of another. Rather, vice-presidents of one organization are most likely to speak to vice-presidents of other organizations, while lawyers of one tend to speak to lawyers of others, bookkeepers of one to bookkeepers of others, and so forth. Thus intergroup communication is facilitated because the people communicating for their groups tend to share a high degree of similarity of perception with the people of other groups with whom they are likely to communicate. Further, even when people in one group do communicate with people with a different function in another group they probably share so many other common group memberships, the likelihood is that they will have very little difficulty communicating effectively.

This is not to say that problems of intergroup communication do not occur. Clearly they do, and one of the most common reasons they do is precisely because the other people, with whom we are communicating, share so many group memberships with us that we tend to forget that there are some perceptions we do not share. Recall from our discussion of interpersonal communication that if the other person with whom we are communicating is clearly different from us in some way we are much more likely to recognize that differences could exist, and hence we tend to be much more precise and careful in our discussion with them. It is when they look and sound so much like us that we become "sloppy" and simply take for granted that they will know what we mean when we say something, regardless of the topic. That's undoubtedly the most usual cause for both interpersonal and intergroup communication breakdown. The constant reminder that no two individuals can communicate 100 percent effectively—regardless of how many group perceptions they share—should help us communicate more effectively because we will try harder.

If we don't know their group very well that is the time it behooves us to find out more about them. Do we know who comprises their group? Do we know which codes members of their group know? Do we have individuals within our own group who understand their codes? After all, if it is we who want to communicate with them, it is we who will have to do something.

We spoke earlier about the network of people that runs through different groups. If we consider that network in our discussion of intergroup communication, we can realize that someone in group A probably knows well, and trusts, if not someone directly from group B, then someone else, who knows someone else, who knows someone in group B. If the Pool study is correct, and everyone knows everyone else within six steps within our country, it is not unreasonable to assume that at least a few people in our group either will know a few people directly in B or can get a message there within fewer than six steps. Interestingly enough, the people in the leadership positions in our group probably know more people in leadership positions in other groups than anyone else in our group. They know who it is they know, and they usually do use that knowledge to achieve their purposes. There are elite restaurants and clubs in every major city of the world to facilitate exactly this kind of contact. The leadership of most groups join such clubs precisely because they know that is where they can meet and speak informally with the leadership of most other groups. Most *inter*group (as well as *intra*group) communication is conducted informally. Lawyers and accountants for each group may have to sit down later and draw up the documents that will formally ratify the agreements that were reached informally over lunch or at the golf club, but the initial agreements are usually informally arrived at. To overlook those elite communication networks is to overlook how most *inter*group communication in most countries of the world actually function. We will discuss this further in the next chapter.

In discussing interpersonal communication I pointed out the importance of establishing trust by establishing common identities. So too in *intergroup* communication, it is possible to "build identity bridges" to the other group. Remember, the more of those bridges we can build, the more trust we are likely to engender.

If the relationship is hostile, and we can't ask them directly the questions to which we need answers, there is always the possibility of going to people from a third group (who are more familiar with them than we are) and asking those people what they can tell us about "them." Admittedly that is not as good a method as direct communication, but once again, some information may be better than none. Also, once again, it is wise to be cautious and screen the answers received from people from the third group for biases toward "them" that the third-group people might consciously or subconsciously harbor.

As we have said repeatedly in this work, any relationship in which there is a lack of trust makes communication extremely difficult. However, as we have also said, one needn't give up. Indeed, if it is important enough that Alpha and Beta do communicate well, one way to proceed might be through a third party. That is, if

Beta and Gamma have a fairly open relationship between themselves, then perhaps it is worth the risk of distortion (discussed earlier) to have members of Alpha transmit their messages to Beta through Gamma, with Beta also transmitting messages to Alpha through Gamma.

Even though it is often the difficulty of trying to open communication between groups who do not trust each other that gets the headlines in most newspapers—and consumes most of our attention and effort when we are involved in such a situation—let's not lose sight of the fact that most communication that occurs on a day-to-day basis in this world actually does occur between people and groups who know and trust each other. Just think for a moment of the myriad of groups to which you belong. Then realize that someone from virtually every one of those groups—this very day—probably communicates with a host of other people from other groups. But the vast majority of those communications will take place between people who share some identities in common, and they will probably be

R = Reader

FIGURE 7.3 "Daisy chain" of people who know and trust each other.

between people who know and trust one another. If you yourself did not speak to a businessman or a soldier or a blue-collar worker or a foreigner (or whatever) today, chances are very great that someone from one of the groups of which you are a part did. Chances also are that the two who spoke were people who knew and trusted each other. Life really can be depicted as a kind of "daisy chain." In the center is you–the reader. (See Figure 7.3.) Each of the petals represents another of the groups to which you belong. And while you yourself may not have spoken to the butcher, the baker, or the candlestick maker today, chances are that some-one from one of the groups to which you belong did. Chances also are that the person who did knew and trusted the person he or she communicated with. It is precisely this factor that makes most intergroup communications as successful as they are.

The diffusion of innovation and the transfer of technology   The transfer of technology is, in reality, merely a subset of the subject of the diffusion of innova-tion between groups–which, in itself, is nothing but a subset of the problem of intergroup (or intercultural) communication. It implies interpreting into culturally relevant language and transmitting to people in another culture a specific set of ideas that make sense in one culture. The two cultures in question could be formal organizations like bureaucracies, private business firms, or whole societies. The process is the same; the only thing that differs is the level of analysis.

The problem is that sometimes ideas that have specific meanings–and make sense–when related to a whole series of interrelated perceptions, attitudes, values, and beliefs in one group, may simply not make sense in another group. Take, for example, the whole belief system sometimes referred to as "the Protestant work ethic" in Western industrial cultures. This concept implies an acceptance of the notion that it is a positive value to work hard for long hours to accumulate more money than the individual actually needs in order to live so that he or she can save and invest that extra money, in order to make still more money. In many cultures that simply does not make sense. "Why do we need all that extra money?" some-one in that other culture might ask. "Does it make one any happier just to accumu-late money?" "What is the use of having money if you are not going to spend it for things that will make you happy?" "Does working hard and making excess money give you more time to spend with your family?" "Does it give you time to enjoy the beauty of nature or poetry?" "Does it earn you merit in heaven–or with the gods?" "If not, why do it?"

It is very difficult to explain the positive aspects of that Protestant work ethic to people who don't share it. What is more, the questions asked above imply a great deal about what is considered important in that other culture, and none of those values are addressed by telling people they would be better off if they only worked harder.

Add to this the fact that the overwhelming majority of us have a built-in aver-sion to change. There seems to be a built-in disposition for most of the people in the world to resist change of any sort. Almost all of us are more comfortable with "the way we have always done things" than with trying "new ways of doing things." Old and customary ways of doing anything are familiar and hence are comfortable. They don't provoke anxiety. We have done them "this way" a thousand times and are accustomed to them. We know what to expect. Doing things differently requires extra effort, risk, and anxiety. Of course we don't like to change our ways—particularly if we think they "work"—whatever that may mean to us. And this is true whether we are talking about learning how to type instead of writing by hand, or learning to use a word processor instead of a typewriter, or whatever. Change, for most people, is "scary." Yet every innovation, whatever it may be and whoever we may be, requires us to change our way of doing something.

A fascinating study of how innovations are communicated across cultural barriers, done by Everett M. Rogers, gave some hint of how the process of cultural innovation works in any group.[10] One of the more revealing findings was that the process was the same whether the innovation was introducing "new math" into the school system of Allegheny County, Pennsylvania, or teaching inhabitants of a village in Peru to boil water.

What Rogers found was that people in any group could be subdivided into several categories: innovators, early adapters, early majority, late majority, and laggards. (See Figure 7.4.) He also found that he could categorize each of these types of people. The innovators were usually the smallest portion of any adapting population. They were the more cosmopolitan types in the group—the one word the author used to describe them was *venturesome.*[11] They were the ones who were willing to experiment and take risks. They were also the ones in the group with most ties to other groups. Thus it would be they who were most likely to be exposed to new ideas and not be afraid of them.

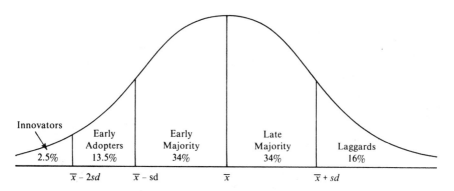

FIGURE 7.4 Adopter categorization on the basis of innovativeness. The innovativeness dimension, as measured by the time at which an individual adopts an innovation or innovations, is continuous. However, this variable may be partitioned into five adopter categories by laying off standard deviations from the average time of adoption. Reprinted with permission of The Free Press, a Division of Macmillan, Inc. from *Diffusion of Innovations,* 3rd ed., by Everett M. Rogers. Copyright © 1962, 1971, 1983 by The Free Press.

Earlier Rogers argued that

> An obvious principle of human communication is that the transfer of ideas occurs most frequently between two individuals who are alike, similar or homophilous. *Homophily* is the degree to which pairs of individuals who interact are similar in certain attributes, such as beliefs, education, social status, and the like. In a free-choice situation, when an individual can interact with any one of a number of other individuals, there is a strong tendency for him to select someone who is most like him — or herself.[12]

In other words, the innovator in any group is likely to be the person in that group who shares the greatest degree of cultural similarity with the person from another group who is introducing the innovation. What is more, whether and/or how quickly the innovation will be adopted in the group as a whole will depend, in part, on whether the innovators are seen by at least part of our group (the early adopters in particular) as being more like "one of us" or more like "one of them." If the innovators are viewed as too different from us—not sharing enough of our important values—we may reject the idea the innovator was willing to adopt as "inappropriate for our groups."

That is, what the Rogers study showed was that the only times a change was widely adopted was when the "respectable people," the "pillars of their communities," adopted the change. If the opinion leaders of their communities adopted the change (and became early adopters), then there was some likelihood that others would. If these people did not adopt, there was virtually no chance that an innovation would be adopted. Now, as far as I can see, this is an extremely important finding. Every group probably has some people who are more venturesome than others. In these kinds of situations the informal decision-makers for the group, so to speak, are not the innovators but rather the opinion leaders—the "respectable people." Other people look to them—for whatever reasons—before adopting new ideas. In terms discussed in chapter 4, they have status, and because of that status other people will do and think what they do and think. Thus, borrowing from the Rogers study, if we want to explore how decisions are made and/or adopted in groups, we had better identify both the innovators and the opinion leaders. If we want to influence some other group to adopt some innovations or to change their attitudes and values, we had better figure out how to change the attitudes and values of the innovators *and* opinion leaders of the other group.

Another crucially important aspect in the transmission of ideas or innovations from one group to another is the question of translating the idea into language and values that are culturally acceptable to the second group. Two examples come to mind to illustrate my point. The first is the story about Sam Green and the Indians of Guatemala, which I told in the section on "perceptions of reality" in chapter 1. The second was told to me many years ago by a representative of the United Nations World Health Organization (WHO). He told of an attempt WHO had made to spray a particular village in India to kill the mosquitoes that were responsible for spreading malaria. When the senior representative of WHO in the district tried to get the permission of the village headman to spray, the headman refused on the grounds that (a) killing any life was bad and (b) malaria was a disease sent by God; it had always existed and always would, and there was no use having man interfere in the workings of nature. The headman simply would not give his permission. But another young Indian WHO worker asked the headman whether they had trouble sleeping at night because of all the mosquitoes around, and the headman responded that, yes, the mosquitoes were a terrible problem. When the young Indian suggested that they could spray the breeding grounds of the mosquitoes so as to eliminate the problems, and that way people could sleep, the headman consented enthusiastically. He recognized that it still meant killing the mosquitoes, but somehow killing them in order for people to be able to sleep better was so positive a value as to make killing them worthwhile.[13]

The point of both those examples is that if one wants to communicate an idea from one group to another, it is important to translate the message into cultural language and values that are acceptable to the second group.

PROPOSITIONAL SUMMARY FOR CHAPTER 7

Intragroup perceptions and identities: The more we know about our own group perceptions and identities, the better communicators we should become. But do we have a clear, conscious image of our own group perceptions and behaviors? Do we know our own group cultures? Who are the individuals who comprise our group? Do we know who makes decisions for our groups? Do we know which values are most important to members of our group in different contexts? Are we aware of the conflicts and potential conflicts in our group values? We should try to find answers to these and similar questions if our group is to be more effective in dealing with other groups.

Intragroup power: How can we realistically assess our own group power in specific contexts? Do we have enough of the right components of power to achieve our group's goals in different contexts? Are there power struggles going on within our group? How well organized is our group?

Intragroup communication: Which codes do members of our group know? What is our group self-image? Is it realistic? Does trust exist within our group? Are there sufficient channels of communication available to members of our group to communicate with each other? Are members of our group communicating with each other as effectively as they should? What can be done to improve communication within our group?

Intergroup perceptions and identities: What are their group perceptions? The more we know about their group perceptions and identities, the more effective in dealing with their group we should become. But do we have a clear, conscious image of their group perceptions and behaviors? Do we know their group culture? Do we know who comprise the membership of their group? Do we know who makes decisions for their group? Do we know which values are most important to members of their group in different contexts? Are we aware of the conflicts and potential conflicts in their group values? We should try to find answers to these and similar questions if our group is to be more effective in dealing with their group.

Intergroup power: How can we realistically assess their group power in specific contexts? Do they have enough of the right components of power to achieve their group goals in different contexts? Are there power struggles going on within their group? How well organized are they?

Intergroup communication: Most communication between groups occurs among people who share many other group perceptions in common. That is why most intergroup communication is as successful as it is. What can be done to improve communication with their group?

The diffusion of innovation and transfer of technology: The transfer of technology is in reality merely a subset of the subject of the diffusion of innovation between groups—which in itself is nothing but a subset of the problem of intergroup (or intercultural) communication. It implies interpreting into culturally relevant language a specific set of ideas that make sense in one culture and transmitting it to people in another.

NOTES

[1] J. Van Mannen and Edwin Schein, "Toward a Theory of Organization Socialization," quoted in Norman G. Dinges and William S. Maynard, "Intercultural Aspects of Organizational Effectiveness," in Dan Landis and Richard W. Brislin, eds., *Handbook of Intercultural Training,* vol. II, *Issues in Training Methodology* (New York: Pergamon Press, 1983), p. 51.

[2] Ibid.

[3] Edgar H. Schein, "Coming to a New Awareness of Organizational Culture," *Sloan Management Review,* vol. 26 (Winter, 1984), 12.

[4] Joseph Luft, *Group Processes: An Introduction to Group Dynamics,* 2nd ed. (Palo Alto, Calif.: National Press, 1970).

[5] William Whyte, *The Organization Man* (New York: Simon and Schuster, 1956).

[6] See US Department of Labor, ed., *Labor-Management Cooperation: Perspectives from the Labor Movement* (Washington, D.C.: US Department of Labor, Bureau of Labor-Management Relations and Cooperative Programs, 1985).

[7] Aaron B. Wildavsky, *Speaking Truth to Power: The Art and Craft of Policy Analysis* (Boston: Little, Brown and Co., 1979).

[8] Robert A. Pitts and John D. Daniels, "Aftermath of the Matrix Mania," in *The Colombia Journal of World Business,* vol. XIX, no. 2 (Summer, 1984), 48–54.

[9] I am indebted to Professor Allyn Morrow of the University of Massachusetts, Boston, for this insight in a personal communication to the author.

[10] Everett M. Rogers, *Diffusion of Innovations,* 3rd ed. (New York: Free Press, 1981).

[11] Ibid. See particularly chapter 7.

[12] Ibid., p. 18.

[13] Personal communication.

CHAPTER EIGHT
INTRA- AND INTERNATIONAL COMMUNICATION

A nation is a formal group, like any other formal group, but with two major differences. Like any other formal group, a nation is a formal organization with specific goals (usually to look after the safety and welfare of its population) and formal communication patterns between its leadership and the rest of the population.

One thing that distinguishes a nation from all other groups is that it recognizes no legal authority above it. Therefore, it feels free to make any decisions it chooses concerning its own population within its own boundaries. Those decisions can and often do include anything the government of a nation feels that it has the power to enforce—including decisions about the life and death of its members. No other group legally has that authority, and very few other groups take that prerogative, even illegally. The second characteristic of nations that distinguishes them from other groups is that they see themselves as being the "sole *legitimate* repository of force" within their own boundaries, and as having the "right" to use force against individuals, groups, and nations—even outside their boundaries—whenever they alone decide that it is in their interest to do so and when they feel that they have sufficient power to do so. No other group claims that right.

Aside from those two characteristics, however, a nation can be viewed in exactly the same terms as any other formal organization. The nation is sometimes larger than most other groups but certainly not always. Approximately two dozen nations have populations smaller than the number of people who work for the General Motors Corporation.

A nation usually has many subgroups within it, many of whom identify on certain issues and in certain contexts more closely with other groups living in other nations than they do with some of the other groups that live in the same nation. Indeed, what makes international communication so interesting to study is the fact that many communications across national boundaries are *less* intercultural than are many of the communications that occur among groups in the same nation. That is, a communication about a problem in physics, for example, between two physicists from different countries may often be far less intercultural than would be a communication on the same subject between the physicist and say a longshoreman from the same country. That having been said, however, to the degree that both the longshoreman and the physicist identify with the symbols of their nation, any communication between nationals of the same country on a subject concerning the nation would be *intra*cultural, while any communication between them and someone from another country on a subject concerning national interest would almost automatically be *inter*cultural.

INTRANATIONAL

Intranational Perceptions and Identities

Just as we have to determine the universe of the members of a group in order to accurately determine the collective group culture, so too do we have to determine the universe of all of the groups in any nation to determine that state's national culture. Also, just as we have to determine who the dominant members of any group are so that we can determine the extent to which their personal cultures have become the dominant group culture, so too do we have to determine which are the dominant groups in any nation to determine the degree to which their group cultures have become the predominant national culture. Often a nation is so large and contains so many very different groups, with so many conflicting values and attitudes, that the task is not an easy one. Still it is not an impossible one either.

For exactly the same reasons as in the *intra*personal and *intra*group sections, I think that it is extremely important for each state to make conscious and explicit exactly what its attitudes and values actually are (and what the attitudes and values of the groups that comprise the nation are) and to deal with those findings realistically. That is, so many nations believe the myths about themselves and propagate them that I think only rarely do they look at themselves realistically and actually try to separate what is myth from what is reality. For example, for over a century Americans have lived by the myth that ours was a land of equality for all. Only when there was rioting in our streets in the 1960s did we start to examine that myth and ask ourselves whether that equality actually extended to our nonwhite population. It was only when we began to consciously look that white Americans found what had been known to black Americans and others for years.[1]

I submit that there are realities about every country that are known to others but about which citizens of the country are themselves unaware. Further, any country would be better off by consciously putting itself in touch with those realities before they emerge as riots in the streets, precisely because it could deal with the problems, if only it weren't blind to them. Exactly the same holds true for information in the unknown areas.

Let us begin by asking ourselves which are the groups that comprise our state, and then ask some questions about *their* attitudes and values. Just as no individual belongs to all, and only, the same groups as any other individual, so too no nation contains within it all, and only, the same groups as any other nation. A country that is primarily agricultural will undoubtedly be composed predominantly of groups associated with agriculture. An industrial country will have a host of heavy, light, and high-technology industries, with all that means in terms of industrial workers, foremen, managers, technicians, and the host of other formal and informal groups associated with those industries. Few predominantly agricultural countries will have any of those groups within their boundaries—and therefore will not have the perceptions, attitudes, and values associated with those industries. The same can be said for religious, racial, ethnic, and/or tribal groups, and all other group identities that might be present in any nation. The point is to start by making as complete an inventory as possible of all of the groups that are present in our country.

In the first place, many states in the international system are not "nations" as the political scientist uses the term. This is not the place for a long scholarly essay on the difference between a state and a nation in the strict sense, but at least a few words on the subject would not be out of order. Many scholars today make a distinction between a state and a nation. In that view a nation is a state whose residents have but one common identity as members of that state: "We who live in this nation are unique in the world. There are no others like us." Most of the residents of many of the countries of the world do not have that common identity. Many of them view some other groups living within the same state as more of an enemy than some people living in a different state.

Walker Connor claims that there are only twelve "true" nations in the world, if *nation* is defined to mean "essentially homogeneous from an ethnic viewpoint."[2] That means that fewer than 10 percent of all of the countries in the world are ethnically homogeneous. Other scholars would dispute that ethnic homogeneity is the sole criterion for national identity. Be that as it may, his point is well taken. Certainly ethnic identity is very important. But it should be observed that of the twelve states he considered nations in 1971 (when he did his research), three of them were divided into separate states: North and South Korea, North and South Vietnam, and East and West Germany.

Now the point of this rather long discussion is that to the degree that the citizens of any state recognize only one ethnic identity and automatically associate that identify with their nation—and only with their nation—clearly the citizens of that state will have a much higher loyalty than could be obtained by citizens who did not see the state as being synonymous with "us." There is no unity like ethnic unity. With one ethnic identity there will be more trust, communication will be better, there will be greater sharing of common perceptions, attitudes, and values, and indeed the state will be "better organized." That is precisely why every state is trying so hard to become a nation.

Once we have identified the groups that exist in the state, we are then in a position to ask some questions about the groups themselves. For example, we could ask the questions about needs/values and attitudes of each of the groups on issues affecting the functioning of the state. Most of us usually just take that functioning for granted.

I suspect that in every nation there are some groups that simply do not accept the way the nation currently functions and, given the opportunity, would like to change it. That is inevitable. The nation would be in a much stronger position if it knew about these "different" attitudes and values before they exploded into violence of one sort or another. But in virtually every state there is a prevalent attitude—as there is in almost every formal organization—not to "rock the boat," not to look for trouble. Thus the government officials of most states proceed to govern with their heads buried deep in the myths that they have enunciated about how "good" things are. Only when a segment of the population takes to the streets —as workers did in Poland in 1981, or as blacks did in America in the 1960s, or as French students did in 1968—do the governments of these countries begin to face the reality that "something is wrong." The trouble is that often by the time those different attitudes and values have erupted into violence it is sometimes too late for the governments of those countries to do much about it. Indeed, succeeding governments are the ones that often have to try to cope with the debris left by the previous government. If an assessment of group attitudes and values were undertaken early enough by governments, and if an effort were made to try to incorporate some of those attitudes and values into those that prevail as state policy, I suspect that many governments would be able to govern longer—and more peacefully—than they do now.

There is no one set of attitudes and values to which all of the groups in any country subscribe. On the other hand, there are within each country predominant attitudes and values on a whole range of issues. Though it is rarely, if ever, written down anywhere—as such—each nation has a kind of "official view" on everything from what the proper functions of government ought to be, through how resources produced in the country ought to be divided among the various groups within the country, to who the enemies are, both within and without the national boundaries.

Decision-making functions go on in every nation. I say functions (plural) because I don't mean just governmental decisions, although that is certainly an important part. Most of the decisions that have great impact on a nation are made *not* by the government but by the people who are in positions to make private decisions daily that affect large numbers of people in very important ways. The decision of a large corporation to invest—or not to invest—in a particular country (or in a particular part of a particular country) can have a profound impact on that country.

The decision of a union to demand—or not to demand—higher wages or better working conditions can have an enormous impact on inflation and working conditions in that nation. Every country, regardless of size, has people within it—and sometimes from outside—who are in a position to make the kinds of decisions, for purely private reasons, that can profoundly affect the lives and well-being of large numbers of people in that nation. These people are normally called the elite. Now, in assessing the perceptions and identities of a nation, it is very important to assess the perceptions and identities of the elite of the country who will be making all of those important decisions. In order to do that, we first have to identify them. After we have identified who the elites are, then we can assess their perceptions and identities. We will get to that shortly.

Every nation, regardless of size, contains so many different groups, each with their own identities and values on so many different issues, that there is always going to be attitude and value conflict within the state. As we said earlier, that is normal. The difficulty arises when one group (or a coalition of groups) within the nation is imposing its attitudes and values on the rest of the country—and some other groups within the country decide to do something about it. As long as most groups accept that other group's value system passively (and it is truly amazing just how long so many groups passively accept other groups' definitions of national interest), there is no immediate problem. The problem arises either when they find, for whatever reason, that the divergence between their own values and the values of the dominant group or groups have become intolerable, or when they feel their own group power is sufficiently strong—vis-à-vis the dominant group—to challenge them.

I argued earlier that every group's attitudes and values will reflect group self-interest. That becomes particularly apparent on the national level, where there are very big "prizes" at stake. The dominant group or groups almost always define national interest in such a way that their own group interests are very well served, indeed. The question that every dominant group faces is how to get or keep enough control of the government so that there will be governmental protection of their needs and values. Usually they make sure that some of the members of the primary elite of the dominant subsectors of the nation have a loud voice within the government of the country. Look at virtually any country of the world and you will find that a large proportion of the primary governmental elite—including bureaucratic and military subsets—is made up of primary elites of other important subsets of the country. And that is as true in democratic states as it is in totalitarian states of both the left and the right.

Different states take different approaches to the problem of value and attitude conflict. Democratic states are supposed to be more receptive to the needs, wishes, and desires of the groups that constitute the nation than dictatorial regimes are. Yet there is evidence that some very repressive regimes are attuned to the values of the groups within their borders and try to give them as much as they possibly can in order to keep them contented.

Regardless of the type of regime in power, in any country the strong likelihood is that the attitudes and values that are articulated as the values of the nation will, in fact, be the attitudes and values of the most dominant groups. What I am arguing here, however, is that it is in the long-term interest of the government of every country to look closely at the needs, values, and attitudes of the groups that comprise the nation and to consciously try to fulfill those values before the deprived groups feel that they have to "take to the hills" or "to the streets" to fight violently for their values.

Intranational Power

The traditional view of national power in international affairs has usually stressed the importance of military capability. While those political scientists were willing to recognize that not every international interaction required military power, their general view was that "when the chips are down, it is military power that counts."[3] Thus, when analyzing the power of any nation, they usually asked questions about the natural resources available (which could be mobilized in a war effort); the number of people within the national boundaries (who could be conscripted to fight a war); the industrial capacity of a country (to be able to produce the most advanced weapons); the geography of the country (Was it large and therefore presumably unconquerable? Was it mountainous and therefore difficult to invade?), and so the list went.

Indeed, it is because some nations so overrated the importance of military power that they underrated the importance of other components of power. Because the Japanese had more military equipment than the U.S. in 1941 they were willing to risk war. What they did not realize is that wealth does not necessarily mean the number of weapons in one's arsenal but rather the ability to produce them when they are needed. Since 1945 the Japanese have been able to achieve virtually all of their goals for a Japanese-dominated "Asian co-prosperity sphere" in Asia by using economic instruments of power, as opposed to the military instruments they tried to use prior to that.

Be that as it may, historically many countries have been wrong in their assessment of their own power. That is why approximately one-half of the nations that fight wars lose them. If they knew that they were going to lose, they probably would not have fought in the first place. Not only is it important that countries correctly assess their own power potential and the power potential of their adversaries, they have to be absolutely certain that they are using the *appropriate components* to achieve their objectives. If they ignore any critical component or are wrong in their assessment of which would work best in which context, they run the very real danger of not being able to achieve their goals.

One question that is important for every state to assess correctly is the power relationships within the country. Are there power struggles going on among different groups within the elite? Are there power struggles between the elite and the masses? Are there struggles between different groups in the masses? All of these questions fall under the component of organization. To the degree that we have more group conflict–of whatever sort–we are "less organized." To the degree that we have less, we are "better organized." To the degree that communication is good within the state, and all groups can be mobilized to put effort into achieving a common goal–whatever it is–that nation is "well organized." To the degree that communication between and among the groups is bad and there is no common identity as members of "the nation," that state is poorly organized.

Intranational Communication

Some years ago I published an essay in which I suggested a way of identifying the elites of each of the major segments of a country.[4] Allow me to present that model here and to expand upon it, showing its impact on *intra*national intercultural communication. Later in this chapter I will show how that model helps identify major *inter*national communication networks. In that earlier work I argued, as I have done here, that it is important to identify all of the important groups in each of the states one is looking at. Within each of the sectors that one identifies one can probably identify those individuals who make the most important decisions within that sector. Many political scientists in the past have chosen to look at an entire state as simply one big pyramid with the elite at the top. That is an approach with which I disagree.

Regardless of form of government, every country has a governmental sector, which is relatively easy to identify. Within that sector, one could determine who the people are who make the most important decisions–those that affect the most people. I would call those people the primary elite of the governmental sector. Within that same sector, upon investigation it is not too difficult to identify those others who also make decisions that are important but not quite as important as the primary governmental elite. Those I would call secondary and tertiary governmental elites. For example, within the United States it is fairly safe to argue that the president, his most influential advisers (who might or might not include specific cabinet members), the heads of the most powerful standing committees of Congress, and the members of the Supreme Court probably constitute the primary governmental elite in this country. The other members of Congress, the next highest level of federal judges, and powerful governors would probably constitute the secondary governmental elite, and so on. In a country like this it is sometimes difficult to determine exactly who fits where in the governmental elite, but one would be surprised at the degree of consensus one would find if, for example, one were to ask a panel of American government experts to do the analysis for us.

Every country also has a bureaucratic sector. Although they are officially a part of the government, in fact, we know enough about how most bureaucracies operate to know that they ought to be considered as a separate subset of the governmental elite. The primary bureaucratic elite subset would be the heads of the various departments. (That those same people might also be included in the governmental elite–and in other subsets as well–need not disturb us at all. Indeed the measure of any one individual's influence may be the number of different subsets in which she or he appears at the top.) In England it is a little easier to identify the ranking of these people because the British assign more accurate rankings to their bureaucratic elite. That is, any bureaucratic officer who is "superscale I" would be a primary bureaucratic elite. In any event, for every country of the world it is possible to identify primary, secondary, and tertiary bureaucratic elites.

In short, what I am suggesting is that we go through this exercise for every functional subset in every country. For example, with but few exceptions every country has a political sector (which may or may not be distinct from the governmental sector), a military sector, an agricultural sector, a commercial/industrial sector, a labor sector, a religious sector, an intellectual sector, a social aristocracy (official or unofficial), and so on. Some may be far more important in some countries than they are in others, to be sure, but they are almost all there in some degree. There are also in every country some groups that are unique to that country alone. For example, if one wants to study Nigeria, one had better ask questions about Hausa, Ibo, and Yoruba (tribal) elites as well as about all of the other major tribal groups in the country. In America one probably ought to ask questions about black-American elites, and also about the whole gamut of so-called hyphenated Americans (Irish-American, Polish-American, and so on). Those groups are country specific—unique to that country alone (more or less)—and every country has them.

Now, if one wanted to be very specific, some sectors really should be divided even further by functions. For example, in certain situations (like at budget time) the military is far less likely to see itself as "the military"—and much more likely to see itself as "army," "air force," "navy," "marines," and so on. The degree of specificity one chooses to examine in most cases would depend on the depth of analysis being undertaken. There is one sector—the commercial/industrial sector—that it probably does pay to break down that way in most countries. The reason is that in so many developing countries a large sector of the primary commercial/industrial elite is foreign. What is more, even in our own country there are marked differences between heavy industry, commerce, and finance, for example.

In any event, each sector can be viewed as a pyramid. At the top are the primary elite of that sector. They are the people who exercise the most influence *within that sector, at least.* Directly below them are the secondary elite, and below them are the tertiary elite. One could, of course, keep going, but let us stop there.

Now, by drawing a pyramid of each of these subsectors of society and then tilting them so that all of the tops touch, one gets a diagram like Figure 8.1.

Looking at our own country this way enables us, I think, to get a good "conceptual fix," so to speak, on the kinds of groups whose attitudes and values are critical to examine and also to look at the communication patterns. That is, we can ask what the attitudes and values are of the governmental elite on a particular set of issues, and we will know which other groups we also have to ask. What is more, we can ask, within the primary elite, for example, What major attitudinal and value differences do we find? Are they more similar than different? If so, how? Of course it depends on the issue and on the context, but if they are similar, I suggest that one would have a quite homogeneous elite. Most primary elites, however, are not

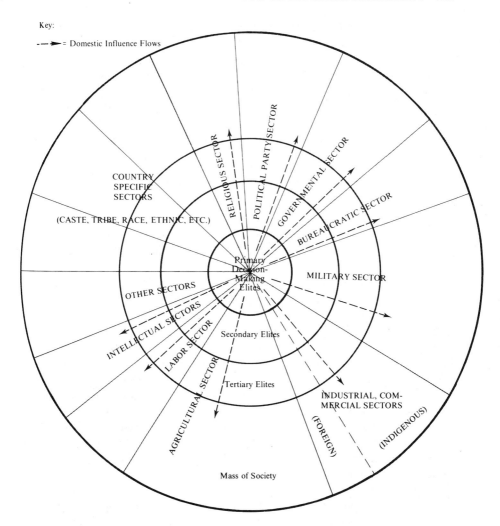

Key:
- - -➤ = Domestic Influence Flows

FIGURE 8.1 A way of viewing elites of individual states. Marshall R. Singer, "Foreign Policy of Small Developing States," from *World Politics,* edited by James N. Rosenau, Kenneth W. Thompson, Gavin Boyd. Copyright © 1976 by The Free Press, a Division of Macmillan, Inc. Reproduced by permission of the publisher.

homogeneous. Each normally views the world from the perspective of their own group and personal self-interest. Thus in virtually every country one has got to expect to find some attitude—and value—conflict. The interesting questions from our perspective are: How are those conflicts resolved? What are the communication channels?

Equally important to examine are the channels of communication in the nation among the various primary elites and between primary elites and governmental elites. Also interesting are the questions of whether adequate communication channels exist between the primary elite of each group and the rank and file (or masses) at the bottom of that pyramid. If the channels of communication exist, there is at least the possibility that those channels will be used and internal mistrust and misperception will be minimized. If those channels do not exist, it is inevitable that mistrust will flourish at every level of the pyramid. It is almost equally as inevitable that unless there is adequate two-way communication, the people at the top of the pyramid will become so alienated from attitudes and values of the people in the middle and at the bottom that ultimately they will be replaced by others who have kept communication channels open and hence who more accurately reflect the attitudes and values of the lower groups. Interestingly enough, most modern totalitarian governments are very aware of the need for adequate communication channels with every section of their population, and they usually build those channels directly into the political-party system that they construct.[5]

Go back to what was said in previous chapters about all of us tending to look to "people we know and trust" either when we are confused about what attitudes to adopt on a particular issue or which value to rank in what order. Now let's look at who it is that we are most likely to know and trust in the light of what was said about these functional sectors of society. If I am a farmer, I am most likely to associate with other farmers. If I am a banker, I associate all day with other bankers. I probably also socialize with them in the evening. If I am a religious Catholic . . . We have been through all of this before, and there is no need to repeat it here. But what is important from the perspective of personal influence is to note how influence tends to stay within the confines of our own groups. Who are those "respectable people" we trust? They are the dominant people in our own groups. We do tend to look *up* the social and economic ladder in terms not only of fashion but also of ideas. We tend *not* to look to others who are in the same position in their lives as we, but in different functional or ethnic pyramids. Why should I be impressed by what "they" wear, do, or think? But one of us who just happens to be above me in rank, now that is another matter entirely.

Or put the statement the other way. In every country the people at the top will tend to have most influence within their own group. The pope and cardinals will have most influence among Catholics; a general will have most influence among his officers in the same branch of the service; an intellectual will have most influence among fellow intellectuals. The farther up in the pyramid one goes, the more crossing over there tends to be in terms of associations and communication patterns. At the top of the commercial/industrial sector of society it is very likely indeed that the heads of corporations will not only see other heads of corporations at work, but will also live near each other and belong to the same social clubs. At every level of analysis in which empirical research has been done, be it personal, group, or national, the findings have been the same: influence seems to flow from the top down. What is more, people at the bottom tend to associate and communicate more with other people at the bottom—of their own subset—while people at the top tend to associate, and communicate more, with other people at the top— not necessarily staying exclusively within their own subset. Thus if I wanted to send a message (using the personal-influence model presented earlier) to someone in my own state but at the top of a group of which I was not a member, I would speak to someone above me—in my group. He in turn would probably speak to someone above him—in his group—who in turn would speak directly to the person I wanted to reach in the different group. The intended recipient would eventually receive the message from "one of us," however defined.

INTERNATIONAL

International Perceptions and Identity

Once again, everything that was said previously about getting to know our own nation applies here as well. If we are going to interact with other countries— and we do all the time—we might as well have as accurate an understanding of them as is possible. In order for us to do that, we simply have to try to get to understand their national cultures, and while it may be difficult, it is not impossible. Interestingly enough, I believe that most of the more powerful countries recognize the importance of understanding other cultures and hence devote an enormous amount of time, energy, and resources trying to accomplish exactly that.

It is truly amazing how much information about their perceptions and identities is actually "open" and available to anyone with the resources to find out. In almost every country it is not at all difficult to identify the major ethnic, linguistic, religious, tribal, occupational, ideological, and other groups. Nor is it very difficult in most to identify who the elites of each of those groups are. Admittedly, there is a bit more difficulty in identifying the leadership in some "closed" societies, and certainly it is often very difficult to identify the leadership of some secret organizations that exist in many countries. But aside from those exceptions, information about the leadership of the vast majority of the groups in most societies is available to almost anyone with the time and resources.

What is more, it is usually not at all difficult to determine the predominant attitudes, values, and beliefs of various groups in the country. The leaders of each of the groups are continually extolling the virtues of their group perception—both for the benefit of their own groups and for the world to see. All one has to do is look carefully, and one can probably discover what they are. The problems come when we don't trust them, or when these values are so completely alien to our own that we just don't understand them. For example, the mistrust that has existed between the United States and the Soviet Union since the Bolshevik revolution in 1918, and particularly since the end of World War II, has been profound. Each side is convinced that the other is out to destroy them. Thus each side tends to interpret what they do or say as proof that the other is not to be trusted. Different administrations in both the U.S. and the USSR have been either more or less trusting of the other side depending on the ideological biases they brought with them on assuming the governing position, but no government since 1945 has really trusted the other side. Thus no government has accurately assessed the perceptions of the leaders of the other country. Those within each administration who have been less biased and have tried to point out to the authorities that their perceptions of the other might be skewed have usually been discounted as being naive or just plain untrustworthy. Alas, Ralph White was so correct! Recall what he said about misperceptions in conflict situations. On the international scene, particularly during times of intense conflict and mistrust, all of those forms of misperception operate to distort our assessment of their national perceptions and identities. We are usually absolutely certain that they simply cannot be trusted: nothing they say or do can lessen that mistrust precisely because we see them as being "diabolic." Invariably, of course, we are the virtuous ones, with justice, truth, and God all on our side. We generally have a total lack of empathy for their needs and values, and because of selective inattention, virile self-image, and military overconfidence, are often totally incapable of accurately assessing whether we have enough of the right components of power to achieve our own goals. There has never been an intense conflict situation between states when this attitude of mistrust and lack of empathy has not been the case. All of this notwithstanding, the fact is that the information that each side needs to make a correct assessment of the other is there and is for the most part available. All one has to do is to interpret it correctly. But as I have said repeatedly throughout this work, that is extremely difficult to do when there is a high degree of mistrust. Thus the tensions exist and feed upon themselves.

The U.S./USSR tensions are clearly not the only ones that poison understanding. Each intense conflict situation one can name, whether it be North and South Korea, El Salvador, Nicaragua, Arab/Israel, India/Pakistan, North and South Ireland, Britain and Argentina, Cuba/U.S. . . . the list goes on and on. Would that there were an easy solution to the problem. There is not. All that is possible is that in every one of these conflict situations the less mistrusting members of our nation —who are nonetheless still trusted by the prevailing groups in our nation—must keep trying to interpret *their* perceptions as dispassionately as possible and to get that information to the decision makers in *our* country (in a form they can understand) as dispassionately as possible. If enough trusted observers of "them" report the same thing to our decision makers often enough, maybe, just maybe, the decision makers will eventually understand. They probably will not, but the stakes are high enough, and important enough to make the exercise worthwhile.

International Power

Wealth, organization, information, status, and will, may all mean somewhat different things on the national level than they meant on the personal or group levels, but the principle is exactly the same. In trying to assess the power of our own nation to achieve any particular goal it may have, it is as crucial to correctly assess whether we have *enough* of the *right* components for that particular international relationship. It takes two to have a relationship of any sort, and power relationships between nations are no exception. We must examine that relationship in the context of the situation and ask all those questions not only about our own power capabilities but about theirs as well.

When authors wrote about international affairs twenty-five years ago, they often overlooked the fact that every interaction between two entities implied a relationship and a specific context. Thus some authors—including me—wrongly argued, for example, that wealth alone could be used as an indicator of a nation's power. Following the logic of that argument, one would be led to the conclusion that because the United States was perhaps fifty times more wealthy than Czechoslovakia, and the Soviet Union only twelve or thirteen times as wealthy as Czechoslovakia, the United States should be able to exercise much more influence in Czechoslovakia than the USSR. That, of course, simply is not the case. One must accurately determine the nature of the relationship between the actors and the context in which that relationship is occurring in order to determine relative power relationships.

The mistrust we discussed in the last section, which leads us to so much misinterpretation with regard to their national perceptions also leads us to misperception in our assessment of their national power. That is precisely why countries have historically been so wrong in assessing their enemy's power capabilities. That is why nations have been so willing to allow their conflicts to lead to war. And that is why approximately one-half of them have lost. Even when they "win," states usually discover that the cost was far higher than they initially anticipated. Indeed, if they had correctly assessed their adversary's power capability before they went to war, they might have decided that the reward of winning simply was not worth the cost.

I am absolutely convinced that this miscalculation is probably the single most common cause of war. No country has yet devoted the resources necessary to make an accurate assessment of both their own and the adversary nation's power. Countries are willing to spend literally hundreds of billions of dollars building military arsenals and on secret intelligence reports about the weapons in their adversary's arsenal, but they don't even spend millions trying to determine whether they are building strength in the *right* components. Earlier I indicated just how difficult it is to get to know them well enough to accurately assess other individual and group power capabilities. There is more danger when nations do a poor job of assessing because nations are the only groups that believe they have the right to kill others to achieve their goals.

But most of the day-to-day relations between nations are not conflictual. Every day students from one country go to another country to study. Every day businesspeople from one country do business in other countries. Every day literally thousands of transactions are conducted across national boundaries, and only the very smallest percent of those are conflictual. Now, those transactions do not happen in a random fashion. Rather, they are highly patterned, and the patterns have to do with international power disparities.

International power, however it is measured, is not at all evenly distributed. The United States alone accounts for over 30 percent of the mobilized wealth of the world. The U.S. together with the USSR, Japan, West Germany, Britain, and

France account for more than two-thirds of the world's mobilized wealth.[6] Of the five hundred largest corporations in the world, all but a handful are located in either North America, Western Europe, or Japan. With perhaps only one or two exceptions—if that—the top one hundred universities in the world are located in those three places. Probably upwards of 90 or 95 percent of all the information sent out to the world via international news agencies is disseminated from those three places. No matter which indicator of international power one chooses to examine, virtually all seem to be located in the same places.

Recall from our discussion of power in chapter 4 that one of its more interesting properties is that it tends to attract. People want some of those components of power. They want information; they want education; they want wealth. In order to get those things they often have to go to where those things are. Thus, for example, if one wants a great university education, one has no choice but to go to one of the world's great universities. To be sure, one can acquire good education at any number of the thousands of universities that now exist in the world, but a truly great education can normally be had only at a great university. In the course of acquiring any education, one's attitudes, values, and perceptions will be markedly influenced, there is no doubt. In acquiring that education in a country other than your own, those perceptions will be even more markedly influenced. Yet if a superb education is what you desire—and if you have both the money and the brains to get it—you have to go to the best university that will admit you. That usually means a university in a country in the Northern Hemisphere.

The same is true on indicator after indicator. Those same Northern Hemisphere countries have more of what most of the people in the world want, and so a vast number of people allow themselves to be influenced in the process of trying to acquire whatever it is that they want.

International Communication

Communication between nations falls into essentially two categories: (a) official transactions between the government of one country and either the government of another or international organizations and (b) unofficial transactions between and among private individuals, groups, and organizations.

Until about two decades ago most writers in the field of international affairs would have argued that the only "actors" in the international system that mattered were the governments of nations. Each independent country was presumed to be equally sovereign, and the official representatives of states could deal only with the official representatives of other states. Only the government of a country could bring a case against another country before the International Court of Justice at The Hague. Since it is the government of every nation that makes official foreign policy and decides matters as major as war or peace, it was simply assumed that all other *inter*national interactions were less important than the transactions of one government with another.

That particular individuals and groups within a country affect the actions of

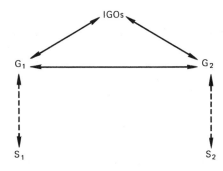

FIGURE 8.2 From Robert O. Keohane and Joseph S. Nye, Jr., *Transnational Relations and World Politics,* (Cambridge, Mass.: Harvard University Press), 1972, p. xiii. Reprinted by permission of the publisher.

its government (including its relations with other governments) never was doubted. But the relations of one government to another was thought to be strictly in the hands of official governmental representatives. Keohane and Nye have diagrammed the traditional view of *inter*national affairs. (See Figure 8.2.)

When governments do communicate with each other on an official level it is normally through representatives of their foreign offices (we call it the State Department in the U.S.), or through the international division of other governmental departments (for example, the Departments of Commerce, Agriculture, and Labor). Of course, the various branches of the military and intelligence communities have communications with their counterparts in other governments.

In the past twenty years scholars have increasingly come to realize that "the nation" is not the only "actor" in the international system. Indeed, they have come to recognize that many individuals, groups, and organizations in one country often interact directly with people, groups, organizations, and agencies of governments in another—without going through formal diplomatic channels.

Keohane and Nye have diagrammed these interactions. (See Figure 8.3.) They call them transnational to distinguish them from official government-to-government interactions.[7] They define *transnational interactions* as those in which at least one of the parties was not an official government representative. Now, while I don't particularly like the term, the fact is that it is being widely used in the literature and, so I will use it here. More important than the term is the fact that scholars have finally come to appreciate that (a) many more of these transnational inter-

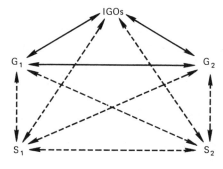

FIGURE 8.3 From Robert O. Keohane and Joseph S. Nye, Jr., *Transnational Relations and World Politics,* (Cambridge, Mass.: Harvard University Press), 1972, p. xiv. Reprinted by permission of the publisher.

actions occur across national boundaries than do formal diplomatic communications, and (b) these interactions cumulatively probably have as great an impact—if not greater—upon relations between states than do formal governmental communications. It took scholars a long time to accept that basic fact of life, but there is now general agreement that this is so. After all, a private giant corporation in one of the more developed countries can make a decision (for purely private, profit motives) to substitute a synthetic product in place of the raw material currently used and utterly destroy the economies of many raw-material-producing countries. Or a private corporation (again for pure profit motives) could make the decision to invest—or not to invest—in a particular developing country and therefore have an enormous impact on the economy of that country.

Foreign aid from the more powerful countries rarely accounts for more than 3 or 4 percent of the gross domestic product (GDP) of any receiving country, but private trade between corporations in the powerful countries and corporations in the developing countries often accounts for between 10 and 20 percent of the latter's GDP. In some cases that trade has accounted for as much as 40 percent of a developing country's GDP.[8]

But it is not just private trade or investments that have an impact on people in different countries. So does working or going to school or doing any of the things that millions of people from the less developed countries do in the more highly developed countries every day of the year. Some go home and often try to turn their countries into replicas of the more developed countries in which they studied or worked. But it does work both ways. People from the more developed countries who study or work in the developing countries very often carry back with them some of the values, attitudes, and world views of the people they have studied and worked among in the developing countries. At the very least, the countries in which they studied or worked become and remain salient to them. We could go on and on citing cases of transnational interactions. The important points to be made are

1. There are many more transnational interactions between peoples, groups, and organizations across national borders than there are official governmental interactions.

2. These transnational ties may be far more important in affecting the lives of the people in both countries on a day-to-day basis than most official government-to-government communications.

3. All *inter*national communications—whether official or unofficial—tend to covary in almost exactly the same, predictable ways. That is, just as within corporate hierarchies most *inter*national communications occur among the countries at the top of the international hierarchy, fewer occur between countries at the top and those in the middle, even fewer occur between those at the top and those at the bottom, and almost none occur between those at the bottom of each of the different hierarchies.

Let me expand a bit on this third point. Johan Galtung has described the world *inter*national system as being very similar to a feudal system.[9] At the top are a few of what he describes as "top-dog" nations—the really powerful countries. Below them, in graded fashion, are the weaker states, which form a part of the top-dog sphere of influence. At the very bottom of each hierarchy are the weakest countries which he calls "underdog" nations. Basically I accept this view of the world system, but with some modifications. In Galtung's view there are only two top-dog countries, the U.S. and the USSR. In *Weak States* I modified that to include Japan, the United Kingdom, and France—not because the latter two are still top-dog nations but because historically they have been, and they still have influence in their former colonies disproportionate to the amount of influence they have in the rest of the world. If the European Economic Community ever were to get its political-unification "act" together, it would become one of the major top-dog countries of the world. It hasn't, and probably will not, but it is the vehicle through which West Germany exercises much of its influence. China may some day become a top-dog state, but that day is probably a minimum of fifty years away. Regardless of which states one might want to include as top dog, geographically the international system would look something like that presented in Figure 8.4. Each of the circles represents a state. The larger circles are the most powerful states. The pie-shaped wedges within each of these states represents functional subsectors of that society. (See Figure 8.1, for more detail.) The rectangles, partially in the states and partially out, represent the multinational corporations (MNCs). They are drawn partially in and partially out because I believe that may represent reality more than drawing them completely in or completely out. When the interests of the MNC coincide with the interests of the state, I believe that the MNC behaves as though it were within the state. But when the interests of the MNC conflict with the interests of the state, I believe that the MNC, as much as it can get away with, behaves as though it were operating outside state jurisdiction.

Most communications occur within each top-dog state's "sphere of influence," so to speak. Indeed, that is particularly true if we view the U.S. and USSR as the only two top-dog states, as Galtung does. If we include the U.K., France, West Germany, Japan, and maybe some day China, as I would, then we see that most interactions, both official and unofficial, occur among top-dog states. The second greatest number of communications occur among the top-dog states and the "middle-dog" states within their own sphere. While even fewer occur among those at the top and those at the very bottom, the fewest number of communications occur among countries at the bottom of different spheres. Thus there are virtually no transactions among, say, Costa Rica, Bulgaria, Chad, and Burma.

Let us look for a moment at the implications of this for *international* communication. Yes, there are official communications among all the major countries of the world. In actual fact, however, it is the big powers that communicate (officially) with most of the rest of the world. The weak countries simply cannot afford to have embassies and consulates in any but those few countries that are the most important to them. Usually they have embassies in the capitals of each of the major powers (because each of the major powers is important to them), in the capitals of a few middle powers (usually the ones that are in their geographic region or the

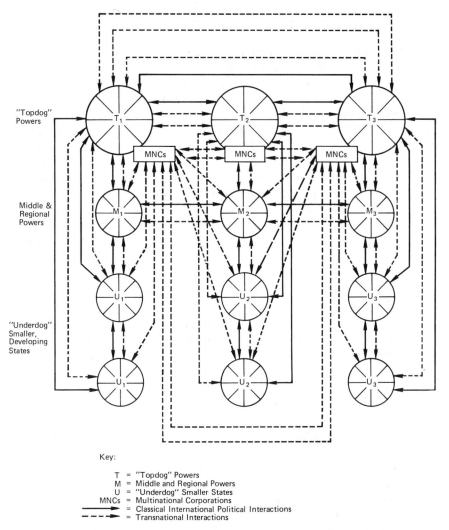

Key:

T   =   "Topdog" Powers
M   =   Middle and Regional Powers
U   =   "Underdog" Smaller States
MNCs =   Multinational Corporations
————▶ =   Classical International Political Interactions
– – –▶ =   Transnational Interactions

FIGURE 8.4

middle powers of their sphere), and some in the capitals of their neighbors. That's it. That is literally more than they can afford, either in terms of money or trained manpower. The big powers on the other hand, not only have embassies in virtually every capital of the world but also have consulates in all the major cities in all the countries with which they have diplomatic relations. It would appear that a major exception to this rule is sports. That is one area in which weaker countries seem to have more interaction among themselves than they do with the major powers.

International mass communication and the "new world-information order"
Whether one looks at mail flows, telephone calls, and telegraph messages received; at where newspapers, magazines, and books are published and where they are sent;

at origins of films and TV and radio shows; the pattern is almost identical. Most interchanges occur among the most powerful. Fewer occur among the less powerful, least occur among the least powerful. Or look at the amount of foreign trade, the number of nongovernmental visitors who go abroad or are received (whether they travel for study, business, or pleasure, they are carriers, or potential carriers, of messages). In sum, look at every conceivable unofficial channel of communication, and the pattern is virtually the same: most communications occur at the top of the hierarchy—among the most powerful countries—least occur among countries at the bottom.

The overwhelming preponderance of ideas, information, and values flow from the big powers of the Northern (highly developed) Hemisphere to the Southern (less developed) Hemisphere.

In *Weak States* I did an analysis of international news flows. What I found then was that in every major power there is an international news-gathering and dissemination agency (we call them wire services) that operates in a vast number of other countries. In the United States there are not one but two such news agencies (United Press International—UPI—and the Associated Press—AP). In the United Kingdom there is Reuters; in France, Agence France-Presse (AFP); and in the Soviet Union, Tass. Each of these international news agencies has reporters in virtually every major city of the world—as well as part-time "stringers" in other places —who monitor information and send it back to the home office for processing, editing, and distribution to subscribers around the world. The pattern of the countries whose media subscribe to those services—as with other indicators I investigated—is not at all random. Media in the major countries (and most of the middle-sized countries), as might be expected, buy virtually all the services they can get. Media in the smaller countries, however, cannot afford to subscribe to all of the services. What I found in 1970 when I was doing the research for *Weak States* was that in many of the smaller countries that were once British colonies media still subscribed to only one service, and that service was Reuters; in many of the French colonies subscribers took only AFP; in many of the smaller countries in Latin America and the Carribean, subscribers took only AP or UPI; while in Eastern European countries the wire service was predominantly Tass. Since then there has not been a comparable study done, to the best of my knowledge, but updates of research I have done recently, on the basis of incomplete data, seem to indicate that, generally, the same picture prevails. There has been some growth of regional news agencies like Press Trust of India (PTI) in India and South Asia, Middle East News Agency (MENA) in Egypt and the rest of the Middle East, and Kyodo and Jiji in Japan and South East Asia, to be sure, but basically there has been no major change in the earlier pattern.

What that means in practice is that if an event occurs in, say, Nigeria, (for example, the overthrow of the democratically elected government by a military leader) it is reported back to London by a Reuters reporter in Lagos (often British); to Paris by an AFP reporter (probably French); to Moscow by a Tass reporter (almost always Russian); and to New York by both AP and UPI reporters (usually American). Those wire services, in turn, report the event—as interpreted through the political and cultural lenses that their reporters have learned to wear by being socialized into their respective systems—to all the countries who subscribe to their service. Thus the people and policy makers in Accra, just four hundred miles away, get the news not from Lagos but from London, four thousand miles away, via British reporters and editors, giving British interpretations, values, and biases, while readers in Budapest and Ulan Bator and all the other Tass-receiving countries, get the news from Russian reporters, as viewed from the Soviet perspective. The same is true for Latin America and AP and UPI reporters and Francophone Africa and French reporters.

What is more, it is not just the overthrow of a democratic government that is reported. Rather, it is anything that sells news in the capitalist press—usually sensationally bad news, in other words. More often than not, nothing is reported to have happened in most of the countries of the world unless there is an earthquake, hurricane, flood, or some other disaster. If you doubt this get this morning's newspaper —wherever you may live—and check it. If you are lucky and live in a major city where international news is regularly reported, there may be stories about things that happened in half a dozen to a dozen countries around the world. In the mid 1980s, at least one of them would have been about killings or bombings or kidnappings in Lebanon, one would have been about starvation in Africa, and one about rioting between blacks and whites in South Africa. Your newspaper might also have said something about guerrillas in Central America and some sort of terrorism in the Middle East. In the early 1970s it would have had at least one story about Vietnam. In the later 1970s there would have been one about fighting between Protestants and Catholics in North Ireland. For most papers, in most cities, that will be it. If you are fortunate enough to get the *New York Times,* the *Washington Post,* the *Los Angeles Times,* the *Wall Street Journal,* or the *Christian Science Monitor* every day, you will see a story about political conditions in some country you hear about once every two or three years—unless of course they have a civil war or natural disaster. It is not that nothing is happening in any of those hundred-some other countries of the world. It's just that it is not getting reported. Good news doesn't "sell." No one is interested in knowing that the crops in some little-known country are much better this year than anticipated. Everyone will want to read about it if the crop failed and thousands are dying of starvation. That's just the way it is.

On the other hand, if you can get your hands on a paper from one of the developing countries—not an easy thing to do in most American cities—you will see that if it is a former French colony, a great deal is reported about what is going on in France, the U.S., and the USSR, while if it is a paper from a former British colony, there will be a great deal reported about Prince Charles and Princess Diane (as in the U.S.) as well as stock quotations on the London market and probably even the cricket scores as well as what is going on in the U.S. and the USSR. People in the Southern Hemisphere are subjected to literally hundreds of times as much information about—and from—the Northern Hemisphere as they are about what is going on right next door. Worse yet, they feel that what the big capitalist news agencies report is neither the news about themselves they would like other people to receive nor the news they want to read about others. No wonder the Southern Hemisphere countries are demanding a reordering of the flow of information. They want a "new world-information order," which will tell the north more about them and will tell them more about each other. The problem is how to get what they want. None of the countries individually has the facilities to collect the information that the big powers do. Nor do they have the money to buy the information, even if the big news agencies offered it. Because most of the developing countries have government-controlled presses, we in capitalist northern countries feel that what they want us to hear about them is only propaganda, and what they want to let in from the north is only the information that they want their populations to receive. We in the north reject that as interfering with the "free flow of information." They see it as interfering with capitalist sensationalism. It is a conflict of values that is not likely to be resolved soon. Increasingly, however, developing countries are restraining what foreign journalists in their countries can report—and, indeed, in some cases they are refusing to allow foreign journalists in at all. Power being what it is, and the southern countries having neither the wealth nor the organization of the north, it is not likely that they will soon acquire the information they want. While the readers of our newspapers may not have the information about the southern countries that the southern countries would like them to have, you can be sure that our policy makers, public and private—just by subscribing to all of the wire services of the world (which they do)—have far more information about the southern countries than the latter have about us.

Just to put the magnitude of the problem in perspective, reflect for a moment on the fact that until now I have been discussing only international news services. The same situation—or in many cases worse yet—prevails whether one discusses radio, books, professional journals, TV programs, movies, and—probably the most serious of all for the twenty-first century—information available via computers. Is it any wonder that many southern countries feel that their cultures are being totally inundated by information, values, and beliefs from the north? Theoretically, they can choose among American, Japanese, British, French, German, and Russian information and values, but it is a lot cheaper to show TV programs or read books that don't have to be translated, and those in the educated portions of their populations, at least, probably read only one of the major northern languages—if that. What is more, because the elite of those countries are likely to be perceptually tied to just one northern country, the likelihood is that they will know, and therefore choose for translation into the native languages, only the information and cultural outpouring of that one northern country.

The countries of the Southern Hemisphere may very rightly feel that their native cultures are being inundated by the northern cultures, but there does not appear to be a great deal they can do to stop it. Calls for a new world-information order notwithstanding, it is not likely that anything will happen in the next few decades that will reverse the trend. Indeed, if anything, it is most likely to get a lot worse (from their point of view) before it gets better.

Interelite international communication   Now expand to a world view as shown in Figure 8.5 the elite model I presented in Figure 8.1. Each nation can be viewed from the same perspective. There is in every country a governmental sector, a bureaucratic sector, a military sector, an agricultural sector, a religious sector, a commercial/industrial sector, a labor sector, an intellectual sector, and so on. When transnational interactions occur they occur between *people* from the bureaucratic elite in one country and the bureaucrats in another, the intellectual elite in different countries, the labor elite in different countries, and so on. When students come to the U.S. to study from all over the world they are studying in the U.S., yes, but specifically they are studying with, and getting to know and trust, the American intellectual elite. When American students and professors go abroad to study or teach they meet other people from other groups in the countries to which they have gone, but primarily they are interacting, and establishing communication networks, with intellectuals in those countries.

To see how this works in practice let's take a closer look at communication among the international military. A high percent of all the military officers of all of the weaker countries of the world have been trained at military institutions in either the U.S., Britain, France, or the USSR. In some cases the figure is as high as 100 percent. Indeed, in some countries one simply cannot get promoted to the rank of colonel unless he has studied at a military institution abroad. While members of the military study in those powerful countries, they learn military strategy and how to use the latest military hardware, to be sure. But they learn far more than that. They also learn from their teachers (who are themselves almost always officers in the military of a major power) to view the world as the teachers, themselves, view it. Regardless of the subject, no teacher can teach without conveying his or her attitudes, values, and world view. The students at these academies very quickly learn who are the "good guys" of the world. They also learn who the enemy is. But more than that, while they are at these institutions, studying these subjects, they are also living in the host country. Therefore, they are learning "our" cultural language (indeed almost all instruction at these institutions are in the verbal language of the host country) as well as a great deal about "us." They may not like everything they see and hear, but they will certainly learn to discriminate between what they like and what they do not like much more clearly than they could have before they came. What is more, they are bound to make friends among their classmates. Some of their friends will undoubtedly be other foreign officers in training, studying at the school. Many more are likely to be officers in training from the host country itself. Those friendships are almost always for life.

The foreign officer goes home and pursues a career in his own military establishment. Having been selected for training overseas he is likely to get promoted. Within a few years there is a strong possibility that he will be in the primary military elite of his country. While his former classmates from major powers may not have gotten promoted quite as quickly as he did, there is every reason to assume that at least some of his classmates would have done at least fairly well in their own

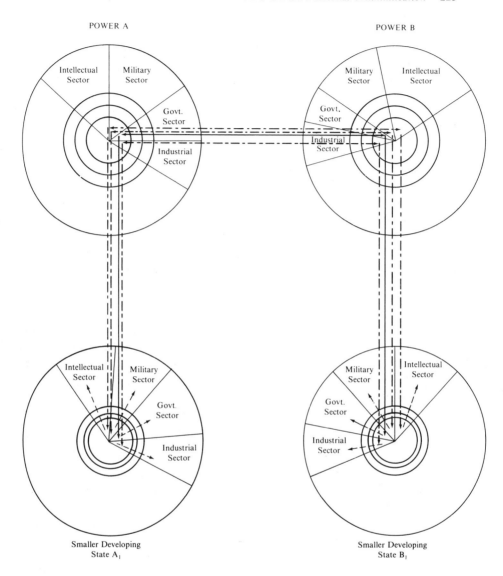

POWER A

POWER B

Smaller Developing
State A₁

Smaller Developing
State B₁

Key:

⟶ = Classical International Political Interactions
—·—·▸ = Transnational Interactions
----▸ = Domestic Influence Flows

FIGURE 8.5 A way of viewing international elite communication. Marshall R. Singer, "Foreign Policy of Small Developing States," from *World Politics,* edited by James N. Rosenau, Kenneth W. Thompson, Gavin Boyd. Copyright © 1976 by The Free Press, a Division of Macmillan, Inc. Reproduced by permission of the publisher.

military establishments. The host-country officers may not have made primary elite status, but they probably made secondary elite. What is more, there is every possibility that the teachers at these academies have themselves been promoted, by this time, perhaps, to the primary elite level.

Let us say there is a message that the government of the host power wants to send to the government of the weaker state. Given that there are official diplomatic representatives there, we could tell our ambassador to give the message to their foreign minister. Official? Yes. Effective? Probably not. Wouldn't it be more effective for our government to give the message to our General Threestar (the former classmate or professor of foreign General Quatrostar) and ask him to pass the message along? Indeed it would be. General Threestar can address foreign General Quatrostar by his first name and over dinner at the club can tell General Quatrostar what he is thinking. (It would be foolish for him to say it was a "message from my government to your government." It would be much more effective for a friend to let his friend know how he felt about something.) While there is clearly no certainty, there is just as clearly a good likelihood that General Quatrostar will be duly impressed by the message and will go to his own foreign minister or prime minister (who very well could be a cousin) and say, "Now look here Pedro . . . " Just think how much more effective that can be.

Or take an example from the international business community. This was reported to me as having actually occurred when S. W. R. D. Bandaranaike was elected prime minister of Ceylon in 1956. He was elected on a pledge to nationalize the British-owned tea plantations in his country. Since the Lipton Tea Company was concerned about his actually going ahead and carrying out his election pledge, a senior executive from Lipton (a British company) could have gone to a senior person in the British Foreign Office and have had the British ambassador in Ceylon tell the prime minister that Britain did not approve. They could have, but why should they? It was much more effective to have the Lipton man in Britain talk to the British Lipton man in Ceylon and let him know how worried the company was and what measures they were contemplating in retaliation, in the event that it happened. The British Lipton man in Ceylon (who had lived there many years and knew everyone of any importance in the commercial sector in Ceylon) went to his old Ceylonese friend, who had gone to school in Britain and whose family owned hundreds of acres of tea plantations in Ceylon and who actually *was* related to the new prime minister. Whether the conversation took place at the club or at one of their homes, I cannot say. What was reported to me, however, was the gist of the conversation, which went something like this: "Ranjit (name is changed), I'm terribly worried. I'm telling you this in strictest confidence, you understand, only because we have been friends for so many years. I've just had a visit from Mr. Teasipper from our London office. He tells me that Lipton is making plans to switch all of their production to Uganda if the nationalization goes through. In fact, he tells me that Lipton intends to organize a British boycott of all Ceylon tea. What do you think we ought to do? I certainly would hate to see your family business ruined."

I do not have any details on the conversation between "Ranjit" and the prime minister, but since almost 90 percent of Ceylon's foreign exchange, at that time, was earned by the sale of tea to Britain, it was not very surprising that the prime minister soon thereafter claimed that he had misunderstood and that, of course, nothing would be done that in any way could jeopardize Ceylon's foreign-exchange earnings.

Now those are only two examples. Repeat them several thousand times *every day,* and one begins to see the magnitude of the importance of personal influence in the conduct of *inter*national communication.

Most international communications are not random. They occur between people who share, at least, some common group identities. Aside from missionaries, Peace Corps volunteers, and anthropologists, most people who go to another country (for other than tourism) are most likely to interact most intensely with people in those countries who belong to, at least, some of the same groups they do. The more of those identities they share, obviously, the easier those communications will be. The danger is to forget that just because we share some group perceptions in common does not mean we will share all. Yes General Threestar may be able to talk about military strategy matters fairly easily with General Quatrostar, but he may have a much more difficult time discussion religion, marriage, or the democratic process.

International diplomacy Viewed in its proper perspective, international diplomacy is really just a specific subset of all international negotiations.[10] We have just seen in the section on interelite international communication that when international negotiations are among businesspeople, the military, intellectuals, or diplomats from two or more different countries, at least they may share the business, military, intellectual, or diplomatic group cultures in common, and thus the exchange may be somewhat less intercultural than one might have at first expected. However, one should not lose sight of the fact that there is still a major intercultural component in most international negotiations, and that aspect is very often neglected.

Negotiation and diplomacy are as old as humanity itself. As long as people have tried to coexist with one another they have had to negotiate who was going to get, or do, what, how, and on what terms. In the diplomacy that occurred between nations in earlier times, a diplomat had to have the complete confidence of the king, emperor, or whatever government he represented because he usually couldn't go back home "to check signals" during the negotiations. It simply would have taken too long. Thus the person actually doing the negotiating usually had a wide latitude of discretion to strike "the best deal possible." In modern times, with modern telecommunication and transportation facilities available, the actual negotiators of *most* international negotiations actually have very little discretionary power. In some cases virtually every word of an agreement must be cleared by the specialists at the home office. In some ways that makes the modern diplomat very little else but a high-class errand boy shuttling messages back and forth from the bargaining table to the home office. On the other hand, assuming that both of the parties to the negotiation are, roughly, equally equipped with professional staff back home, it puts the actual negotiations very much in the hands of specialized technocrats who know what questions to ask and what pitfalls to avoid.

In most negotiations between the representatives of the less developed countries and either diplomats of the more highly developed countries or businesspeople from the highly developed countries, the LDC negotiator is at a distinct disadvantage since he often does not have the expert assistance or vast amounts of technical information available to the representative of the more highly developed nation. Every day representatives of some less developed country conduct negotiations with representatives of either business or some branch of government from one of the more developed countries, and every day the representative of the LDC is forced to make decisions based on inadequate information and/or inadequate understanding of the implications of the agreement he is trying to negotiate.

But leave aside for the moment the question of inadequate information. To the degree that both parties to the negotiation have skilled technocrats who can study the details of the proposals being made, the cultural gap between the negotiators is lessened, and agreement, at least on what the terms mean, should be easier to arrive at. Indeed, there is some hard evidence to indicate that the more technical the subject being negotiated and the more it is left to technocrats to do the negotiating, the more likely it is that agreement will be reached.[11] That is, of course, because both sides will more likely be speaking the same technical language. The more "political" the subject becomes—or the broader it becomes—the more it is open to different cultural interpretations.

Let's go back to the differences that have to be dealt with. Yes, the businessperson or diplomat from country A will try to get the best possible "deal" in the negotiation with his counterpart that he possibly can. But (a) the definition of what the "best possible deal" actually is may itself be subject to differing cultural interpretations; (b) how he goes about arriving at that "deal" will be conditioned by the cultures of which he is a part; and (c) how that deal is implemented will also depend on the cultural definition of what each party understood the deal to have meant. Although there are power questions that ought to be addressed, let's concentrate first on the cultural considerations.

Let's start with a definition of what is the best possible deal. Since each of the parties to a negotiation brings with her her own collection of group identities and perceptions, it is inevitable that each of the parties will interpret incoming messages from the other party at least somewhat differently. Thus none of the parties really will be sharing the same information. Recall that each of us assumes that our motives are honorable, and thus we make assumptions about ourselves in the negotiations that it is just not reasonable to assume the other parties will make. What is more, depending on how conflictual the subject being negotiated is, it is entirely possible that the other party will make assumptions about us that are quite far from the picture we have of ourselves.

Further there is every likelihood that even the same words we use will have different meanings in our cultural language, if not in our verbal language. When the businessperson talks about "fair profit" is he or she talking about 7 percent, 20 percent, or 100 percent? Depending on the industry and the culture, all might be "fair." When the diplomat talks about reducing offensive weapons, what weapons is he talking about? Very often the same weapons both of us have in our arsenals are viewed by me as being "defensive" when I have them pointed at you, but as "offensive" when you have them pointed at me. Of course we both want "peace with honor," but your definition of what is honorable for me may be very different from my definition of what I consider honorable.

Certainly most of the perhaps hundred (or even thousands) of international negotiations that are conducted every day are not conflictual. Both parties to the negotiation see something to be gained for themselves (however they define that something) and thus decide to enter into negotiations. Also, let us not exaggerate the degree of the problem. Many, if not most, of the negotiations probably go quite well, and both (or all) parties are quite satisfied. But a certain proportion of the negotiations do not go well, and at least a substantial part of the reason they do not is the cultural differences among the negotiators; how they go about making the deal will be conditioned by the culture of which they are a part.

Recall Robert Kaplan's argument in the previous chapter about the different thought processes of different linguistic groups. Now imagine a negotiation between an American trying to get from point A to point B by taking the most direct linear route and his Chinese counterpart also trying to get to point B but by indirection rather than linear thinking. How frustrating for both of the negotiators.

Years ago Edward C. Stewart developed for use in training sessions a wonderful series of scenarios of negotiations between an American and what he called his "contrast American." [12] The contrast American was a professional actor who had been trained to internalize a whole series of values, attitudes, and beliefs that were virtually diametrically opposite to those held by most Americans. The American who was attending the training session was asked in the scenario to try to negotiate some specific objective. Almost always in these training sessions the American would begin by trying to come directly to the point of his visit, while "Mr. Khan" would inquire about the American's health, his family, how he liked the country, and a whole host of questions that would help Mr. Khan get to know the American better. The poor unsuspecting Americans in these training sessions would very quickly get terribly frustrated as they began to realize that Mr. Khan simply refused to address the question the way the Americans wanted to. The example may exaggerate what happens in most real-life situations (precisely because both the negotiators probably do share at least some cultural values in common), but it illustrates the nature of the problem. Indeed, when the person one is negotiating with is clearly as different as Mr. Khan, it may be easy to recognize the cultural differences and try consciously to compensate for them. When, however, in so many other ways the negotiator seems so much like us, we are sometimes caught off guard, so to speak, and we simply forget that differences probably will arise somewhere along the negotiating process.

Stewart also tells us that Americans prefer to reason inductively. That is, they prefer to start with the specific data and then to draw their inferences from those data. Europeans, on the other hand, prefer to reason deductively. That is, they prefer to start with a total logical or theoretical conceptualization and then to reason on the basis of that logical construct, drawing in data only where it is appropriate to the logical argument. (The reader may notice that my own thought patterns tend to follow the European model more than the inductive model that Stewart has categorized as being typically American. To me that just illustrates the problem with trying to group everyone into those very large categories.) Be that as it may, regardless of how we label them, there is no question that some people are more comfortable with inductive logic while others prefer deductive. When you have a negotiation between two individuals preferring those differing styles of reasoning, discontent with the other party is virtually assured.

American culture also contains the myth about the positive nature of openness in negotiations. "Open covenants, openly arrived at," President Wilson insisted, as did a later president, Harry Truman, in setting up the United Nations. The problem is that when your constituents can hear what you propose to give away, in order to reach agreement, the probability is that no agreement at all will be reached. As a matter of fact, virtually nothing of any substance or importance is ever agreed upon in most of those official UN debates precisely because of that openness. Rather, diplomats meet behind closed doors or in the corridors, reach their private agreements, and then publicly announce the agreements that were reached.

Attitudes toward time are another factor that often enter into intercultural negotiations. Many different cultures teach that the best way to reach an agreement is to give the matter sufficient time. In those cultures people are in no rush to reach agreements. They are perfectly prepared to wait out their adversaries in a negotiation. They know full well that particularly the American (who feels that "time is money") may very well agree to certain terms if they just wait long enough.

Some nationalities prefer to arrive at decisions collectively—sharing responsibility for whatever decision is arrived at equally—while in other cultures only the person at the top can make the decision, and thus all major (and many minor) decisions have to be made by that person alone.

In some cultures it is just not polite to say no to someone. Thus they say yes to whatever is being asked, but when the negotiator goes home thinking he has an agreement he finds that the other side had no intention of doing what they said they would do.

Some cultures are more conflictual than others. In those societies it is okay to ask for a great deal more than you expect to get, expecting the other party to fight you by asking for far more than they expect to get. When the direct confrontation is finished, each side winds up with more or less what they anticipated. But other cultures are nonconflictual or conflict-avoidant. Negotiators from those cultures are likely to go in with minimal expectations, expecting the other side also to make minimal requests and for consensus to emerge. When someone from the former culture negotiates with someone from the latter, agreement might be reached on paper, with the former being very happy at "how much we got," but the latter party will probably never implement the agreement. That leads us to the next point: how the deal is implemented.

If the parties to an international agreement have understood the words and concepts used in the agreement the same way, implementing the agreement may not be too much of a problem. Frequently, however, the same words mean very different things to the different parties. Thus it often happens that the ink is hardly dry on an international agreement before one of the parties is accusing the other of "bad faith" in not implementing the agreement as agreed upon. The problem is of course, that the words notwithstanding, very little may actually have been agreed upon in a negotiation because neither side was aware that the same words meant different things. That is why it is often so necessary to have built-in mechanisms in many international agreements either to have disagreements arbitrated by some neutral third party or to have mechanisms set up to discuss what has gone wrong and how to correct the situation. What this usually means, in practice, is a process of ongoing negotiation (continual feedback, in my terms) to settle problems as both sides come to realize that a problem exists—and often that is known only when one tries to implement agreements one thought had been reached.

Sometimes there is no mechanism built into an agreement to insure a method of resolving differences in interpretation as the agreement is being implemented. If the process is between very unequal partners, and the weaker partner feels that it is being taken advantage of by the way the agreement is being implemented—but that it is helpless to do anything about it—a great deal of counterdependence can build up. Often the weaker party seethes for perhaps several years, and then, when conditions permit it—for whatever reasons—the weaker party "blows up," so to speak, and simply terminates the agreement. Often the stronger has no idea why such an action was taken because it was unaware of just how angry the weaker was becoming. At that point it sometimes happens that conditions are so strained that no new negotiations are possible. At still other times the stronger finally gets the message that something went wrong and agrees to a renegotiation.

Despite everything that has been said in these pages about how difficult it is to communicate effectively across cultural barriers in countries other than their own, the fact is that hundreds of thousands of people do it every day. And I suggest that while almost all of them may have experienced at least some difficulty communicating at least some of the time, a large majority of these people have been able to communicate relatively successfully. I submit that it's not that all of those people who do so are intuitively better communicators than those who do not (although there may be some merit in the argument that those who are willing to take the risk just might be). Rather, I suggest that the reason they are relatively so successful is that the people with whom they must communicate most intensely day to day do share a good number of cultures in common with them. Thus many of their most important communications internationally may not have been nearly as intercultural as one might have expected them to be. The more all of us continue to work and go to school and live in countries other than our own, the less intercultural these communications are likely to be in the future.

ENDPIECE

What I have attempted to do in these chapters is to show how the concepts I have been talking about could be applied on the personal, group, and national levels. I have raised a great many questions, it is true, but the questions that I have raised have all been very general. There really is not a great deal of choice in a work that tries to paint with as broad a brush as I have attempted to do here. If practitioners or researchers in intercultural communication have found anything that I have said in these pages stimulating enough to make them want to try to apply those concepts themselves, the questions they ask will have to be much more specifically related to the particular intercultural communication they are interested in. What I have hoped to do is to suggest the kinds of questions that have to be asked at each level of analysis. I hope that the exercise has enough interest for students of intercultural communication to motivate them to go out and actually try to apply these concepts themselves in their daily living. If only one of the concepts I have raised proves useful in making intercultural communication more effective for just one reader, this exercise will not have been in vain.

PROPOSITIONAL SUMMARY FOR CHAPTER 8

A nation: A nation is a formal group, like any other formal group, with only two major differences. Like any other formal group, a nation is a formal organization with specific goals (usually to look after the safety and welfare of its population) and formal communication patterns between its leadership and the rest of the population. What distinguishes a nation from all other groups is that it recognizes no legal authority above it. Another characteristic of nations that distinguishes them from other groups is that they see themselves as being the "sole legitimate repository of force" within their own boundaries and as having the "right" to use force against individuals, groups, and nations—even outside their boundaries—whenever they alone decide that it is in their interest to do so and when they feel that they have sufficient power to do so. No other group claims that right.

Intranational perceptions and identities: The more we know about our own national perceptions and identities, the better communicators we should become. But do we have a clear, conscious image of our own national perceptions and behaviors? Do we know our own national culture? What are the groups that comprise our nation? Do we know who makes decisions for our nation? Do we know which values are most important to groups in our nation in different contexts? Are we aware of the conflicts and potential conflicts in our national values? We should try to find answers to these and similar questions if our nation is to be more effective in dealing with other nations.

Intranational power: How can we realistically assess our own national power in specific contexts? Do we have enough of the right components of power to achieve our national goals in different contexts? Are there power struggles going on within our nation? How well organized is our nation?

Intranational communication: What codes do members of our nation know? What is our national self-image? Is it realistic? Does trust exist in our nation? Are there sufficient channels of communication available for groups in our nation to communicate with each other? Are groups in our nation communicating with each other as effectively as they should be? What can be done to improve communication in our nation?

International perceptions and identities: What are their national perceptions? The more we know about their national perceptions and identities, the more effective in dealing with their nation we should become. But do we have a clear, conscious image of their national perceptions and behaviors? Do we know their national culture? Do we know what groups comprise their nation? Do we know who makes decisions for their nation? Do we know which values are most important to members of their nation in different contexts? Are we aware of the conflicts and potential conflicts in their national values? We should try to find answers to these and similar questions if our nation is to be more effective in dealing with their nation.

International power: How can we realistically assess their national power in specific contexts? Do they have enough of the right components of power to achieve their national goals in different contexts? Are there power struggles going on in their nation? How well organized are they?

International communication: What codes do members of their nation know? What is their national self-image? Does trust exist between our nation and theirs? If not, generally, does trust exist between a particular individual in our nation and someone in theirs? Are there sufficient channels of communication available between their nation and ours? Are members of our nation communicating as effectively with them as they should? What can we do to improve communication between our nations?

International mass communication and the "new world-information order": Regardless of which form of mass communication one looks at—radio, television, news agencies, books, films, whatever—the picture is the same: news and information tend to travel from the more powerful countries in the Northern Hemisphere to weaker countries in the Southern Hemisphere. Because leaders in the weaker countries do not like what—and how little—is reported about them, and because they are afraid that their national cultures are being inundated by "Western cultural values and ideas" they are demanding a "new world-information order" to redress this situation.

Interelite international communication: Communication among elites from one country to another is not random. For the most part businesspeople from one country tend to speak primarily with businesspeople from other countries. The same is true for politicians, the military, religious leaders, intellectuals, labor-union leaders, or most other groups. What this means in practice is that many international communications among elites are probably less intercultural than one might at first suspect. That is because even if they do not share national cultural values and language, they probably do share their functional group language and values.

International diplomacy: International diplomacy is really just a specific subset of all international negotiations. While the people who actually do the negotiating may share many cultural values and perceptions with their counterparts from other countries, there are often still major differences in national perceptions and values that must not be ignored.

NOTES

[1] Gunnar Myrdal, *An American Dilemma: The Negro Problem and Modern Democracy* (New York: Harper and Row, 1944).

[2] Walker Connor, "Nation Building or Nation Destroying," *World Politics* 24 (April 1972), 320.

[3] See, for example, John G. Stoessinger, *The Might of Nations: World Politics in Our Time* (New York: Random House, 1962); or Inis L. Claude, Jr., *Power and International Relations* (New York: Random House, 1962).

[4] Marshall R. Singer, "Foreign Policy of Small Developing States," in James Rosenau, Kenneth Thompson, and Gavin Boyd, eds., *World Politics* (New York: Free Press, 1976), pp. 263–90.

[5] See, for example, the path-breaking work on Soviet communication channels done many years ago by Alex Inkeles, *Public Opinion in Soviet Russia: A Study in Mass Persuasion* (Cambridge: Harvard University Press, 1950).

[6] For country data, see *World Bank Annual Report, 1977* (Washington, D.C.: World Bank, 1977); and *World Bank Atlas: Population, Per Capita Product and Growth Rates* (Washington, D.C.: World Bank, 1976). For business firms see *Fortune* magazine, May and August 1976.

[7] Robert O. Keohane and Joseph S. Nye, Jr., *Transnational Relations and World Politics* (Cambridge: Harvard University Press, 1972).

[8] Singer, *Weak States;* see chapter 6, "Economic Ties."

[9] Johan Galtung, "East-West Interaction Patterns," *Journal of Peace Research* (1966), 146–77.

[10] See, for example, Glen Fisher, *The Cross-Cultural Dimension in International Negotiation* (Washington, D.C.: School of Area Studies, Foreign Service Institute, U.S. Department of State, 1980).

[11] Karl Keiser, "Transnational Politics: Toward a Theory of Multinational Politics," *International Organization* 25, no. 4 (Autumn 1971), 790–817.

[12] Edward C. Stewart, *American Cultural Patterns: A Cross-Cultural Perspective* (Chicago: Intercultural Press, 1972).

BIBLIOGRAPHY

INTERCULTURAL COMMUNICATION BOOKS

ABELSON, R. P., E. ARONSON, W. J. McGUIRE, T. M. NEWCOMB, M. J. ROSENBERG, and P. H. TANNENBAUM, *Theories of Cognitive Consistency: A Source Book.* Chicago: Rand McNally & Co., 1968.

AKIN, JOHNNYE, ALVIN GOLDBERG, GAIL MYERS, and JOSEPH STEWART, eds., *Language Behavior: A Book of Readings in Communication.* The Hague: Morton, 1970.

ALLPORT, F. H., *Theories of Perception and the Concept of Structure.* New York: John Wiley & Sons, 1955.

ALLPORT, G. W., and L. POSTMAN, *The Psychology of Rumor.* New York: Holt, Rinehart & Winston, 1947.

ALMOND, GABRIEL A., *The American People and Foreign Policy.* New York: Praeger Publishers, 1960.

ALTHEN, GARY, *The Handbook of Foreign Student Advising.* Chicago: Intercultural Press, 1983.

ARGYLE, MICHAEL, *Bodily Communication.* New York: International Universities Press, 1975.

ASANTE, MOLEFI KETE, EILEEN NEWMARK, and CECIL A. BLAKE, eds., *Handbook of Intercultural Communication.* Beverly Hills, Calif.: Sage Publishing Co., 1979.

BANDLER, RICHARD, and JOHN GRINDER, *Frogs into Princes: Neuro-Linguistic Programming.* Moab, Utah: Real People Press, 1979.

BEM, DARYL J., *Beliefs, Attitudes, and Human Affairs.* Belmont, Calif.: Brooks/Cole Publishing Co., 1970.

BENEDICT, RUTH, *Patterns of Culture,* 1934. Reprint. New York: New American Library, 1959.

BERELSON, BERNARD, and GARY A. STEINER, *Human Behavior: An Inventory of Scientific Findings.* New York: Harcourt, Brace & World, 1964.

BERLO, DAVID K., *The Process of Communication.* New York: Holt, Rinehart & Winston, 1960.

BERRY, JOHN W., *Human Ecology and Cognitive Style: Comparative Studies in Cultural and Psychological Adaptation.* Beverly Hills, Calif.: Sage Publications, 1974.

——, and P. R. DASEN, eds., *Culture and Cognition: Readings in Cross Cultural Psychology.* London: Methuen & Co., 1974.

BERRY, J. W., and W. J. LONNER, eds., *Applied Cross-Cultural Psychology.* Amsterdam: Swets and Zeitlinger, 1975.

BIDDLE, BRUCE J., *Role Therapy: Expectations, Identities and Behaviors.* New York: Academic Press, 1979.

BIRDWHISTELL, RAY L., *Kinesics and Context: Essays on Body Motion Communication.* Philadelphia: University of Pennsylvania Press, 1970.

BJORN-ANDERSEN, NIELS, ed., *Information Society: For Richer, For Poorer.* New York: North-Holland Publishing Co., 1982.

BOULDING, KENNETH E., *The Image* (6th ed.). Ann Arbor: University of Michigan Press, 1968.

BLUBAUGH, JON A., and DORTHY L. PENNINGTON, *Crossing Difference: Inter-Racial Communication.* Columbus, Ohio: Charles E. Merrill Publishing Co., 1976.

BRISLIN, RICHARD W., *Cross-Cultural Encounters: Face-to-Face Interaction.* New York: Pergamon Press, 1981.

——, *Culture Learning: Concepts, Applications and Research.* Honolulu: East-West Center and University Press of Hawaii, 1977.

——, ed., *Topics in Culture Learning,* vol. IV. Honolulu: East-West Center, 1976.

——, and PAUL PEDERSON, *Cross-Cultural Orientation Programs.* New York: Gardner Press, 1976.

BROADBENT, D. E., *Perception and Communication.* London: Pergamon Press, 1958.

CANTRIL, HADLEY, *The Pattern of Human Concerns.* New Brunswick, N.J.: Rutgers University Press, 1966.

CASMIR, FRED L., ed., *International and Intercultural Communication Annual,* vol. I. Falls Church, Va.: Speech Communication Association, 1974.

——, ed., *International and Intercultural Communication Annual,* vol. II. Falls Church, Va.: Speech Communication Association, 1975.

——, ed., *International and Intercultural Communication Annual,* vol. III. Falls Church, Va.: Speech Communication Association, 1976.

CASSE, PIERRE, *Training for the Cross-Cultural Mind* (2nd ed.). Washington, D.C.: Society for Intercultural Education, Training and Research, 1981.

——, *Training for the Multicultural Manager.* Washington, D.C.: Society for Intercultural Education, Training and Research, 1982.

CHERRY, COLIN, *On Human Communication: A Review, a Survey and a Criticism.* Cambridge: MIT Press; and New York: John Wiley & Sons, 1957. Reprint. New York: Science Editions, 1961.

CLEVENGER, JR., THEODORE, and JACK MATTHEWS, *The Speech Communication Process.* Glenview, Ill.: Scott, Foresman and Co., 1971.

COMBS, JAMES E., and MICHAEL W. MANSFIELD, eds., *Drama in Life: The Uses of Communication in Society.* New York: Hastings House, 1976.

——, and FATHI S. YOUSEF, *An Introduction to Intercultural Communication.* Indianapolis: Bobbs-Merrill, 1975.

CONDON, JOHN C., *With Respect to the Japanese: A Guideline for Americans.* Yarmouth, Maine: Intercultural Press, 1984.

CORNISH, EDWARD, ed., *Communications Tomorrow: The Coming of the Information Society.* Bethesda, Md.: World Future Society, 1982.

DANCE, FRANK E. X., ed., *Human Communication Theory.* New York: Holt, Rinehart & Winston, 1967.

DANIEL, NORMAN, *The Cultural Barrier: Problems in the Exchange of Ideas.* Edinburgh: University Press, 1975.

DAVEY, WILLIAM G., *Intercultural Theory and Practice: A Case Method Approach.* Washington, D.C.: Society for Intercultural Education, Training and Research, 1981.

DEESE, J., *The Structure of Associations in Language and Thought.* Baltimore: Johns Hopkins Press, 1966.

DE RIVERA, JOSEPH H., *The Psychological Dimension of Foreign Policy.* Columbus, Ohio: Charles E. Merrill Publishing Co., 1968.

DEUTSCH, KARL W., *Nationalism and Social Communication: An Inquiry into the Foundations of Nationality.* Cambridge: Technology Press of MIT; and New York: John Wiley & Sons, 1953.

——, *The Nerves of Government.* New York: Free Press, 1963.

DILTS, ROBERT, JOHN GRINDER, RICHARD BANDLER, LESLIE C. BANDLER, JUDITH DE LOZIER, *Neuro Linguistic Programming:* vol. I, *The Study of the Structure of Subjective Experience.* Cupertino, Calif.: Meta Publications, 1980.

DODD, CARLEY H., *Perspectives on Cross-Cultural Communication.* Dubuque, Iowa: Kendall/Hunt Publishing Co., 1977.

EKMAN, PAUL, *The Face of Man: Expressions of Universal Emotions in a New Guinea Village.* New York: Garland STPM Press, 1980.

——, *Universals and Cultural Differences in Facial Expressions of Emotion.* Lincoln: University of Nebraska Press, 1971.

ERIKSON, ERIK H., *Identity and the Life Cycle.* New York: W. W. Norton & Co., 1979.

FAST, JULIUS, *Body Language.* New York: Pocketbooks, 1971.

FERGUSON, HENRY, *Manual for Multi-Cultural Education* (2nd ed.). Yarmouth, Me.: Intercultural Press, 1986.

FESTINGER, LEON, *A Theory of Cognitive Dissonance.* Stanford, Calif.: Stanford University Press, 1957.

FISHER, GLEN, *American Communication in a Global Society.* Norwood, N.J.: Ablex Publishing Co., 1979.

——, *International Negotiation: A Cross-Cultural Perspective.* Chicago: Intercultural Press, 1980.

FISCHER, HEINZ-DIETRICH, and J. C. MERRILL, eds., *International Communication: Media, Channels, and Functions.* New York: Hastings House Publishers, 1970.

——, *International and Intercultural Communication.* New York: Hastings House Publishers, 1976.

FITZGERALD, THOMAS K., ed., *Social and Cultural Identity: Problems of Persistence and Change.* Athens: University of Georgia Press, 1974.

GIFFIN, KIM, and BOBBY R. PATTON, *Fundamentals of Interpersonal Communication.* New York: Harper & Row, 1971.

GLENN, EDMUND S., and CHRISTINE GLENN, *Man and Mankind and Communication Between Cultures.* Norwood, N.J.: Ablex Publishing Co., 1981.

GORDON, THOMAS, *P.E.T.: Parent Effectiveness Training.* New York: New American Library, 1970.

GROVE, CORNELIUS LEE, *Communications across Cultures: A Report on Cross-Cultural Research.* Washington, D.C.: National Education Association of the U.S., 1976.

GUDYKUNST, WILLIAM B., ed., *Intercultural Communication Theory: Current Perspectives* (which is also *International and Intercultural Communication Annual,* vol. VII). Beverly Hills, Calif.: Sage Publications, 1983.

——, and YOUNG KIM, eds., *Methods for Intercultural Communication Research* (which is also *International and Intercultural Communication Annual,* vol. VIII). Beverly Hills, Calif.: Sage Publications, 1984.

HAGEN, EVERETT E., *On a Theory of Social Change: How Economic Growth Begins.* Homewood, Ill.: Dorsey Press, 1962.

HAIGH, ROBERT W., GEORGE GERBNER, and RICHARD B. BYRNE, *Communication in the Twenty-First Century.* New York: John Wiley & Sons, 1981.

HALL, EDWARD T., *Beyond Culture.* New York: Anchor Press/Doubleday, 1976.

——, *The Hidden Dimension.* Garden City, N.Y.: Doubleday & Co., 1966.

——, *The Silent Language.* Greenwich, Conn.: Fawcett Publications, 1959.

HARMS, LEROY STANLEY, *Intercultural Communication.* New York: Harper & Row, 1973.

HARPER, ROBERT G., ARTHUR N. WIENS, and JOSEPH D. MATARAZZO, *Nonverbal Communication: The State of the Art.* New York: John Wiley & Sons, 1978.

HARRINGTON, MICHAEL, *The Other America: Poverty in the United States.* New York: Macmillan, 1962.

HARRIS, PHILIP R., and ROBERT T. MORAN, *Managing Cultural Differences.* Houston: Gulf Publishing Co., 1983.

——, *Managing Cultural Synergy.* Houston: Gulf Publishing Co., 1982.

HOIJER, HARRY, ed., *Language in Culture.* Chicago: University of Chicago Press, 1954.

HOMAUS, G. C., *The Human Group.* New York: Harcourt, Brace, 1950.

HOOPES, DAVID S., ed., *Readings in Intercultural Communication.* Vol. V, *Intercultural Programming.* Pittsburgh: Intercultural Communications Network, 1976.

——, and PAUL VENTURA, eds., *Intercultural Sourcebook: Cross-Cultural Training Methodologies.* Chicago: Intercultural Press, 1979.

INKELES, ALEX, *Public Opinion in Soviet Russia: A Study in Mass Persuasion.* Cambridge: Harvard University Press, 1950.

ISAACS, HAROLD, *Idols of the Tribe: Group Identity and Political Change.* New York: Harper & Row, 1977.

——, *Scratches on Our Minds: American Images of China and India.* New York: J. Day Co., 1958.

JAIN, NEMI C., ed., *International and Intercultural Communication Annual,* vol. IV. Falls Church, Va.: Speech Communication Association, 1977.

——, ed., *International and Intercultural Communication Annual,* vol. V. Falls Church, Va.: Speech Communication Association, 1979.

——, ed., *International and Intercultural Communication Annual,* vol. VI. Falls Church, Va.: Speech Communication Association, 1982.

JERVIS, ROBERT, *Perception and Misperception in International Politics.* Princeton, N.J.: Princeton University Press, 1976.

JUSSAWALLA, MEHEROO, *Bridging Global Barriers: Two New International Orders, NIEO, NWIO.* Honolulu: East-West Communication Institute, 1981.

KELLER, JOSEPH, *Intercommunity Understanding: The Verbal Dimension.* Washington, D.C.: University Press of America, 1977.

KELLEY, HAROLD H., and JOHN W. THIBAUT, *The Social Psychology of Groups.* New York: John Wiley & Sons, 1959.

KELLY, GEORGE, *A Theory of Personality: The Psychology of Personal Constructs.* New York: W. W. Norton, 1963.

KELMAN, HERBERT C., ed., *International Behavior: A Social-Psychological Analysis.* New York: Holt, Rinehart & Winston, 1965.

KEOHANE, ROBERT O., and JOSEPH S. NYE, *Transnational Relations and World Politics.* Cambridge: Harvard University Press, 1972.

KEY, WILSON BRYAN, *Subliminal Seduction: A Media's Manipulation of a Not So Innocent America.* New York: New American Library, 1973.

KILPATRICK, FRANKLIN P., ed., *Explorations in Transactional Psychology.* New York: New York University Press, 1961.

KLINEBERG, OTTO, *The Human Dimension in International Relations.* New York: Holt, Rinehart & Winston, 1964.

KNAPP, MARK L., *Nonverbal Communication in Human Interaction* (2nd ed.). New York: Holt, Rinehart & Winston, 1978.

KOHLS, L. ROBERT, *Developing Intercultural Awareness: A Learning Module Complete with Lesson Plan, Content, Exercises and Handouts.* Washington, D.C.: Society for Intercultural Education, Training and Research, 1981.

LANDIS, DAN, and RICHARD W. BRISLIN, eds., *Handbook of Intercultural Training.* Vol. II, *Issues in Training Methodology.* New York: Pergamon Press, 1983.

LASSWELL, HAROLD D., *Politics: Who Gets What, When, How.* New York: McGraw-Hill Book Co., 1936.

——, *Power and Personality.* New York: W. W. Norton & Co., 1948.

——, and ABRAHAM KAPLAN, *Power and Society: A Framework for Political Inquiry.* New Haven, Conn.: Yale University Press, 1950.

LAWRENCE, CHARLES R., ed., *Man, Culture and Society*. New York: Brooklyn College Press, 1962.

LERNER, DANIEL, *The Passing of Traditional Society: Modernizing the Middle East*. Glencoe, Ill.: Free Press, 1958.

LEVITT, HAROLD, *Managerial Psychology* (2nd ed.). Chicago: University of Chicago Press, 1964.

―――, and LOUIS R. PONDY, eds., *Readings in Managerial Psychology* (2nd ed.). Chicago: University of Chicago Press, 1963.

LEWIS, OSCAR, *Five Families: Mexican Case Studies in the Culture of Poverty*. New York: New American Library, 1959.

LIPPITT, GORDON L., and DAVID S. HOOPES, *Helping Across Cultures*. Washington, D.C.: International Consultants Foundation, 1978.

LITTLEJOHN, STEPHEN W., *Theories of Human Communication*. Columbus, Ohio: Charles E. Merrill Publishing Co., 1978.

LLOYD, BARBARA B., *Perception and Cognition: A Cross-Cultural Perspective*. Baltimore: Penguin Books, 1972.

LUFT, JOSEPH, *Group Processes: An Introduction to Group Dynamics* (2nd ed.). Palo Alto, Calif.: National Press, 1970.

―――, *Of Human Interaction*. Palo Alto, Calif.: National Press, 1969.

MAKLER, HARRY, ALBERT MARTINELLI, and NEIL SMELSER, eds., *Many Voices, One World: Communication and Society Today and Tomorrow: Towards a New More Just and More Efficient World Information and Communication Order, Report by the International Commission for the Study of Communication Problem*. New York: Uniput, 1980.

MALLOY, JOHN T., *Dress for Success*. New York: P. H. Weyden, 1975.

MATTHEWS, ELLEN, *Culture Clash*. Chicago: Intercultural Press, 1982.

McCALL, GEORGE J., and J. L. SIMMONS, *Identities and Interactions: An Examination of Human Associations in Everyday Life* (rev. ed.). New York: Free Press, 1978.

McCLELLAND, DAVID C., *The Achieving Society*. Princeton, N.J.: D. Van Nostrand Co., 1961.

MEHRABIAN, ALBERT, *Silent Messages: Implicit Communication of Emotions and Attitudes* (2nd ed.). Belmont, Calif.: Wadsworth Publishing Co., 1981.

MILLER, JAMES G., *Living Systems*. New York: McGraw-Hill Book Co., 1978.

MISRA, BHABAGRAHI, and JAMES PRESTON, eds., *Community, Self, and Identity*. The Hague: Mourton, 1978.

MORAIN, GENELLE, *Kinesics and Cross-Cultural Understanding*. Arlington, Va.: Center for Applied Linguistics, 1978.

MORTENSON, DAVID, *Basic Readings in Communication Theory*. New York: Harper & Row, 1973.

MORRIS, DESMOND, PETER COLLETT, PETER MARSH, and MARIE O'SHAUGHNESSY, *Gestures*. New York: Stein & Day, 1979.

NISBETT, RICHARD, and LEE ROSS, *Human Inference: Strategies and Shortcomings of Social Judgment*. Englewood Cliffs, N.J.: Prentice-Hall, 1980.

NORTHRUP, F. S. L., and H. H. LIVINGSTON, *Cross-Cultural Understanding: Epistemology in Anthropology*. New York: Harper & Row, 1964.

OSGOOD, C. E., WILLIAM H. MAY, and MURRAY S. MIRON, *Cross-Cultural Universals of Affective Meaning*. Urbana: University of Illinois Press, 1975.

PARSONS, TALCOTT, *The Social System*. Glencoe, Ill.: Free Press, 1951.

―――, and EDWARD A. SHILS, eds., *Toward a General Theory of Action*. Cambridge: Harvard University Press, 1951.

PARSONS, TALCOTT, R. F. BALES, and E. A. SHILS, *Working Papers in the Theory of Action*. Glencoe, Ill.: Free Press, 1953.

PEDERSON, PAUL, ed., *Readings in Intercultural Communication*. Vol. IV, *Cross-Cultural Counseling*. Pittsburgh: Intercultural Communications Network, 1974.

POOL, ITHIEL DE SOLA, WILBER SCHRAMM, FREDRICK W. FREY, NATHAN MAC-COBY, and EDWIN B. PARKER, eds., *Handbook of Communication*. Chicago: Rand McNally, 1973.

PRICE-WILLIAMS, D. R., ed., *Cross-Cultural Studies*. Englewood Cliffs, N.J.: Prentice-Hall, 1969.

PROSSER, MICHAEL H., *The Cultural Dialogue: An Introduction to Intercultural Communication*. Boston: Houghton Mifflin, 1978.

——— , ed., *Intercommunication among Nations and Peoples*. New York: Harper & Row, 1973.

PUSCH, MARGARET D., ed., *Multicultural Education: A Cross-Cultural Training Approach*. Chicago: Intercultural Press, 1981.

PYE, LUCIEN W., ed., *Communication and Political Development*. Princeton, N.J.: Princeton University Press, 1963.

REDFIELD, ROBERT, *Peasant Society and Culture*. Chicago: University of Chicago Press, 1956.

RENWICK, GEORGE, *Evaluation Handbook for Cross-Cultural Training and Multicultural Education*. La Grange Park, Ill.: Intercultural Press.

RICH, ANDREA L., *Interracial Communication*. New York: Harper & Row, 1974.

RIESMAN, DAVID, with NATHAN GLAZER and REVEI DENNY, *The Lonely Crowd: A Study of the Changing American Character*. New Haven, Conn.: Yale University Press, 1961.

ROBINSON, GLEN O., ed., *Communication for Tomorrow: Policy Perspectives for the 1980's*. New York: Praeger Publishers, 1978.

ROBERTSON, ROLAND, and BURKHART HOLZNER, eds., *Identity and Authority: Explorations in the Theory of Society*. New York: St. Martin's Press, 1980.

ROGERS, EVERETT M., *Diffusion of Innovations* (3rd ed.). New York: Free Press, 1983.

ROGERS, EVERETT M., and REKHA AGARWALA-ROGERS, *Communication in Organizations*. New York: Free Press, 1976.

ROGERS, EVERETT M., and F. FLOYD SHOEMAKER, *Communication of Innovations: A Cross-Cultural Approach*. New York: Free Press, 1971.

ROKEACH, MILTON, *The Nature of Human Values*. New York: Free Press, 1973.

——— , *The Open and Closed Mind: Investigations into the Nature of Belief Systems and Personality Systems*. New York: Basic Books, 1960.

ROSENBLITH, W. A., ed., *Sensory Communication*. New York: John Wiley & Sons, 1961.

RUHLY, SHARON, *Orientations to Intercultural Communication*. Chicago: Science Research Associates, 1976.

SAMOVAR, LARRY A., *Understanding Intercultural Communication*. Belmont, Calif.: Wadsworth Publishing Co., 1981.

——— , and RICHARD E. PORTER, *Intercultural Communication: A Reader* (4th ed.). Belmont, Calif.: Wadsworth Publishing Co., 1985.

SCHILLER, HERBERT I., *Communication and Cultural Domination*. New York: International Arts and Sciences Press, 1976.

SEELYE, H. NED, *Teaching Culture Strategies for Intercultural Communication*. Lincolnwood, Ill.: National Textbook Co., 1984.

——— , and V. LYNN TYLER, *Intercultural Communicator Resources*. Provo, Utah: Brigham Young University, 1977.

SEGALL, M. H., D. T. CAMPBELL, and M. J. HERSKOVITS, *The Influence of Culture on Visual Perception*. Indianapolis: Bobbs-Merrill, 1966.

SHANNON, C. E., and WARREN WEAVER, *The Mathematical Theory of Communication*. Urbana: University of Illinois Press, 1949.

SIEGMAN, ARON W., and STANLEY FELDSTEIN, *Nonverbal Behavior and Communication*. New York: Halsted Press, 1978.

SINGER, MARSHALL R., *Weak States in a World of Powers: The Dynamics of International Relationships*. New York: Free Press, 1972.

SITARAM, K. S., and ROY R. COGDELL, *Foundation of Intercultural Communication*. Columbus, Ohio: Merrill Publishing Co., 1976.

SMITH, ALFRED G., *Communication and Culture*. New York: Holt, Rinehart & Winston, 1966.

SMITH, ANTHONY, *The Geopolitics of Information: How Western Culture Dominates the World*. New York: Oxford University Press, 1980.

SMITH, ELISE C., and LOUISE FIBER LUCE, eds., *Toward Internationalism: Readings in Cross-Cultural Communication.* Rowley, Mass.: Newbury House Publishers, 1979.

SMITHERMAN, GENEVA, *Talkin and Testifyin: The Language of Black America.* Boston: Houghton Mifflin Co., 1977.

SPROTT, W. J. H., *Human Groups.* Harmondsworth, England: Penguin Books, 1958.

STEINER, SHARI, *The Female Factor: Women in Western Europe, a Cross-Cultural Perspective.* Chicago: Intercultural Press, 1977.

STEWART, EDWARD C., *American Cultural Patterns: A Cross-Cultural Perspective.* Chicago: Intercultural Press, 1972.

STEWART, JOHN, and GARY D'ANGELO, *Together: Communicating Interpersonally.* Reading, Mass.: Addison-Wesley Publishing Co., 1976.

SZALEY, LORAND B., and JAMES E. DEESE, *Subjective Meaning and Culture: An Assessment through Word Associations.* New York: Halsted Press, 1978.

TAGUIRI, R., and L. PETROLLO, *Personal Perception and Interpersonal Behavior.* Stanford, Calif.: Stanford University Press, 1958.

TAYLOR, HOWARD F., *Balance in Small Groups.* New York: A. Van Nostrand Reinhold, 1970.

THIBAUT, J. W., and H. H. KELLY, *The Social Psychology of Groups.* New York: John Wiley & Sons, 1959.

TRIANDIS, HARRY C., *The Analysis of Subjective Culture.* New York: John Wiley & Sons, 1972.

UTTAL, W. R., *The Psychology of Sensory Coding.* New York: Harper & Row, 1973.

VETTER, JR., CHARLES T., *Citizen Ambassadors.* Provo, Utah: David M. Kennedy International Center, 1983.

WEITZ, SHIRLEY, ed., *Non-Verbal Communication: Readings with Commentary.* Oxford: Oxford University Press, 1974.

WHORF, BENJAMIN L., *Language, Thought and Reality: Selected Writings of Benjamin Lee Whorf,* edited by J. B. Carroll. Cambridge: MIT Press, 1956.

WILENTZ, JOAN S., *The Senses of Man.* New York: Thomas Y. Crowell Co., 1968.

WIENER, NORBERT, *Cybernetics.* Cambridge: Technology Press of MIT; and New York: John Wiley & Sons, 1948.

—— , *Human Use of Human Beings.* New York: Houghton Mifflin Co., 1964.

WOLFGANG, AARON, ed., *Nonverbal Behavior: Applications and Culture Implications.* New York: Academic Press, 1979.

JOURNAL ARTICLES AND CHAPTERS IN BOOKS

ABE, HIROKO, and RICHARD L. WISEMAN, "A Cross-Cultural Confirmation of the Dimensions of Intercultural Effectiveness," *International Journal of Intercultural Relations* 7, no. 1 (1983).

ADLER, PETER S., "Beyond Cultural Identity: Reflections on Cultural and Multicultural Man," in Larry A. Samovar and Richard E. Porter, *Intercultural Communication: A Reader* (4th ed.). Belmont, Calif.: Wadsworth Publishing Co., 1985.

ANDERSEN, JANIS F., "Educational Assumptions Highlighted from a Cross-Cultural Comparison," in Larry A. Samovar and Richard E. Porter, *Intercultural Communication: A Reader* (4th ed). Belmont, Calif.: Wadsworth Publishing Co., 1985.

ARKOFF, ABE, FALAK THAVER, and LEONARD ELKIND, "Mental Health and Counseling Ideas of Asian and American Students," in Paul Pedersen, ed., *Readings in Intercultural Communication.* Vol. IV, *Cross-Cultural Counseling.* Pittsburgh: Intercultural Communications Network, 1974.

ASUNCION-LANDE, NOBELEZA C., "Implications of Intercultural Communication for Bilingual and Bicultural Education," in Fred L. Casmir, ed., *International and Intercultural Communication Annual,* vol. II. Falls Church, Va.: Speech Communication Association, 1975.

BADAMI, MARY KENNY, "Interpersonal Perceptions in a Simulation Game of Intercultural Contact," in Fred L. Casmir, ed., *International and Intercultural Communication Annual,* vol. I. Falls Church, Va.: Speech Communication Association, 1974.

BALDASSINI, JOSE G., and VINCENT F. FLAHERTY, "Acculturation Process of Colombian Immigrants into the American Culture in Bergen County, New Jersey," *International Journal of Intercultural Relations* 5, no. 2 (1981).

BARNA, LA RAY M., "Stumbling Blocks in Intercultural Communication," in Larry A. Samovar and Richard E. Porter, *Intercultural Communication: A Reader* (4th ed.). Belmont, Calif.: Wadsworth Publishing Co., 1985.

BARNLUND, DEAN C., "Communication in a Global Village," in Larry A. Samovar and Richard E. Porter, *Intercultural Communication: A Reader* (4th ed.). Belmont, Calif.: Wadsworth Publishing Co., 1985.

——, "The Cross-Cultural Arena: An Ethical Void," in Larry A. Samovar and Richard E. Porter, *Intercultural Communication: A Reader* (4th ed.). Belmont, Calif.: Wadsworth Publishing Co., 1985.

——, "A Transactional Model of Communication," in Johnnye Akin, Alvin Goldberg, Gail Myers, and Joseph Stewart, eds., *Language Behavior: A Book of Readings in Communication.* The Hague: Morton, 1970.

——, and NAOKI NOMURA, "Decentering Convergence, and Cross-Cultural Understanding," in Larry A. Samovar and Richard E. Porter, *Intercultural Communication: A Reader* (4th ed.). Belmont, Calif.: Wadsworth Publishing Co., 1985.

BENNETT, JANET, "Transition Shock: Putting Culture Shock in Perspective," in Nemi C. Jain, ed., *International and Intercultural Communication Annual,* vol. IV. Falls Church, Va.: Speech Communication Association, 1977.

BENSON, PHILIP G., "Measuring Cross-Cultural Adjustment: The Problem of Criteria," *International Journal of Intercultural Relations* 2, no. 1 (1978).

BERRY, ELIZABETH, JOAN B. KESSLER, JOHN T. FODOR, and MASAKATSU WATO, "Intercultural Communication for Health Personnel," *International Journal of Intercultural Relations* 7, no. 4 (1983).

BLOOMBAUM, MILTON, JOE YAMAMOTO, and QUINTON JAMES, "Cultural Stereotyping among Psychotherapists," in Paul Pedersen, ed., *Readings in Intercultural Communication.* Vol. IV, *Cross-Cultural Counseling.* Pittsburgh: Intercultural Communications Network, 1974.

BORDEN, GEORGE A., and JEAN M. TANNER, "The Cross-Cultural Transfer of Educational Technology: A Myth," *International Journal of Intercultural Relations* 7, no. 1 (1983).

BOXER, MARILYN J., "Are Women Human Beings? Androcentricity as a Barrier to Intercultural Communication," in Larry A. Samovar and Richard E. Porter, *Intercultural Communication: A Reader* (4th ed.). Belmont, Calif.: Wadsworth Publishing Co., 1985.

BRASHEN, HENRY M., "Research Methodology in Another Culture: Some Precautions," in Fred L. Casmir, ed., *International and Intercultural Communication Annual,* vol. II. Falls Church, Va.: Speech Communication Association, 1975.

BREIN, MICHAEL, and KENNETH H. DAVID, "Intercultural Communication and the Adjustment of the Sojourner," in Paul Pedersen, ed., *Readings in Intercultural Communication.* Vol. IV, *Cross-Cultural Counseling.* Pittsburgh: Intercultural Communications Network, 1974.

BRIGGS, NANCY E., and GLENN R. HARWOOD, "Training Personnel in Multinational Businesses: An Inoculation Approach," *International Journal of Intercultural Relations* 6, no. 4 (1982).

BRISLIN, RICHARD W., "Prejudice in Intercultural Communication," in Larry A. Samovar and Richard E. Porter, *Intercultural Communication: A Reader* (4th ed.). Belmont, Calif.: Wadsworth Publishing Co., 1985.

BROOME, BENJAMIN J., "Facilitating Attitudes and Message Characteristics in the Expression of Differences in Intercultural Encounters," *International Journal of Intercultural Relations* 5, no. 3 (1981).

BRUNEAU, TOM, "The Time Dimension in Intercultural Communication," in Larry A. Samovar and Richard E. Porter, *Intercultural Communication: A Reader* (4th ed.). Belmont, Calif.: Wadsworth Publishing Co., 1985.

BURGOON, MICHAEL, JAMES P. DILLARD, and NOEL E. DORAN, "Cultural and Situational Influences on the Process of Persuasive Strategy Selection," *International Journal of Intercultural Relations* 6, no. 1 (1982).

BURK, JERRY L., "The Effects of Ethnocentrism upon Intercultural Communication," in Fred L. Casmir, ed., *International and Intercultural Communication Annual,* vol. III. Falls Church, Va.: Speech Communication Association, 1976.

——— , "Intercultural Communication Vistas: Description, Concept, and Theory," in Fred L. Casmir, ed., *International and Intercultural Communication Annual,* vol. II. Falls Church, Va.: Speech Communication Association, 1975.

CARMICHAEL, CARL W., "Cultural Patterns of the Elderly," in Larry A. Samovar and Richard E. Porter, *Intercultural Communication: A Reader* (4th ed.). Belmont, Calif.: Wadsworth Publishing Co., 1985.

CLARK, M. L., and WILLIE PEARSON, JR., "Racial Stereotypes Revisited," *International Journal of Intercultural Relations* 6, no. 4 (1982).

CLARK, ROBERT R., "African Healing and Western Psychotherapy: Meetings between Professionals," *International Journal of Intercultural Relations* 6, no. 1 (1982).

CLARKE, CLIFFORD H., "Personal Counseling across Cultural Boundaries," in Paul Pedersen, ed., *Readings in Intercultural Communication.* Vol. IV, *Cross-Cultural Counseling.* Pittsburgh: Intercultural Communications Network, 1974.

CLINE, REBECCA J., and CAROL A. PUHL, "Gender, Culture, and Geography: A Comparison of Seating Arrangements in the United States and Taiwan," *International Journal of Intercultural Relations* 8, no. 2 (1984).

CONDON, E. C., "Cross-Cultural Inferences Affecting Teacher-Pupil Communication in American Schools," in Fred L. Casmir, ed., *International and Intercultural Communication Annual,* vol. III. Falls Church, Va.: Speech Communication Association, 1976.

CUSHMAN, DONALD, and GORDON C. WHITING, "An Approach to Communication Theory: Towards Consensus on Rules," *Journal of Communication* 22 (September 1972).

DANIEL, JACK, "The Poor: Aliens in an Affluent Society: Cross-Cultural Communication," in Larry A. Samovar and Richard E. Porter, *Intercultural Communication: A Reader* (4th ed.). Belmont, Calif.: Wadsworth Publishing Co., 1985.

DA SILVA, EDGAR J., "Microbial Technology: Some Social and Intercultural Implications in Development," *International Journal of Intercultural Relations* 8, no. 4 (1984).

DEETZ, STANLEY, "Metaphor Analysis," in William B. Gudykunst and Young Yun Kim, eds., *Methods for Intercultural Communication Research.* Beverly Hills, Calif.: Sage Publications, 1984.

DELGADO, MELVIN, "Cultural Consultation: Implications for Hispanic Mental Health Services in the United States," *International Journal of Intercultural Relations* 6, no. 3 (1982).

DIAMOND, C. T. PATRICK, "Understanding Others: Kellyian Theory, Methodology and Applications," *International Journal of Intercultural Relations* 6, no. 4 (1982).

DOUGLAS, DONALD G., "The Study of Communication Messages and the Conflict Over Global Eco-Patience," in Fred L. Casmir, ed., *International and Intercultural Communication Annual,* vol. II. Falls Church, Va.: Speech Communication Association, 1975.

DYAL, JAMES A., and RUTH Y. DYAL, "Acculturation Stress and Coping: Some Implications for Research and Education," *International Journal of Intercultural Relations* 5, no. 4 (1981).

EAKINS, BARBARA WESTBROOK, and R. GENE EAKINS, "Sex Differences in Nonverbal Communication," in Larry A. Samovar and Richard E. Porter, *Intercultural Communication: A Reader* (4th ed.). Belmont, Calif.: Wadsworth Publishing Co., 1985.

EDGERTON, ROBERT B., and MARVIN KARNO, "Mexican-American Bilingualism and the Perception of Mental Illness," in Paul Pedersen, ed., *Readings in Intercultural Communication.* Vol. IV, *Cross-Cultural Counseling.* Pittsburgh: Intercultural Communications Network, 1974.

EDWARDS, WALTER F., "Some Linguistic and Behavioral Links in the African Diaspora: Cultural Implications," *International Journal of Intercultural Relations* 5, no. 2 (1981).

ESFANDIARI, M , and J. HAMADANIZADEH, "An Investigation of the Iranian's Attitudes towards Goals of Education," *International Journal of Intercultural Relations* 5, no. 2 (1981).

EVERETT, JAMES E., BRUCE W. STENING, and PETER A. LONGTON, "Stereotypes of the Japanese Manager in Singapore," *International Journal of Intercultural Relations* 5, no. 3 (1981).

FARMER, HELEN S., NAYEREH TOHIDI, and ELISABETH R. WEISS, "Study of the Factors Influencing Sex Differences in the Career Motivation of Iranian High School Students," *International Journal of Intercultural Relations* 6, no. 1 (1982).

FEARING, FRANKLIN, "An Examination of the Conceptions of Benjamin Whorf in the Light of Theories on Perception and Cognition," in *Language in Culture,* edited by Harry Hoijer, Chicago: University of Chicago Press, 1954.

FLEMINGS, CORINNE K., "National and International Conferences Relating to International and Intercultural Communication," in Fred L. Casmir, ed., *International and Intercultural Communication Annual,* vol. III. Falls Church, Va.: Speech Communication Association, 1976.

FLORIAN, VICTOR, "Cross-Cultural Differences in Attitudes towards Disabled Persons: A Study of Jewish and Arab Youth in Israel," *International Journal of Intercultural Relations* 6, no. 3 (1982).

FOLB, EDITH A., "Vernacular Vocabulary: A View of Interracial Perceptions and Experiences," in Larry A. Samovar and Richard E. Porter, *Intercultural Communication: A Reader* (4th ed.). Belmont, Calif.: Wadsworth Publishing Co., 1985.

——— , "Who's Got the Room at the Top? Issues of Dominance and Nondominance in Intracultural Communication," in Larry A. Samovar and Richard E. Porter, *Intercultural Communication: A Reader* (4th ed.). Belmont, Calif.: Wadsworth Publishing Co., 1985.

FRIDERES, JAMES, and S. GOLDENBERG, "Ethnic Identity: Myth and Reality in Western Canada," *International Journal of Intercultural Relations* 5, no. 2 (1981).

FYANS, LESLIE J., JR., BARBARA KREMER, FARIDEH SALILI, and MARTIN L. MAEHR, "The Effects of Evaluation Conditions on 'Continuing Motivation': Study of the Cultural Personological and Situational Antecedents of a Motivational Pattern," *International Journal of Intercultural Relations* 5, no. 1 (1981).

GO, MAE JEAN, "Quantitative Content Analysis," in William B. Gudykunst and Young Kim, eds., *Methods for Intercultural Communication Research.* Beverly Hills, Calif.: Sage Publications, 1984.

GRAHAM, MORRIS A., "Acculturative Stress among Polynesian, Asian and American Students on the Brigham Young University—Hawaii Campus," *International Journal of Intercultural Relations* 7, no. 1 (1983).

GREY, ALAN L., "The Counselling Process and Its Cultural Setting," in Paul Pedersen, ed., *Readings in Intercultural Communication.* Vol. IV, *Cross-Cultural Counseling.* Pittsburgh: Intercultural Communications Network, 1974.

GUDYKUNST, WILLIAM B., "Intercultural Contact and Attitude Change: A Review of Literature and Suggestions for Future Research," in Nemi C. Jain, ed., *International and Intercultural Communication Annual,* vol. IV. Falls Church, Va.: Speech Communication Association, 1977.

——— , "Toward a Typology of Stranger-Host Relationships," *International Journal of Intercultural Relations* 7, no. 4 (1983).

GUTHRIE, GEORGE M., TOMAS L. FERNANDEZ, and NENITA O. ESTRERA, "Small-Scale Studies and Field Experiments in Family Planning in the Philippines," *International Journal of Intercultural Relations* 8, no. 4 (1984).

HALL, EDWARD T., "Context and Meaning," in Larry A. Samovar and Richard E. Porter, *Intercultural Communication: A Reader* (4th ed.). Belmont, Calif.: Wadsworth Publishing Co., 1985.

HAWES, FRANK, and DANIEL J. KEALEY, "An Empirical Study of Canadian Technical Assistance: Adaptation and Effectiveness on Overseas Assignment," *International Journal of Intercultural Relations* 5, no. 3 (1981).

HECHT, MICHAEL L., and SIDNEY RIBEAU, "Ethnic Communication: A Comparative Analysis of Satisfying Communication," *International Journal of Intercultural Relations* 8, no. 2 (1984).

HEPWORTH, JANICE C., "Some Empirical Considerations for Cross-Cultural Attitude Measurements and Persuasive Communications," in Fred L. Casmir, ed., *International and*

Intercultural Communication Annual, vol. I. Falls Church, Va.: Speech Communication Association, 1974.

HERBERG, DOROTHY C., "Discovering Ethnic Root Behavior Patterns: Towards an Applied Canadian Ethnic Studies," *International Journal of Intercultural Relations* 5, no. 2 (1981).

HOIJER, HARRY, "The Sapir-Whorf Hypotheses," in Harry Hoijer, ed., *Language in Culture.* Chicago: University of Chicago Press, 1954.

HUI, CHI-CHIU HARRY, "Locus of Control: A Review of Cross-Cultural Research," *International Journal of Intercultural Relations* 6, no. 3 (1982).

INGLIS, MARGARET, and WILLIAM B. GUDYKUNST, "Institutional Completeness and Communication Acculturation: A Comparison of Korean Immigrants in Chicago and Hartford," *International Journal of Intercultural Relations* 6, no. 3 (1982).

IVEY, ALLEN E., and SUZANNE JESSOP McGOWAN, "Sociolinguistics: The Implications of a Sociological Approach in Examining the Counseling Relationship," *International Journal of Intercultural Relations* 5, no. 1 (1981).

JEFFRES, LEO W., and K. KYOON HUR, "Communication Channels within Ethnic Groups," *International Journal of Intercultural Relations* 5, no. 1 (1981).

JENSEN, J. VERNON, "Perspective on Nonverbal Intercultural Communication," in Larry A. Samovar and Richard E. Porter, *Intercultural Communication: A Reader* (4th ed.). Belmont, Calif.: Wadsworth Publishing Co., 1985.

JOHNSON, KENNETH R., "Black Kenesics: Some Non-Verbal Communication Patterns in Black Culture," in Larry A. Samovar and Richard E. Porter, *Intercultural Communication: A Reader* (4th ed.). Belmont, Calif.: Wadsworth Publishing Co., 1985.

JUN, SUK-HO, "Communication Patterns among Young Korean Immigrants," *International Journal of Intercultural Relations* 8, no. 4 (1984).

KAPLAN, ROBERT B., "Cultural Thought Patterns in Inter-Cultural Education," *Language Learning* 16, nos. 1 and 2 (1966).

KIM, YOUNG YUN, "Communication and Acculturation," in Larry A. Samovar and Richard E. Porter, *Intercultural Communication: A Reader* (4th ed.). Belmont, Calif.: Wadsworth Publishing Co., 1985.

——, "Intercultural Personhood: An Integration of Eastern and Western Perspectives," in Larry A. Samovar and Richard E. Porter, *Intercultural Communication: A Reader* (4th ed.). Belmont, Calif.: Wadsworth Publishing Co., 1985.

——, "Inter-Ethnic and Intra-Ethnic Communication: A Study of Korean Immigrants in Chicago," in Nemi C. Jain, ed., *International and Intercultural Communication Annual,* vol. IV. Falls Church, Va.: Speech Communication Association, 1977.

——, "Searching for Creative Integration," in William B. Gudykunst and Young Kim, eds., *Methods for Intercultural Communication Research.* Beverly Hills, Calif.: Sage Publications, 1984.

KING, STEPHEN W., "A Taxonomy for the Classification of Language Studies in Intercultural Communication," in Larry A. Samovar and Richard E. Porter, *Intercultural Communication: A Reader* (4th ed.). Belmont, Calif.: Wadsworth Publishing Co., 1985.

KOENIG, EDNA L., "Language and Ethnicity in Intergroup Communication," in Fred L. Casmir, ed., *International and Intercultural Communication Annual,* vol. II. Falls Church, Va.: Speech Communication Association, 1975.

KORZENNY, FELIPE, and KIMBERLY A. NEUENDORF, "The Perceived Reality of Television and Aggressive Predispositions among Children in Mexico," *International Journal of Intercultural Relations* 7, no. 1 (1983).

——, and BETTY ANN GRIFFIS KORZENNY, "Quantitative Approaches: An Overview," in William B. Gudykunst and Young Kim, eds., *Methods for Intercultural Communication Research.* Beverly Hills, Calif.: Sage Publications, 1984.

LA BARRE, WESTON, "Paralinguistics, Kinesics and Cultural Anthropology," in Larry A. Samovar and Richard E. Porter, *Intercultural Communication: A Reader* (4th ed.). Belmont, Calif.: Wadsworth Publishing Co., 1985.

LA FRANCE, MARIANNE, and CLARA MAYO, "Cultural Aspects of Nonverbal Communication: A Review Essay," *International Journal of Intercultural Relations* 2, no. 1 (1978).

LAMPE, PHILIP E., "Ethnicity and Crime: Perceptual Differences among Blacks, Mexican Americans, and Anglos," *International Journal of Intercultural Relations* 8, no. 4 (1984).

——, "Interethnic Dating: Reasons For and Against," *International Journal of Intercultural Relations* 5, no. 2 (1981).

LESSING, ELISE E., CHESTER C. CLARKE, and LISA GRAY-SHELLBERG, "Black Power Ideology: Rhetoric and Reality in a Student Sample," *International Journal of Intercultural Relations* 5, no. 1 (1981).

LEWIS, SASHA GREGORY, "Sunday's Women: Lesbian Life Today," in Larry A. Samovar and Richard E. Porter, *Intercultural Communication: A Reader* (4th ed.). Belmont, Calif.: Wadsworth Publishing Co., 1985.

MAEHR, MARTIN L., and ANTON LYSY, "Motivating Students of Diverse Sociocultural Backgrounds to Achieve," *International Journal of Intercultural Relations* 2, no. 1 (1978).

MARTIN, JUDITH N., "The Intercultural Reentry: Conceptualization and Directions for Future Research," *International Journal of Intercultural Relations* 8, no. 2 (1984).

MASLOW, A. H., "A Theory of Human Motivation," in Harold J. Levitt and Louis R. Pondy, eds., *Readings in Managerial Psychology* (2nd. ed.). Chicago: University of Chicago Press, 1963.

MATSUMOTO, DAVID, and HIROMU KISHIMOTO, "Developmental Characteristics in Judgements of Emotion from Nonverbal Vocal Cues," *International Journal of Intercultural Relations* 7, no. 4 (1983).

MEEHAN, ANITA, and GLYNIS BEAN, "Tracking the Civil Rights and Women's Movements in the United States," *International Journal of Intercultural Relations* 5, no. 2 (1981).

MENDENHALL, MARK, GARY ODDOU, and DAVID V. STIMPSON, "Enhancing Trainee Satisfaction with Cross-Cultural Training Programs via Prior Warning," *International Journal of Intercultural Relations* 6, no. 4 (1982).

MILLER, MILTON, ENG-KUNG YEH, A. A. ALEXANDER, MARJORIE KLEIN, KWO-KWA TSENG, FIKRE WORKNEH, and HUNG-MING CHU, "The Cross-Cultural Student: Lessons in Human Nature," in Paul Pedersen, ed., *Readings in Intercultural Communication.* Vol. IV, *Cross-Cultural Counseling.* Pittsburgh: Intercultural Communications Network, 1974.

MORTEN, GEORGE, and DERALD WING SUE, "Minority Group Counseling: An Overview," in Larry A. Samovar and Richard E. Porter, *Intercultural Communication: A Reader* (4th ed.). Belmont, Calif.: Wadsworth Publishing Co., 1985.

NEEL, ROBERT G., OLIVER C. S. TZENG, and CAN BAYSAL, "Comparative Studies of Authoritarian-Personality Characteristics across Culture, Language and Methods," *International Journal of Intercultural Relations* 7, no. 4 (1983).

NEWMARK, EILEEN, and MOLEFI K. ASANTE, "Perception of Self and Others: An Approach to Intercultural Communication," in Fred L. Casmir, ed., *International and Intercultural Communication Annual,* vol. II. Falls Church, Va.: Speech Communication Association, 1975.

NILAN, MICHAEL S., "Development Communication Expectations in Occupational Contexts: A Comparison of U.S. and Foreign Graduate Students," *International Journal of Intercultural Relations* 5, no. 2 (1981).

NOMURA, NAOKI, and DEAN BARNLUND, "Patterns of Interpersonal Criticism in Japan and the United States," *International Journal of Intercultural Relations* 7, no. 1 (1983).

NWANKWO, ROBERT L., "International and Intercultural Communication Annual Minoritarianism and Ethnic Groups Communication," in Fred L. Casmir, ed., *International and Intercultural Communication Annual,* vol. II. Falls Church, Va.: Speech Communication Association, 1975.

——, and HUMPHREY A. REGIS, "The Perception of Transcendent Interest: Communication and Identification in an Emergent Community," *International Journal of Intercultural Relations* 7, no. 4 (1983).

PALMER, MARK T., and GEORGE A. BARNETT, "Using a Spatial Model to Verify Language Translation," in William B. Gudykunst and Young Kim, eds., *Methods for Intercultural Communication Research.* Beverly Hills, Calif.: Sage Publications, 1984.

PEDERSEN, ANNE B., and PAUL B. PEDERSEN, "The Cultural Grid: A Personal Cultural Orientation," in Larry A. Samovar and Richard E. Porter, *Intercultural Communication: A Reader* (4th ed.). Belmont, Calif.: Wadsworth Publishing Co., 1985.

PEDERSEN, PAUL, "International Conferences: Significant Measures of Success," *International Journal of Intercultural Relations* 5, no. 1 (1981).

—— , "The Transfer of Intercultural Training Skills," in Larry A. Samovar and Richard E. Porter, *Intercultural Communication: A Reader* (4th ed.). Belmont, Calif.: Wadsworth Publishing Co., 1985.

PENNINGTON, DORTHY L., "Intercultural Communication," in Larry A. Samovar and Richard E. Porter, *Intercultural Communication: A Reader* (4th ed.). Belmont, Calif.: Wadsworth Publishing Co., 1985.

PETTERSEN, DUANE D., "Language and Information Processing: An Approach to Intercultural Communication," in Fred L. Casmir, ed., *International and Intercultural Communication Annual,* vol. III. Falls Church, Va.: Speech Communication Association, 1976.

POOL, ITHIEL DE SOLA, "Communication Systems," in Ithiel De Sola Pool, Wilber Schramm, Frederick W. Frey, Nathan Maccoby, and Edwin B. Parker, eds., *Handbook of Communication.* Chicago: Rand McNally, 1973.

—— , and MANFRED KOCHEN, "Contacts and Influence," *Social Networks* 1 (1978/79).

PORTER, RICHARD E., and LARRY A. SAMOVAR, "Approaching Intercultural Communication," in Samovar and Porter, *Intercultural Communication: A Reader* (4th ed.). Belmont, Calif.: Wadsworth Publishing Co., 1985.

PRICE-WILLIAMS, D., "Cross-Cultural Studies," in Brian M. Foss, ed., *New Horizons in Psychology.* Baltimore: Penguin Books, 1966. Reprinted in Larry A. Samovar and Richard E. Porter, eds., *Intercultural Communication: A Reader* (2nd ed.). Belmont, Calif.: Wadsworth Publishing Co., 1976.

PRUITT, FRANCE J., "The Adaptation of African Students to American Society," *International Journal of Intercultural Relations* 2, no. 1 (1978).

RAMSEY, SHEILA J., "Nonverbal Behavior: An Intercultural Perspective," in Molefi Kete Asante, Eileen Newmark, and Cecil A. Blake, eds., *Handbook of Intercultural Communication.* Beverly Hills, Calif.: Sage Publishing Co., 1979.

—— , "To Hear One and Understand Ten: Nonverbal Behavior in Japan," in Larry A. Samovar and Richard E. Porter, eds., *Intercultural Communication: A Reader* (4th ed.). Belmont, Calif.: Wadsworth Publishing Co., 1985.

RENWICK, GEORGE W., "Intercultural Communication: State-of-the-Art Study," in Nemi C. Jain, ed., *International and Intercultural Communication Annual,* vol. V. Falls Church, Va.: Speech Communication Association, 1979.

RICH, YISRAEL, YEHUDA AMIR, and RACHEL BEN-ARI, "Social and Emotional Problems Associated with Integration in the Israeli Junior High School Motivational Pattern," *International Journal of Intercultural Relations* 5, no. 3 (1981).

RIPPLE, RICHARD E., GAIL A. JAQUISH, H. WING LEE, and JOHN SPINKS, "Intergenerational Differences in Descriptions of Life-Span Stages among Hong Kong Chinese," *International Journal of Intercultural Relations* 7, no. 4 (1983).

RUBEN, BRENT D., "Human Communication and Cross-Cultural Effectiveness," in Larry A. Samovar and Richard E. Porter, eds., *Intercultural Communication: A Reader* (4th ed.). Belmont, Calif.: Wadsworth Publishing Co., 1985.

RUHLY, SHARON, "The Major Triad Revisited: A Potential Guide for Intercultural Research," in Fred L. Casmir, ed., *International and Intercultural Communication Annual,* vol. III. Falls Church, Va.: Speech Communication Association, 1976.

RUSZKOWSKI, ANDREW, "Role of the Holy See Observer to the United Nations as Intercultural Communication," in Fred L. Casmir, ed., *International and Intercultural Communication Annual,* vol. III. Falls Church, Va.: Speech Communication Association, 1976.

ST. MARTIN, GAIL M., "Intercultural Differential Decoding of Nonverbal Affective Communication," in Fred L. Casmir, ed., *International and Intercultural Communication Annual,* vol. III. Falls Church, Va.: Speech Communication Association, 1976.

SALILI, FARIDEH, MARTIN L. MAEHR, and LESLIE J. FYANS, JR., "Evaluating Morality and Achievement: A Study of the Interaction of Social Cultural and Developmental Trends," *International Journal of Intercultural Relations* 5, no. 2 (1981).

SARBAUGH, L. E., "An Overview of Selected Approaches," in William B. Gudykunst and Young Kim, eds., *Methods for Intercultural Communication Research.* Beverly Hills, Calif.: Sage Publications, 1984.

—— , "A Systematic Framework for Analyzing Intercultural Communication," in Nemi C.

Jain, ed., *International and Intercultural Communication Annual,* vol. V. Falls Church, Va.: Speech Communication Association, 1979.

SARETT, CARLA J., "Observational Methods," in William B. Gudykunst and Young Kim, eds., *Methods for Intercultural Communication Research.* Beverly Hills, Calif.: Sage Publications, 1984.

SARMAD, ZOHREH, "Pattern of Some Measured Mental Abilities among Persian Bilingual and Monolingual Children," *International Journal of Intercultural Relations* 5, no. 4 (1981).

SCHEIN, EDGAR H., "Coming to a New Awareness of Organizational Culture," *Sloan Management Review* 26 (Winter 1984).

SCHNEIDER, MICHAEL J., and WILLIAM JORDAN, "Perception of the Communicative Performance of Americans and Chinese in Intercultural Dyads," *International Journal of Intercultural Relations* 5, no. 2 (1981).

SECHREST, LEE, TODD L. FAY, and S. M. ZAIDI, "Problems of Translation in Cross-Cultural Communication," in Larry A. Samovar and Richard E. Porter, eds., *International Communication: A Reader* (4th ed.). Belmont, Calif.: Wadsworth Publishing Co., 1985.

SHAMIR, BOAS, "Some Differences in Work Attitudes between Arab and Jewish Hotel Workers," *International Journal of Intercultural Relations* 5, no. 1 (1981).

SHUTER, ROBERT, "Naturalistic Field Research," in William B. Gudykunst and Young Kim, eds., *Methods for Intercultural Communication Research.* Beverly Hills, Calif.: Sage Publications, 1984.

——, and JUDITH FITZGERALD MILLER, "An Exploratory Study of Pain Expression Styles among Blacks and Whites," *International Journal of Intercultural Relations* 6, no. 3 (1982).

SINGER, MARSHALL R., "Culture: A Perceptual Approach," *Vidya,* no. 3 (Spring 1969).

SMITH, ALFRED G., "Taxonomies for Planning Intercultural Communication," in Nemi C. Jain, ed., *International and Intercultural Communication Annual,* vol. V. Falls Church, Va.: Speech Communication Association, 1979.

SMUTKUPT, SURIYA, and LA RAY M. BARNA, "Impact of Nonverbal Communication in an Intercultural Setting: Thailand," in Fred L. Casmir, ed., *International and Intercultural Communication Annual,* vol. III. Falls Church, Va.: Speech Communication Association, 1976.

SPRANG, ALONZO, "Counseling the Indian," in Paul Pedersen, ed., *Readings in Intercultural Communication.* Vol. IV, *Cross-Cultural Counseling.* Pittsburgh: Intercultural Communications Network, 1974.

STANBACK, MARSHA HOUSTON, and W. BARNETT PEARCE, "Talking to 'the Man': Some Communication Strategies Used by Members of 'Subordinate' Social Groups," in Larry A. Samovar and Richard E. Porter, eds., *Intercultural Communication: A Reader* (4th ed.). Belmont, Calif.: Wadsworth Publishing Co., 1985.

STAROSTA, WILLIAM J., "On Intercultural Rhetoric," in William B. Gudykunst and Young Kim, eds., *Methods for Intercultural Communication Research.* Beverly Hills, Calif.: Sage Publications, 1984.

STEIN, HOWARD F., "Adversary Symbiosis and Complementary Group Dissociation: An Analysis of the U.S./U.S.S.R. Conflict," *International Journal of Intercultural Relations* 6, no. 1 (1982).

STEWART, EDWARD C., "The Survival Stage of Intercultural Communication," in Nemi C. Jain, ed., *International and Intercultural Communication Annual,* vol. IV. Falls Church, Va.: Speech Communication Association, 1977.

SUE, DERALD WING, and STANLEY SUE, "Counseling Chinese-Americans," in Paul Pedersen, ed., *Readings in Intercultural Communication.* Vol. IV, *Cross-Cultural Counseling.* Pittsburgh: Intercultural Communications Network, 1974.

SZALAY, LORAND B., "Intercultural Communication—A Process Model," *International Journal of Intercultural Relations* 5, no. 2 (1981).

TAFOYA, DENNIS W., "Research and Cultural Phenomena," in William B. Gudykunst and Young Kim, eds., *Methods for Intercultural Communication Research.* Beverly Hills, Calif.: Sage Publications, 1984.

TING-TOOMEY, STELLA, "Ethnic Identity and Close Friendship in Chinese-American College Students," *International Journal of Intercultural Relations* 5, no. 4 (1981).

——, "Qualitative Research: An Overview," in William B. Gudykunst and Young Kim, eds.,

Methods for Intercultural Communication Research. Beverly Hills, Calif.: Sage Publications, 1984.

TYLER, VERNON LYNN, "Dimensions, Perspectives and Resources of Intercultural Communication," in Fred L. Casmir, ed., *International and Intercultural Communication Annual,* vol. I. Falls Church, Va.: Speech Communication Association, 1974.

USEEM, JOHN, and RUTH HILL USEEM, "American Educated Indians and Americans in India: A Comparison of the Two Modernizing Roles," *Journal of Social Issues* 24, no. 4 (1968).

VAN MANNEN, J., and EDWIN SCHEIN, "Toward a Theory of Organization Socialization," quoted in Norman G. Ginges and William S. Maynard, "Intercultural Aspects of Organizational Effectiveness," in Dan Landis and Richard W. Brislin, eds., *Handbook of Intercultural Training.* Vol. II, *Issues in Training Methodology.* New York: Pergamon Press, 1983.

VIGLIONESE, PASCHAL C., "Text and Metatext in Hersey's *A Single Pebble* from the Perspective of Intercultural Communication," *International Journal of Intercultural Relations* 6, no. 1 (1982).

WEBER, SHIRLEY N., "The Need to Be: The Socio-Cultural Significance of Black Language," in Larry A. Samovar and Richard E. Porter, eds., *Intercultural Communication: A Reader* (4th ed.). Belmont, Calif.: Wadsworth Publishing Co., 1985.

WEIMANN, GABRIEL, "Images of Life in America: The Impact of American T.V. in Israel," *International Journal of Intercultural Relations* 8, no. 2 (1984).

WHITE, RALPH K., "Misperception and the Vietnam War," *Journal of Social Issues* 22, no. 3 (July 1966).

WOELFEL, JOSEPH, and NICHOLAS R. NAPOLI, "Measuring Human Emotion: Proposed Standards," in William B. Gudykunst and Young Kim, eds., *Methods for Intercultural Communication Research.* Beverly Hills, Calif.: Sage Publications, 1984.

WOLFSON, KIM, and MARTIN F. NORDEN, "Measuring Responses to Filmed Interpersonal Conflict: A Rules Approach," in William B. Gudykunst and Young Kim, eds., *Methods for Intercultural Communication Research.* Beverly Hills, Calif.: Sage Publications, 1984.

WONG-RIEGER, DURHANE, "Testing a Model of Emotional and Coping Responses to Problems in Adaptation: Foreign Students at a Canadian University," *International Journal of Intercultural Relations* 8, no. 2 (1984).

WRENN, C. GILBERT, "The Culturally Encapsulated Counselor," in Paul Pedersen, ed., *Readings in Intercultural Communication.* Vol. IV, *Cross-Cultural Counseling.* Pittsburgh: Intercultural Communications Network, 1974.

WRIGHT, JOSEPH E., "The Implications of Cognitive Science," in William B. Gudykunst and Young Kim, eds., *Methods for International and Intercultural Communication Annual,* vol. VIII. Beverly Hills, Calif.: Sage Publications, 1984.

YAMAMOTO, KAORU, O. L. DAVIS, JR., and GAIL McEACHRON-HIRSCH, "International Perceptions Across the Sea: Patterns in Japanese Young Adults," *International Journal of Intercultural Relations* 7, no. 1 (1983).

YINON, YOEL, and YEHUDA RON, "Ethnic Similarity and Economic Status of the Potential Helper as Determinants of Helping Behavior," *International Journal of Intercultural Relations* 6, no. 3 (1982).

YOUSEF, FATHI S., and NANCY E. BRIGGS, "The Multinational Business Organization: A Schema for the Training of Overseas Personnel in Communication," in Fred L. Casmir, ed., *International and Intercultural Communication Annual,* vol. II. Falls Church, Va.: Speech Communication Association, 1975.

YUM, JUNE OCK, "Network Analysis," in William B. Gudykunst and Young Kim, eds., *Methods for Intercultural Communication Research.* Beverly Hills, Calif.: Sage Publications, 1984.

INDEX

H

Hagen, Everett E., 123
Hall, Edward T., 85, 86, 104
Harrington, Michael, 40, 63
Harvard, 117, 172
Hellenists, 31
Hess, E. H., 74, 103
Heterosexual, 16
  non-verbal communication, 74
Hindi (language), 65
Hindu, 11, 80
Hinduism, 81
Hitler, 19
Holjer, Henry, 7, 36
Holocaust, 169
Holsti, Ole R., 36
Homophily, 197
Homosexual, 89
  non-verbal communication, 74-75
Hoopes, David, 45
Human behavior, politics of, 105-6,
  122

I

Id, 87, 88
Identities:
  Catholic, 16, 51
  equally ranked, 56-57
  involuntary, 158-60
  primary, secondary, and tertiary, 50-53,
    55
  related to censor screens, 80-81
  role, 162, 181
  tribal, racial, 158
  voluntary, 158-62
Identity:
  context determines ranking, 52-53
  ethnic, 158, 203-4
  group(s), 1, 6, 7, 38, 40-42, 170
    continuum of types, 158
    defined, 40, 60
    ranking of them, 49-53, 61, 167-68
    sharing of, 43-46, 61
    types of, 157-62, 175
  male and female, 158-59
  national, 21
  role of communication, 38-63
India(n), 21, 65, 121, 157, 169, 212, 219
Indians, Guatemalan, 33, 34
Individuals, in relation to power, 105-23
Indonesia, 111, 121
Influence, ability to exercise, 105-23
Influence and power, relationship, 106-7
Informal groups, 157, 165, 185 (*see also*
  Groups, small)

Information:
  about ourselves that is conscious, 137-38
  basic and specific, as component of power,
    113-17, 123
  free flow of, 221
  manifest and latent, 115-17
  Order, New World, 218-21, 231
  overload, 114, 115
Ingram, Harrington, 132
Inkeles, Alex, 232
Innovation, diffusion of, 195-98, 199
Inquisition, 31
Intercultural communication:
  everything you always wanted to know
    about it but were afraid to ask, 1-248
  relationship to political science, 109-10
Interdependence, psychological, 140-41
Intergroup communication(s), 2-3, 192-95,
  199
Intergroup perceptions and identities,
  188-90, 199
Intergroup power, 190-92, 199
International communication(s), 3, 54, 66,
  214-18, 231
International communication, interelite,
  222-25, 232
International Court of Justice, 214
International diplomacy, 225-30, 232
International mass communication, 218-21,
  231
International negotiations, 225-30
International news flows, 218-21
International perceptions and identity,
  211-12, 231
International power, 212-14, 231
International Society for Educational,
  Cultural and Scientific Interchanges
  (ISECI), 178
International system, 215, 217, 218
Interpersonal communication, 2, 3, 24, 66,
  138-53, 154, 164-66, 192
  accuracy of, 166
  process, steps in, 148-52, 154
  role of trust in, 148-53
Interpersonal perceptions and identities,
  138-41, 153
Interpersonal power, 140-41, 154
Intimacy:
  change in, with increase in number(s),
    165-66
  level desired in interpersonal
    communication, 144-45
Intra- and intergroup communication,
  177-200
Intra- and international communication,
  201-33
Intra- and interpersonal communication,
  124-55

Parker, Edwin B., 155
Parsimony, law of, in communication process, 145–46
Parsons, Talcott, 157
Patton, Bobby R., 102
Peace Corps, 149, 225
Peasants, 33, 39, 63
Penny Foundation in Guatemala, 34
Perception(s):
  defined, 9, 35
  determinants of:
    environmental, 13–15, 35
    learned, 15–20
    physical, 12–13
  effects on power relationships, 120–22
  environmental determinants of, 13–15, 35
  factors that affect, 12–29
  and human behavior, 8–9
  and identities:
    intergroup, 188–90, 199
    international, 211–12, 231
    interpersonal, 138–41
    intragroup, 178–82, 198
    intranational, 202–6, 230
    intrapersonal, 138–41, 153
  learned determinants of, 15–20
  physical determinants of, 12–13
  role of, in communication, 3–37
  what are they, 9–29
Perceptual groups, 38–40, 60
  defined, 38, 60
Personality, 12, 87
"Personal space," 85
Peru, 196
Philippines, 171
Pitts, Robert A., 200
Pittsburgh, Pa., 37, 44
Pittsburgh, University of, 177
Plato, 44
Poland, Polish, 173, 204
Polish-American(s), 47, 208
Political behavior, 26, 27, 105–6
Political science, relationship to intercultural communication, 109–10
Politics of human behavior, 105–6, 122
Pool, Ithiel de Sola, 148, 149, 155
Porter, Richard E., 36, 102, 104
Postman, L., 81, 82, 103, 155
Poverty, culture of, 40
Power:
  and the ability to coerce, 107–8
  attractive instruments of, 108–9
  capability, individual, 135–36
  component, in every communication relationship, 2–3, 108
  components of, 109–20, 123, 191, 206, 214
    information, basic and specific, 113–17

    organization, formal and informal, 112–13
    status, ascribed and acquired, 117–18
    wealth, material and human, 110–12
    will, conscious and subconscious, 118–20
  defined, 106–7, 122
  and influence, relationship, 106–7
  intergroup, 190–92, 199
  international, 212–14, 231
  interpersonal, 140–41, 154
  as an interpersonal process, 106
  intragroup, 182–84, 198
  intranational, 206–7, 231
  intrapersonal, 135–36, 153
  military, 206
  role in communication, 105–23
  as value to which individuals, groups, and nations aspire, 109, 119
Power is a process, 110
Power is contextual, 107–8, 184
Power is relative, 106–7, 184
Press Trust of India (PTI), 219
Price-Williams, D., 15, 36
Private cues, in communication, 96–97
Propositional summary:
  for chapter 1, 34–36
  for chapter 2, 60–62
  for chapter 3, 99–102
  for chapter 4, 122–23
  for chapter 5, 153–54
  for chapter 6, 175–76
  for chapter 7, 198–99
  for chapter 8, 230–32
Protestants, 220
Protestant work ethic, 195
Psychosomatic illness, 56
Public cues, in communication, 96–97

Q

Quality Circles, 186
Quality of Work Life Committees, 186

R

Racial group, 158, 166
Ramsey, Sheila, 83, 104
Reality, perceptions and misperceptions of, 29–34, 35
Rebellion, while in teens, 6
Red Cross, 17
Redfield, Robert, 63
Relationship development in communication theory, 68, 69
Religious believers and nonbelievers, 160
Republican, 81